SKILLS & VALUES:
INTELLECTUAL PROPERTY

SKILLS & VALUES: INTELLECTUAL PROPERTY

Courtney G. Lytle
Adjunct Professor of Law
Emory University School of Law

Library of Congress Cataloging-in-Publication Data

Perry, Courtney Lytle.
  Skills & values. Intellectual property / Courtney Lytle Perry.
     p. cm.
  Includes index.
  ISBN 978-1-4224-7844-8 (soft cover)
  1. Intellectual property—United States. I. Title. II. Title: Intellectual property.
III. Title: Skills and values.
  KF2980.P46 2011
  346.7304'8—dc22

                                                          2011007639

Editorial Offices
121 Chanlon Rd., New Providence, NJ 07974 (908) 464-6800
201 Mission St., San Francisco, CA 94105-1831 (415) 908-3200
www.lexisnexis.com

MATTHEW◆BENDER   (Pub.3305)

Summary of Contents

PART I

Copyright

Chapter 1:   Hope, Change and Infringement **3**

Copyright – Fair use. Students analyze a fact pattern based on the Obama campaign poster infringement issue. Optional memorandum drafting exercise.

Chapter 2:   Jumping Through Hoops **15**

Copyright — Copyright Registration. Students complete on-line Copyright Application.

Chapter 3:   How Many Years Can a Mountain Exist? **17**

Copyright — Term and Termination of Transfers. On-line quiz covering various aspects of copyright duration under 1976 and 1909 Acts.

Chapter 4:   My Sweet Lord **43**

Copyright — Infringement and Independent Creation. Students draft an original judicial opinion addressing the infamous *My Sweet Lord* infringement case. Optional oral argument exercise.

Chapter 5:   Trash, Treasure and Tacky **51**

Copyright — Useful items. On-line pictorial review of copyrightability of various useful and functional items.

PART II

Trademark

Chapter 6:   Versus **59**

Trademark — Infringement and Likelihood of Confusion.   On-line collection of marks from trademark lawsuits. Students analyze the marks and try to predict the holding and reasoning.

Chapter 7: Waya Soap **69**

Trademark — Registration. Students analyze the relative strengths of a new mark and complete an on line Trademark Application. Optional Opposition Proceeding Exercise.

Chapter 8: By Any Other Name. **85**

Trademark — Famous Name Dispute and Domain Name Rights. Students research and analyze client's rights in response to a "cease and desist" letter.

PART III

Applied IP: Licensing And Software Protection

Chapter 9: Copyleft and Licensing **99**

Copyright — Creative Commons, GNU and Standard Licensing. Students review three different examples of license agreements and compare the different strategies and protections.

Chapter 10: CyberAlchemy **165**

Patent/Copyright — Protecting Software Rights. Students analyze a fact pattern involving a start up Software Company and devise a strategy for protecting the company's IP. Optional client interview exercise.

Chapter 11: Where No Man Has Gone Before. **191**

Trademark — Name and Likeness Protection. Students review a client's concerns regarding product endorsement and revise a draft agreement to reflect desired terms.

Chapter 12: Legacy of the Cluefall **201**

Copyright /Trademark — Licensing and Negotiation. Students are assigned to opposing sides in a negotiation for rights to create video games based on successful novels. Optional contract drafting exercise.

PART IV

Patent

Chapter 13: FlingWing **233**

Patent — Standards and Application. Students analyze a client's invention for patentability and review a file of prior art.

Chapter 14: Building A Better Mousetrap **295**

Patent — Patent Abuse. Students review some unlikely patents collected on line and complete an online search for similar interesting patents.

Chapter 15: Ersatz University. **303**

Patent/Combined IP — Protection Strategy. Students review overall business plan of an on line university and provide advice for modifying potential infringing activity and developing a protection strategy for corporate IP.

Table of Contents

PART I COPYRIGHT **1**

**Chapter 1: Hope, Change and Infringement —
Fair Use and Derivative Works** **3**

Overview: Copyright Infringement, Fair Use and Derivative Works 3
 1. Copyright Law in the Digital Era 3
 2. Fair Use Defense to Copyright Infringement 4
  A. The First Factor: The Purpose and Character of the Use 7
  B. The Second Factor: The Nature of the Copyrighted Work 9
  C. The Third Factor: The Amount Used 9
  D. The Fourth Factor: The Effect on the Market 10
  E. Balancing the Factors 10
Exercise 11
Assignment 13

**Chapter 2: Jumping Through Hoops — Copyright
Registration** **15**

Exercise 15

**Chapter 3: How Many Years Can A Mountain
Exist? Copyright Term and
Termination of Transfers** **17**

Overview: Duration of Copyright 17
 1. The Politics of Term Limits — Copyright Style 17
  A. Lawrence Lessig on *Eldred v. Ashcroft* 17
  B. Justice Ginsburg on *Eldred v. Ashcroft* 25
 2. The Mechanics 33
  A. Duration of Copyright 33
   i. Duration of Copyright — 1976 Act 33
   ii. Duration of Copyright — 1909 Act 33
   iii Duration of Copyright — Gap Works 35
  B. Termination of Transfers 36
   i. Section 203 36
   ii. Section 304 37
   iii. Derivative Works and Termination of Transfers 38
 3. Summary of the 1909 Act Rules 39

4. Summary of the 1976 Act Rules 39
5. Important Dates 40
Exercise 41

Chapter 4:   My Sweet Lord — Copyright Infringement . . . 43

Overview: Infringement 43
1. Elements of Infringement 43
    A. Copying — Probative Similarity 44
    B. Illicit Copying — Substantial Similarity 45
2. Independent Creation 47
Exercise 49

Chapter 5:   Trash, Treasure and Tacky — Useful
Items and Copyright 51

Overview : Pictorial, Graphic and Sculptural Works 51
Exercise 55

PART II   TRADEMARK 57

Chapter 6:   Versus — Infringement and Likelihood
of Confusion 59

Overview: Likelihood of Confusion 59
Exercise 68

Chapter 7:   Waya Soap — Trademark Registration 69

Overview: Trademark Registration Standards 69
1. Strength of a Proposed Mark 69
    A. Generic Marks 69
    B. Descriptive Marks 69
    C. Suggestive Marks 70
    D. Arbitrary, Fanciful and Coined Marks 70
2. Doctrine of Foreign Equivalents 70
3. Filing a Trademark Application 74
4. Opposition Proceedings 75
Exercise 77
Waya Soap: Part One 77
Waya Soap: Part Two 79
Waya Soap: Part Three 80

Chapter 8:   By Any Other Name — Domain Name and
Trademark Infringement 85

Overview: Domain Name Disputes 85
1. Primary Source — UDRP 86
2. Primary Source — ACPA/Lanham Act 89

3. Recent Developments 93
Exercise.. 94

PART III   APPLIED INTELLECTUAL PROPERTY: LICENSING AND SOFTWARE PROTECTIONS . . . 97

Chapter 9:   Copyleft and Licensing 99

Overview: Approaches to Licensing.. 99
1. The Creative Commons.. 99
    A. Creative Commons Materials — "About Licenses"..................... 101
    B. The "Legal Deed"... 103
    C. License Agreement... 105
    D. Conclusion.. 110
2. GNU General Public License 111
    A. GNU in a Nutshell 114
    B. The Current Version (3.0) of the GNU GPL 122
3. Copyright License — Standard Approach................................ 134
    A. Traditional Copyright Licensing Issues............................. 134
    B. Traditional Approach License — Lexis/Nexis Form 136
    C. License Drafting Checklist 146
Exercise.. 164

Chapter 10:   CyberAlchemy — Protecting Software: Copyright, Patent and Other Options 165

Overview: Software Protection 165
1. Copyright Protection for Software... 165
    A. Historical Background 166
    B. Current Status 177
2. Patent Protection for Software 178
3. Trade Secret Protection for Software 179
4. Grass Roots Protection Options — Anarchy and Copyleft 180
    A. The GPL Trap 181
5. Ownership of Rights — Employee/Employer Relationships.. 181
    A. Patent Law and Employee Issues 181
    B. Copyright Law and Employee Issues................................ 182
      i. Scope of Employment... 182
      ii. Written Work Made For Hire Agreement.............. 183
6. Client-Focused Legal Advice.. 184
Exercise.. 187
CyberAlchemy: Part One 187
CyberAlchemy: Part Two... 189

Chapter 11:   Where No Man Has Gone Before — Licensing 191

Exercise.. 191

**Chapter 12: Legacy of the Cluefall — Negotiating
             a Licensing Agreement 201**

Overview: Licensing Terms and Negotiation Tactics 201
    1. Negotiation: The Basic Steps 201
        A. Preparation.. 201
        B. Introduction and Information Exchange 203
        C. Offer and Counter-Offer... 204
        D. Agreement 205
Exercise.. 206

PART IV PATENT. 231

Chapter 13: FlingWing — Patent Application 233

Overview: Filing a Patent 233
    1. Patent Standards... 233
        A. Patentable Subject Matter... 233
            i.   Process claims 233
            ii. Product claims 236
        B. Originality 237
            i.   Novelty.. 237
            ii. Utility.. 238
            iii. Non-obviousness 238
    2. Role of the Patent Attorney.. 239
Exercise.. 240

**Chapter 14: Building A Better (or Patenting
             a Worse) Mousetrap — Patent Abuse 295**

Overview: Business Method and Software Patents 295
Exercise.. 297

**Chapter 15: Ersatz University — Patent/Combined
             IP Strategy 303**

Exercise.. 303

PART I

COPYRIGHT

Chapter 1

HOPE, CHANGE AND INFRINGEMENT — FAIR USE AND DERIVATIVE WORKS

OVERVIEW: COPYRIGHT INFRINGEMENT, FAIR USE AND DERIVATIVE WORKS

1. *Copyright Law in the Digital Era*

The Copyright Act, by its very nature, is an attempt to balance the rights of authors against the desire of other authors to use pre-existing works. Especially with the increased tools in today's digital culture, the urge to make an artistic statement based on someone else's work drives much of the current art culture.[1] Harvard Law Professor and professional copyright anarchist Lawrence Lessig has stated that because 70% of young people infringe digital works, it is better to change the laws than have a generation of law breakers.[2]

Part of the problem, as Lessig and his supporters would cast it, is that the rights reserved to an author under the Copyright Act extend beyond a straight prohibition of direct copying. Although ideas are not protected,[3] the Act extends an author's protection significantly by adding the list of rights in Section 106 reserved to the author, including the exclusive right to make derivative works.[4] An author's right, for instance, to write a sequel to her breakthrough novel may be as important as the right to the original text. Similarly, in the absence of European style moral rights, the right to create derivative works protects an author somewhat from having unauthorized and even offensive knock-off works circulated.[5] The right to make derivative works, also called the right of adaptation, is also what preserves to the author the right to make a screenplay from a novel or a Broadway musical from an animated film.

That sort of major recasting of a work is not usually what new "artists" are inclined to infringe. There is not much of a market for illicit Broadway shows or movies pirated from protected novels. Instead, the digital age has created a generation which seems to hold as canon that they should have the right to sample and alter existing works to create new ones.[6]

---

[1] See, Lawrence Lessig, Remix: Making Art and Commerce Thrive in the Hybrid Economy (2008).

[2] *Id.*; see also, Lawrence Lessig, Interview *Colbert Nation.* Comedy Central. (January 8, 2009). Event occurs at 2:16. http://www.colbertnation.com/the-colbert-report-videos/215454/january-08-2009/lawrence-lessig (cited at http://en.wikipedia.org/wiki/Lawrence_Lessig).

[3] *See, e.g., Baker v. Selden,* 101 U.S. 99 (1879).

[4] 17 U.S.C. 106(2).

[5] *See, e.g., Walt Disney Productions v. Air Pirates*, 581 F.2d 751 (9th Cir. 1978), *cert. denied*, 439 U.S. 1132, 59 L. Ed. 2d 94, 99 S. Ct. 1054 (1979).

[6] Professor Lessig discusses and supports this trend at great length in *Remix*, cited *supra*, and in his 2004 book, *Free Culture* as well as in numerous articles and interviews.

Unfortunately for these artists, the law does not support their desires for free artistic expression. One trend, however which has developed along with the digital artists is a broadening of the Fair Use defense to infringement.

2. *Fair Use Defense to Copyright Infringement*

On a basic level, it is important to remember that the fair use defense is exactly that; it is a *defense* to an action for infringement. Although some artists are sufficiently well funded to survive the litigation process and reach the point in the law suit that they can bring up this defense to escape liability for their infringement, for the majority of parties, artist or otherwise, the expense of going so far into a trial is prohibitive. This is important to keep in mind when you are advising a client as to the consequences of a questionable use. For the vast majority of small companies, never mind starving artists, whether they would ultimately prevail on a fair use defense is a purely academic exercise. Keep in mind your clients' financial reality as you advise them; in many cases staying out of trouble is much more valuable than ultimately prevailing at trial.

Aside from the financial realities of trial, however, the doctrine of fair use seems to have developed along lines designed especially for the generation of sampling and remixing digital artists. The idea of transformative use has in many cases seemed to swallow the traditional analysis of the four statutory elements expressed in the code. Copyright scholars realize very quickly that the seemingly straightforward application of four express statutory elements bolstered by an express list of "fair" uses is little more than a seemingly solid layer over a bottomless swamp.

The analysis appears straightforward enough. The Act lists specific uses that will be deemed "fair" and therefore not infringement. Section 107 clearly states that copies of any sort made for the following purposes will not be deemed infringement: "criticism, comment, news reporting, teaching (including multiple copies for classroom use), scholarship, or research, is not an infringement of copyright."[7] The statute clearly states that copies made for one of those purposes are "**not an**

---

[7] 17 U.S.C. 107.

Notwithstanding the provisions of sections 106 and 106A, the fair use of a copyrighted work, including such use by reproduction in copies or phonorecords or by any other means specified by that section, for purposes such as criticism, comment, news reporting, teaching (including multiple copies for classroom use), scholarship, or research, is not an infringement of copyright. In determining whether the use made of a work in any particular case is a fair use the factors to be considered shall include —

(1) the purpose and character of the use, including whether such use is of a commercial nature or is for nonprofit educational purposes;
(2) the nature of the copyrighted work;
(3) the amount and substantiality of the portion used in relation to the copyrighted work as a whole; and
(4) the effect of the use upon the potential market for or value of the copyrighted work.

The fact that a work is unpublished shall not itself bar a finding of fair use if such finding is made upon consideration of all the above factors.

infringement of copyright."[8] The code does not say "may" not be infringement, or "is more likely not to be" infringement; it says such a use is not an infringement.

That at least seems clear enough. Obviously, in some cases, there will be issues of fact whether the specifics of a particular behavior fall within one of the categories, but clear cases of enumerated actions should be safe from infringement. Unfortunately, this is not true. Courts have found ways around the clear statutory language and found infringement and no fair use in a case of a Professor having copies made for use in his class[9] and in a case with researchers making archive copies of technical journal articles to keep in their own research files.[10] In each of those cases, there was an element of commercial impact and a reasonable justification for a finding of infringement without fair use, if it were not for the express language of the statute.

So in an analysis where even the clear and express statutory language can become somehow difficult to apply, it is inevitable that the equitable balancing of four factors will become a swampy marsh of opportunity for clever and persuasive litigators. The factors seem relatively straightforward when viewed objectively, but even a brief study of the application by the courts show that it has not developed that way.

Judge Leval[11] explains the somewhat unfocused evolution of the fair use doctrine:

> What is most curious about this doctrine is that neither the decisions that have applied it for nearly 300 years, nor its eventual statutory formulation, undertook to define or explain its contours or objectives. In Folsom v. Marsh,[12] in 1841, Justice Story articulated an often-cited summary of how to approach a question of fair use: "In short, we must often . . . look to the nature and objects of the selections made, the quantity and value of the materials used, and the degree in which the use may prejudice the sale, or diminish the profits, or supersede the objects, of the original work."[13] The 1976 Copyright Act largely adopted his summary. [footnote omitted] These formulations, however, furnish little guidance on how to recognize fair use. The statute, for example, directs us to examine the "purpose and character" of the secondary use as well as "the nature of the copyrighted work." Beyond stating a preference for the critical, educational, and nonprofit over the commercial, the statute

---

[8]　*Id.* (emphasis added).

[9]　*Princeton University Press vs. Michigan Document Services, Inc.*, 99 F.3rd 1831 (6th Cir. 1996).

[10]　*American Geophysical Union vs. Texaco, Inc.*, 60 F.3d 913 (2d Cir. 1994).

[11]　Hon. Pierre N. Leval, Judge, 2d Cir. *See* http://en.wikipedia.org/wiki/Pierre_N._Leval.

[12]　[n. 5] 9 F.Cas. 342 (C.C.D.Mass.1841) (No. 4901).

[13]　[n. 6] *Id.* at 348.

tells little about what to look for in the "purpose and character" of the secondary use. It gives no clues at all regarding the significance of "the nature of" the copyrighted work. Although it instructs us to be concerned with the quantity and importance of the materials taken and with the effect of the use on the potential for copyright profits, it provides no guidance for distinguishing between acceptable and excessive levels. Finally, although leaving open the possibility that other factors may bear on the question, the statute identifies none.[14]

Curiously, judges generally have neither complained of the absence of guidance, nor made substantial efforts to fill the void. Uttering confident conclusions as to whether the particular taking was or was not a fair use, courts have treated the definition of the doctrine as assumed common ground.

The assumption of common ground is mistaken. Judges do not share a consensus on the meaning of fair use. Earlier decisions provide little basis for predicting later ones. Reversals[15] and divided courts[16] are commonplace. The opinions reflect widely differing notions of the meaning of fair use. Decisions are not governed by consistent principles, but seem rather to result from intuitive reactions to individual fact patterns. Justification is sought in notions of fairness, often more responsive to the concerns of private property than to the objectives of copyright.

Confusion has not been confined to judges. Writers, historians, publishers, and their legal advisers can only guess and pray as to how courts will resolve copyright

---

[14] [n. 8] *See* Harper & Row, Publishers, Inc. v. Nation Enters., 471 U.S. 539, 549 (1985).

[15] [n. 9] Five of the recent leading cases were reversed at every stage of review. In Rosemont Enterprises, Inc. v. Random House, Inc., 256 F.Supp. 55 (S.D.N.Y.), *rev'd*, 366 F.2d 303 (2d Cir.1966), *cert. denied*, 385 U.S. 1009 (1967) — the Howard Hughes case — the Second Circuit reversed a district court injunction. In Universal City Studios, Inc. v. Sony Corp. of America, 480 F. Supp. 429 (C.D.Cal.1979), *rev'd*, 659 F.2d 963 (9th Cir.1981), *rev'd*, 464 U.S. 417 (1984), the court of appeals reversed the district court's finding for the defendant, and was in turn reversed by the Supreme Court. In Harper & Row, Publishers, Inc. v. Nation Enterprises, 557 F. Supp. 1067 (S.D.N.Y.), *modified*, 723 F.2d 195 (2d Cir.1983), *rev'd*, 471 U.S. 539 (1985), the district court's damage award was reversed by the court of appeals, which in turn was reversed by the Supreme Court. In Salinger v. Random House, Inc., 650 F. Supp. 413 (S.D.N.Y.1986), *rev'd*, 811 F.2d 90 (2d Cir.), *cert. denied*, 484 U.S. 890 (1987), and in New Era Publications International v. Henry Holt & Co., 695 F. Supp. 1493 (S.D.N.Y.1988), *aff'd on other grounds*, 873 F.2d 576 (2d Cir.1989), my findings of fair use were rejected on appeal.

[16] [n. 10] In its first two encounters with fair use, the Supreme Court split 4-4 and thus failed to resolve anything. *See* Williams & Wilkins Co. v. United States, 420 U.S. 376 (1975); Columbia Broadcasting Sys. v. Loew's, Inc., 356 U.S. 43 (1958). The Court decided *Sony* by a 5-4 majority, *see Sony*, 464 U.S. 417, and *Nation* by a 6-3 majority, *see Nation*, 471 U.S. 539. In *New Era*, the Second Circuit voted 7-5 to deny en banc review to alter the panel's dicta on fair use. Four judges joined in a concurring opinion, *see New Era*, 884 F.2d at 660 (Miner, J., concurring), and four in a dissenting opinion, *see id*. at 662 (Newman, J., dissenting).

disputes. After recent opinions of the Second Circuit cast-
ing serious doubt on any meaningful applicability of fair
use to quotation from previously unpublished letters,[17]
publishers are understandably reluctant to pay advance
royalties or to undertake commitments for biographical
or historical works that call for use of such sources.[18]

Judge Leval goes on to express optimism that a unified approach to
fair use in the judiciary is possible, although it does not seem to have
occurred in the twenty years since he penned the article. Perhaps by
characterizing the liquid nature of fair use analysis as flexible rather
than unpredictable,[19] it becomes more palatable, but any practitioner
seeking solid guidelines is fated to be frustrated in fair use doctrine.

Nevertheless, in any fair use argument the court will address and
weigh each of the four factors in turn:

A. *The First Factor: The Purpose and Character of the Use*

The first factor is "the purpose and character of the use, including
whether such use is of a commercial nature or is for nonprofit educational purposes."[20] The commercial/noncommercial distinction is a key
one which judges weigh heavily. If a use is commercial in nature, it
seems almost hypocritical for that infringing user to claim privilege
and seek to be excused from the application of the very law intended to
provide financial incentive for authors to create merely so the infringing user can in turn enjoy the financial benefit now denied to the original author. Fair use is not strictly an equitable defense, but fairness
matters in an ad hoc weighing of factors, and it seems unfair to excuse
an infringer's actions so that infringer can turn about and enjoy the
profit denied the original creator.

Purpose and character of the use does not stop with the determination of commercial or non-commercial use. Although it does not appear
in the statute, the idea of transformative/non-transformative use often
seems to swallow the other factors and monopolize a discussion of fair
use. Like the digital remix artists who find great creative and artistic
value in changing existing works rather than creating something new,
the idea of transformative use focuses on the alleged benefit to society
of allowing the adaptation right to be whittled away by the application
of fair use. So long as the underlying work is changed or transformed,
the theory goes, there is such value being added to the work and to
society that the unauthorized taking of the underlying work is justified.

---

[17] [n. 11] *See New Era*, 873 F.2d 576; *Salinger*, 811 F.2d 90.
[18] Pierre N. Leval, *Toward a Fair Use Standard*, 103 HARV. L. REV. 1105, 1105–1107 (1990). Reprinted
      with permission.
[19] Jennifer M. Urban, *Updating Fair Use for Innovators and Creators in the Digital Age: Two Targeted
      Reforms*, Public Knowledge Fair Use White Paper, Samuelslon Law, Technology & Public Policy Clinic,
      UC Berkely School of Law (Feb 15, 2010).
[20] 17 U.S.C. 107.

It is somewhat intellectually comforting to learn that although analysis of transformative characteristics of the challenged use seem to be a recent creation of creative litigators, the concept has a historical tradition and a certain amount of gravity as well. Judge Leval again sheds light on a murky area of analysis:

> I believe the answer to the question of justification turns primarily on whether, and to what extent, the challenged use is *transformative*. The use must be productive and must employ the quoted matter in a different manner or for a different purpose from the original.[21] A quotation of copyrighted material that merely repackages or republishes the original is unlikely to pass the test; in Justice Story's words, it would merely "supersede the objects" of the original.[22] If, on the other hand, the secondary use adds value to the original — if the quoted matter is used as raw material, transformed in the creation of new information, new aesthetics, new insights and understandings — this is the very type of activity that the fair use doctrine intends to protect for the enrichment of society.[23]

> Transformative uses may include criticizing the quoted work, exposing the character of the original author, proving a fact, or summarizing an idea argued in the original in order to defend or rebut it. They also may include parody, symbolism, aesthetic declarations, and innumerable other uses.

> The existence of any identifiable transformative objective does not, however, guarantee success in claiming fair use. The transformative justification must overcome factors favoring the copyright owner. A biographer or critic of a writer may contend that unlimited quotation enriches the portrait or justifies the criticism. The creator of a derivative work based on the original creation of another may claim absolute entitlement because of the transformation. Nonetheless, extensive takings may impinge on creative incentives. And the secondary user's claim under the first factor is weakened to the extent that her takings exceed the asserted justification. The justification will likely be outweighed if the takings are excessive and other factors favor the copyright owner.[24]

---

[21] [n. 29] *See* Cary v. Kearsley, 170 Eng. Rep. 679, 681–82, 4 Esp. 168, 170–71 (1802). In Sony Corp. of America v. Universal City Studios, Inc., 464 U.S. 417 (1984), the dissenters approved this approach, *see id.* at 480 (Blackmun, J., dissenting), but the majority of the Supreme Court rejected it, *see* 464 U.S. at 448–51.

[22] [n. 30] *See* Folsom v. Marsh, 9 F.Cas. 342, 345 (C.C.D.Mass.1841) (No. 4901).

[23] [n. 31] *But cf.* Fisher, *Reconstructing the Fair Use Doctrine*, 101 Harv. L. Rev. 1659, 1768–69 (1988) (using the term "transformative" in a somewhat different sense).

[24] Leval, 103 Harv. L. Rev. at 1111–1112 (emphasis in the original).

Through this analysis, the value of the adapted work eclipses both the value of the original work and the Section 106 adaptation right of the original author. Presumptively, however, the other factors will help to balance this preference for derivative rather than original creation.

B. The Second Factor: The Nature of the Copyrighted Work

The second factor focuses on the nature of the underlying or copyrighted work. A judge looks to see whether the underlying work is the sort of creative or artistic work that lies in the center of copyright and enjoys the strongest protection rather than a more factual or useful work, which enjoys only a thin level of protection. If the underlying work enjoys greater protection, the infringement is less likely to be excused as fair use. This factor looks to how much creativity was involved in the original creation. Poetry will enjoy greater protection under this factor than will instructions for mixing lye soap. A list of personal names appearing in the New York Times Index was protected by copyright, but because it lacked a significant level of creativity, the court did not offer it much protection from an arguably fair use.[25]

Greater protection and a less likely finding of fair use will also be appropriate if the underlying work was created for publication.[26] If it was created with the intention of being a significant work, one may assume the author was more likely to be creating with the intention of relying on the protections offered by the law. A incidental creation, like a personal letter or perhaps a short email setting a time for dinner that evening, seems less deserving of protection than, say, a law school supplement for an intellectual property course which saw its author toiling late into the night in the throes of creativity. Justice Story described the concept as "value of the materials used."[27]

C. The Third Factor: The Amount Used

The third factor is refreshingly quantitative. Here the language is interpreted as it was written. The more of a work that is usurped, the less likely that use is to be excused as fair. For instance, quotations from a noted Judge's article can be safely included in a text book, whereas a complete copy of the article would require advance permission. Of course there is also a qualitative element to this analysis. In *Harper & Row v. Nation Enterprises*,[28] the Court refused to find fair use even where only a short piece of a very long book was copied. Because that section that was taken was the highlight of the entire long work, the Court decided that taking the "essence" of a work does in fact take too much under this factor and will preclude a fair use finding, even if it seems on its face to be qualitatively a small segment of the copyrighted

---

[25] *New York Times Co. v. Roxbury Data Interface*, 434 F. Supp. 217 (D.N.J. 1977).
[26] Leval, 103 Harv. L. Rev. at 1117.
[27] *Folsom v. Marsh*, 9 F. Cas. 342, 344 (C.C.D. Mass. 1841) (No. 4901).
[28] 471 U.S. 539 (1985).

work. Even with these departures from pure numeric calculation, clearly under the third factor, the more that has been taken from the underlying work, the less likely the infringement will be excused as fair use.

D. The Fourth Factor: The Effect on the Market

With the fourth factor, the analysis again becomes deeper and more heavily relied upon for an overall fair use determination. Under the fourth factor, the inquiry focuses on the economic effect on the original author and on the market for the underlying work. If the infringing work is not one that is likely to serve as a substitute for the underlying work, a court is more likely to find fair use. For instance, the reproduction of copyrighted works in a series of thumbnail images shown as search results on a web search engine was a fair use.[29] The works at issue were copyrighted art, and the thumbnails used by the search engine reproduced the entire work in some cases, nevertheless the court found that because the reproduced copy was so small, it would not be a replacement for someone interested in the original work and would accordingly not have any negative impact on the market for the original works.[30]

Emphasizing this factor supports the underlying purpose of copyright. If the ability of the author to profit from the work is harmed by an infringing use, the incentive to create on which copyright is based would be undermined. Because this is the very heart of copyright law and its Constitutional foundations, courts' strong attention to this factor is appropriate.

E. Balancing the Factors

The synthesis of the factors together with any specific case by case issues which a court finds relevant is an ad hoc procedure and is the topic of many learned attempts at clarification or recasting.[31] Copyright expert Nimmer suggests the following: "It may be that no more precise guide can be stated than Joseph McDonald's clever paraphrase of the Golden Rule: 'Take not from others to such an extent and in such a manner that you would be resentful if they so took from you.'"[32]

---

[29] *Kelly v. Arriba Soft Corp.*, 280 F.3d 811 (9th Cir. 2003). *See also Perfect 10, Inc. v. Google, Inc.*, 508 F.3d 1146 (9th Cir. 2007).
[30] *Id.*
[31] *See, e.g.*, Leval, *supra;* 4–13 Nimmer on Copyright § 13.05 at note 32.
[32] 4–13 Nimmer on Copyright § 13.05 at note 33 (citing McDonald, *Non-Infringing Uses,* 9 Bull. Copyright Soc'y 466, 467 No. 355 (1962)).

EXERCISE

TOPIC: Copyright

    i.   Fair Use

    ii. Derivative Works

SKILLS:

    i.   Research

    ii. Critical Reasoning

    iii. Analysis

    iv. Optional drafting

ESTIMATED TIME FOR COMPLETING THIS EXERCISE:

Approximately two hours.

ESTIMATED LEVEL OF DIFFICULTY (1–5): 3—Moderate.
Some original analysis and research required.

One of the partners at your firm, Mike Delphi, just sent you the
following email:

> I just got off the phone with Mona Jackson, who, as you
> know, is on the Board of Xantax Corp., one of our most
> important corporate clients. She is now apparently also
> involved in Rigby Mortiss's campaign for Governor, and
> she has asked me for advice on an intellectual property
> issue relating to the campaign.
>
> The Mortiss campaign wants to use some sort of con-
> temporary folk art look for their campaign theme, and
> they are planning on hiring someone to make a poster of
> the candidate like the popular Obama campaign poster
> by Shepherd Fairey. From the way she was talking, he
> must be some popular urban artist or something, but
> I've never heard of him. She said they had a photo of the
> candidate that is a similar looking head shot to the one
> of Obama in the famous work and that they were hiring
> an artist to make a poster out of it like the Obama Hope
> poster.

She said she heard from a friend on the Obama campaign that there were some infringement issues with the Obama poster, and now she is concerned that her candidate will have troubles as well. I am not familiar with the Obama issue nor with infringement in general, so I will need you to look into both the specific Obama issue and the general law.

What should we advise them in terms of avoiding trouble for the campaign? You may assume this is still in the planning stages, so we need to be able to educate them as to the specific issues as well as offer them advice on how to safely accomplish their goals. Remember the goal in transactional work is to *avoid* rather than *win* lawsuits.

I am having lunch with Mona the day after tomorrow, so I will need a short memo from you outlining each of these issues. Although I am fairly well versed in election law, the last time I thought about infringement was in a survey IP course back in law school. That was many years ago, so please be sure your memo is clear and refreshes my memory on the black letter law as well as the application to this specific issue. When I learn more details on her plans, I may need to get some follow up research from you, but for now I just need to know enough that I can speak intelligently to her concerns over lunch.

Regards

Mike.

ASSIGNMENT

To answer the partner's questions, you need to research the Obama issue so you understand it and all the copyright implications involved, and then apply the conclusions and results from that situation to the one at hand. Although you may not have sufficient detail to come to a conclusive result on all fronts, you should: (a) identify the issues, (b) analyze to the extent you can without too much conjecture and (c) advise the client how best to proceed. As you prepare your answers, keep in mind the purpose of the research and your audience. Be sure you are giving the partner what he needs so he will not feel foolish with an important client.

1. Prepare a legal memorandum for your partner.

2. Be prepared to discuss the issues in class.

After you have written your memorandum, consult the Self-Assessment on the LexisNexis webcourse

Chapter 2

JUMPING THROUGH HOOPS — COPYRIGHT REGISTRATION

EXERCISE

TOPIC: Copyright

    i.   Copyright Registration Process

SKILLS:

    i.   Research (on-line – general and Copyright Office website and processes)

ESTIMATED TIME FOR COMPLETING THIS EXERCISE:

Approximately one hour.

ESTIMATED LEVEL OF DIFFICULTY (1–5): 1—Straightforward.

This exercise is designed as an adventure in exploration. You have heard that filing a copyright is an easy thing. Generally, someone who is basically competent with a computer and the internet can find the right place and complete the filing process without too much difficulty. So now we'll test that theory.

You have just written the great American novel. Or a campy comic book if you'd prefer. You may choose the nature of your forthcoming book; just be sure to specify the details in your answer.

Being a clever law student, you know that it is in your interest to formally file your copyright. When you spoke to the local book store about stocking your book, they were willing to overlook your self-published status, but they insisted that their inventory and bookkeeping systems hinged on all books having an ISBN number.

You don't have a publisher. Well, not yet. You are fairly certain that a bidding war amongst the major publishing houses will commence immediately after you make them aware of your existence, but in the meantime, you want to get the copyright registration taken care of and you want to get the ISBN number assigned so you can get it on at least the local bookseller's shelves.

So the question is, how do you do it? Write a short "how to" summary for both the registration and the ISBN application.

You will also complete a copyright registration form, but do not use the electronic copyright process which requires you to create an account and log in. Instead please fill out and print a copy of the appropriate registration form available on the website without any log-in requirement. Please attach a copy of your completed copyright registration application. Indicate what else you would need to submit (fees, etc.) to complete the filing. Fill out the copyright application with your information or made up information, just so long as it is clear that you have entered the right information in the right places and that the form and information matches your soon-to-be-famous work.

Once you have completed the exercise, consult the Self-Assessment on the LexisNexis webcourse.

Chapter 3

HOW MANY YEARS CAN A MOUNTAIN EXIST? COPYRIGHT TERM AND TERMINATION OF TRANSFERS

OVERVIEW: DURATION OF COPYRIGHT

1. *The Politics of Term Limits — Copyright Style*

Once Upon a Time, copyright professors taught their students how long a copyright lasted and left it at that. It was often linked to Termination of Transfers, a topic which was often painful, but seldom compelling. Whether the term and renewal term approach of the 1909 Act or the single term approach adopted by the 1976 Act, the length of a copyright simply did not occupy a significant place on the syllabus.... At least not until the birth of a vocal public domain activism that viewed any extension of the term of copyright as a violent attack on creative rights.

Once Upon a Time, the name Sonny Bono was associated with a wide variety of things — from Cher to Palm Springs to horrible skiing accidents — but it was not generally connected with controversy.... At least not until his widow helped get the 1998 Copyright Term Extension Act named after him.

So now, the term of copyright and the name Sonny Bono are both related to the public domain furor over the CTEA and the resulting challenge in *Eldred v. Ashcroft*.[1]

Following the *Eldred* decision, which removed any doubt that Congress does indeed have the right to extend copyright terms so long as they are actually limited as required in the Constitution, the issue of duration can again be safely linked to termination of transfers and taught as a straightforward statutory exercise. However, a copyright issue that transforms a straightforward piece of Code into the center of a maelstrom of impassioned argument for a number of years, and ultimately warranted Supreme Court action, is worth a little back-story. To that end, what follows is an excerpt from the attorney for Mr. Eldred (challenging the CTEA) and the Constitutional justifications from the *Eldred* decision.

A. *Lawrence Lessig on Eldred v. Ashcroft*[2]

CHAPTER THIRTEEN: Eldred

In 1995, a father was frustrated that his daughters didn't seem to like Hawthorne. No doubt there was more than one such father, but at

---

[1] 537 U.S. 186 (2003).
[2] Lawrence Lessig, *Free Culture: How Big Media Uses Technology and the Law to Lock Down Culture and Control Creativity,* at 209–228, (2004) (available at: http://www.free-culture.cc/freeculture.pdf).

least one did something about it. Eric Eldred, a retired computer programmer living in New Hampshire, decided to put Hawthorne on the Web. An electronic version, Eldred thought, with links to pictures and explanatory text, would make this nineteenth-century author's work come alive.

It didn't work — at least for his daughters. They didn't find Hawthorne any more interesting than before. But Eldred's experiment gave birth to a hobby, and his hobby begat a cause: Eldred would build a library of public domain works by scanning these works and making them available for free.

Eldred's library was not simply a copy of certain public domain works, though even a copy would have been of great value to people across the world who can't get access to printed versions of these works. Instead, Eldred was producing derivative works from these public domain works. Just as Disney turned Grimm into stories more accessible to the twentieth century, Eldred transformed Hawthorne, and many others, into a form more accessible — technically accessible — today.

Eldred's freedom to do this with Hawthorne's work grew from the same source as Disney's. Hawthorne's *Scarlet Letter* had passed into the public domain in 1907. It was free for anyone to take without the permission of the Hawthorne estate or anyone else. Some, such as Dover Press and Penguin Classics, take works from the public domain and produce printed editions, which they sell in bookstores across the country. Others, such as Disney, take these stories and turn them into animated cartoons, sometimes successfully (*Cinderella*), sometimes not (*The Hunchback of Notre Dame, Treasure Planet*). These are all commercial publications of public domain works.

    ....

As I said, Eldred lives in New Hampshire. In 1998, Robert Frost's collection of poems *New Hampshire* was slated to pass into the public domain. Eldred wanted to post that collection in his free public library. But Congress got in the way.... [I]n 1998, for the eleventh time in forty years, Congress extended the terms of existing copyrights — this time by twenty years. Eldred would not be free to add any works more recent than 1923 to his collection until 2019. Indeed, no copyrighted work would pass into the public domain until that year (and not even then, if Congress extends the term again). By contrast, in the same period, more than 1 million patents will pass into the public domain.

This was the Sonny Bono Copyright Term Extension Act (CTEA), enacted in memory of the congressman and former musician Sonny

Bono, who, his widow, Mary Bono, says, believed that "copyrights should be forever."[3]

Eldred decided to fight this law. He first resolved to fight it through civil disobedience. In a series of interviews, Eldred announced that he would publish as planned, CTEA notwithstanding. But because of a second law passed in 1998, the NET (No Electronic Theft) Act, his act of publishing would make Eldred a felon — whether or not anyone complained. This was a dangerous strategy for a disabled programmer to undertake.

It was here that I became involved in Eldred's battle. I was a constitutional scholar whose first passion was constitutional interpretation. And though constitutional law courses never focus upon the Progress Clause of the Constitution, it had always struck me as importantly different. As you know, the Constitution says, Congress has the power to "promote the Progress of Science ... by securing for limited Times to Authors ... exclusive Right to their ... Writings...."

As I've described, this clause is unique within the power-granting clause of Article I, section 8 of our Constitution. Every other clause granting power to Congress simply says Congress has the power to do something — for example, to regulate "commerce among the several states" or "declare War." But here, the "something" is something quite specific — to "promote ... Progress" — through means that are also specific — by "securing" "exclusive Rights" (i.e., copyrights) "for limited Times." In the past forty years, Congress has gotten into the practice of extending existing terms of copyright protection. What puzzled me about this was, if Congress has the power to extend existing terms, then the Constitution's requirement that terms be "limited" will have no practical effect. If every time a copyright is about to expire, Congress has the power to extend its term, then Congress can achieve what the Constitution plainly forbids — perpetual terms "on the installment plan," as Professor Peter Jaszi so nicely put it.

As an academic, my first response was to hit the books. I remember sitting late at the office, scouring on-line databases for any serious consideration of the question. No one had ever challenged Congress's practice of extending existing terms. That failure may in part be why Congress seemed so untroubled in its habit. That, and the fact that the practice had become so lucrative for Congress. Congress knows that copyright owners will be willing to pay a great deal of money to see their copyright terms extended. And so Congress is quite happy to keep this gravy train going.

---

[3] (n2) 2. The full text is: "Sonny [Bono] wanted the term of copyright protection to last forever. I am informed by staff that such a change would violate the Constitution. I invite all of you to work with me to strengthen our copyright laws in all of the ways available to us. As you know, there is also Jack Valenti's proposal for a term to last forever less one day. Perhaps the Committee may look at that next Congress," 144 Cong. Rec. H9946, 9951–2 (October 7, 1998).

For this is the core of the corruption in our present system of government. "Corruption" not in the sense that representatives are bribed. Rather, "corruption" in the sense that the system induces the beneficiaries of Congress's acts to raise and give money to Congress to induce it to act. There's only so much time; there's only so much Congress can do. Why not limit its actions to those things it must do — and those things that pay? Extending copyright terms pays.

If that's not obvious to you, consider the following: Say you're one of the very few lucky copyright owners whose copyright continues to make money one hundred years after it was created. The Estate of Robert Frost is a good example. Frost died in 1963. His poetry continues to be extraordinarily valuable. Thus the Robert Frost estate benefits greatly from any extension of copyright, since no publisher would pay the estate any money if the poems Frost wrote could be published by anyone for free.

. . . .

Constitutional law is not oblivious to the obvious. Or at least, it need not be. So when I was considering Eldred's complaint, this reality about the never-ending incentives to increase the copyright term was central to my thinking. In my view, a pragmatic court committed to interpreting and applying the Constitution of our framers would see that if Congress has the power to extend existing terms, then there would be no effective constitutional requirement that terms be "limited." If they could extend it once, they would extend it again and again and again.

It was also my judgment that *this* Supreme Court would not allow Congress to extend existing terms. As anyone close to the Supreme Court's work knows, this Court has increasingly restricted the power of Congress when it has viewed Congress's actions as exceeding the power granted to it by the Constitution. Among constitutional scholars, the most famous example of this trend was the Supreme Court's decision in 1995 to strike down a law that banned the possession of guns near schools.

Since 1937, the Supreme Court had interpreted Congress's granted powers very broadly; so, while the Constitution grants Congress the power to regulate only "commerce among the several states" (aka "interstate commerce"), the Supreme Court had interpreted that power to include the power to regulate any activity that merely affected interstate commerce.

As the economy grew, this standard increasingly meant that there was no limit to Congress's power to regulate, since just about every activity, when considered on a national scale, affects interstate commerce. A Constitution designed to limit Congress's power was instead interpreted to impose no limit.

The Supreme Court, under Chief Justice Rehnquist's command, changed that in *United States* v. *Lopez*. The government had argued

important cases or cases that raise issues specific to the circuit as a whole, where the court will sit "en banc" to hear the case. The Court of Appeals rejected our request to hear the case en banc. This time, Judge Sentelle was joined by the most liberal member of the D.C. Circuit, Judge David Tatel. Both the most conservative and the most liberal judges in the D.C. Circuit believed Congress had overstepped its bounds.

It was here that most expected *Eldred* v. *Ashcroft* would die, for the Supreme Court rarely reviews any decision by a court of appeals. (It hears about one hundred cases a year, out of more than five thousand appeals.) And it practically never reviews a decision that upholds a statute when no other court has yet reviewed the statute.

But in February 2002, the Supreme Court surprised the world by granting our petition to review the D.C. Circuit opinion. Argument was set for October of 2002. The summer would be spent writing briefs and preparing for argument.[9]

Professor Lessig speaks as a proponent for creative freedom and is not alone in his strongly held and loudly voiced belief that traditional copyright is an unacceptable constraint on creativity and on the very promotion of "progress" mandated by the Constitution. Unfortunately for his cause, sincerity of belief and general persuasiveness was not, in this instance, sufficient to sway the Court. What follows is an edited selection of the Court's dismissal of the "free rights" petitioner's arguments in the *Eldred* decision:

B. *Justice Ginsburg on Eldred v. Ashcroft*[10]

JUSTICE GINSBERG delivered the opinion of the Court.

(Dissent by: STEVENS; BREYER)

This case concerns the authority the Constitution assigns to Congress to prescribe the duration of copyrights. The Copyright and Patent Clause of the Constitution, Art. I, § 8, cl. 8, provides as to copyrights: "Congress shall have Power ... to promote the Progress of Science ... by securing [to Authors] for limited Times ... the exclusive Right to their ... Writings." In 1998, in the measure here under inspection, Congress enlarged the duration of copyrights by 20 years. Copyright Term Extension Act (CTEA). As in the case of prior extensions, principally in 1831, 1909, and 1976, Congress provided for application of the enlarged terms to existing and future copyrights alike.

Petitioners are individuals and businesses whose products or services build on copyrighted works that have gone into the public domain.

---

9   Lessig, *Free Culture* 210–229. Reprinted by permission.
10   *Eldred v. Ashcroft*, 537 U.S. 186 (2003).

They seek a determination that the CTEA fails constitutional review under both the Copyright Clause's "limited Times" prescription and the First Amendment's free speech guarantee. Under the 1976 Copyright Act, copyright protection generally lasted from the work's creation until 50 years after the author's death. Under the CTEA, most copyrights now run from creation until 70 years after the author's death. Petitioners do not challenge the "life-plus-70-years" time span itself. "Whether 50 years is enough, or 70 years too much," they acknowledge, "is not a judgment meet for this Court." Congress went awry, petitioners maintain, not with respect to newly created works, but in enlarging the term for published works with existing copyrights. The "limited Time" in effect when a copyright is secured, petitioners urge, becomes the constitutional boundary, a clear line beyond the power of Congress to extend. As to the First Amendment, petitioners contend that the CTEA is a content-neutral regulation of speech that fails inspection under the heightened judicial scrutiny appropriate for such regulations.

In accord with the District Court and the Court of Appeals, we reject petitioners' challenges to the CTEA. In that 1998 legislation, as in all previous copyright term extensions, Congress placed existing and future copyrights in parity. In prescribing that alignment, we hold, Congress acted within its authority and did not transgress constitutional limitations.

....

We granted certiorari to address two questions: whether the CTEA's extension of existing copyrights exceeds Congress' power under the Copyright Clause; and whether the CTEA's extension of existing and future copyrights violates the First Amendment. We now answer those two questions in the negative and affirm.

II

A

We address first the determination of the courts below that Congress has authority under the Copyright Clause to extend the terms of existing copyrights. Text, history, and precedent, we conclude, confirm that the Copyright Clause empowers Congress to prescribe "limited Times" for copyright protection and to secure the same level and duration of protection for all copyright holders, present and future.

The CTEA's baseline term of life plus 70 years, petitioners concede, qualifies as a "limited Time" as applied to future copyrights. Petitioners contend, however, that existing copyrights extended to endure for that same term are not "limited." Petitioners' argument essentially reads into the text of the Copyright Clause the command that a time prescription, once set, becomes forever "fixed" or "inalterable." The word "limited," however, does not convey a meaning so constricted. At the time of the Framing, that word meant what it means today: "confined within certain bounds," "restrained," or "circumscribed." Thus understood, a time span appropriately "limited" as applied to future copyrights does not automatically cease to be "limited" when applied to existing copyrights. And as we observe, there is no cause to suspect that purpose to evade the "limited Times" prescription prompted Congress to adopt the CTEA.

To comprehend the scope of Congress' power under the Copyright Clause, "a page of history is worth a volume of logic." History reveals an unbroken congressional practice of granting to authors of works with existing copyrights the benefit of term extensions so that all under copyright protection will be governed evenhandedly under the same regime. As earlier recounted, the First Congress accorded the protections of the Nation's first federal copyright statute to existing and future works alike. Since then, Congress has regularly applied duration extensions to both existing and future copyrights.

Congress' consistent historical practice of applying newly enacted copyright terms to future and existing copyrights reflects a judgment stated concisely by Representative Huntington at the time of the 1831 Act: "Justice, policy, and equity alike forbid" that an "author who had sold his [work] a week ago, be placed in a worse situation than the author who should sell his work the day after the passing of [the] act." The CTEA follows this historical practice by keeping the duration provisions of the 1976 Act largely in place and simply adding 20 years to each of them. Guided by text, history, and precedent, we cannot agree with petitioners' submission that extending the duration of existing copyrights is categorically beyond Congress' authority under the Copyright Clause.

Satisfied that the CTEA complies with the "limited Times" prescription, we turn now to whether it is a rational exercise of the legislative authority conferred by the Copyright Clause. On that point, we defer substantially to Congress.

The CTEA reflects judgments of a kind Congress typically makes, judgments we cannot dismiss as outside the Legislature's domain. As respondent describes, a key factor in the CTEA's passage was a 1993 European Union (EU) directive instructing EU members to establish a copyright term of life plus 70 years. Consistent with the Berne Convention, the EU directed its members to deny this longer term to the works of any non-EU country whose laws did not secure the same extended term. By extending the baseline United States copyright term to life plus 70 years, Congress sought to ensure that American authors would receive the same copyright protection in Europe as their European counterparts. The CTEA may also provide greater incentive for American and other authors to create and disseminate their work in the United States.

In addition to international concerns, Congress passed the CTEA in light of demographic, economic, and technological changes, and rationally credited projections that longer terms would encourage copyright holders to invest in the restoration and public distribution of their works.

In sum, we find that the CTEA is a rational enactment; we are not at liberty to second-guess congressional determinations and policy judgments of this order, however debatable or arguably unwise they may be. Accordingly, we cannot conclude that the CTEA — which continues the unbroken congressional practice of treating future and existing copyrights in parity for term extension purposes — is an impermissible exercise of Congress' power under the Copyright Clause.

B

Petitioners' Copyright Clause arguments rely on several novel readings of the Clause. We next address these arguments and explain why we find them unpersuasive.

1

Petitioners contend that even if the CTEA's 20-year term extension is literally a "limited Time," permitting Congress to extend existing copyrights allows it to evade the "limited Times" constraint by creating effectively perpetual copyrights through repeated extensions. We disagree.

As the Court of Appeals observed, a regime of perpetual copyrights "clearly is not the situation before us." Nothing before this Court warrants construction of the CTEA's 20-year term extension as a congressional attempt to evade or override the "limited Times" constraint.[11] Critically, we again emphasize, petitioners fail to show how the CTEA crosses a constitutionally significant threshold with respect to "limited Times" that the 1831, 1909, and 1976 Acts did not. Those earlier Acts did not create perpetual copyrights, and neither does the CTEA.

2

Petitioners dominantly advance a series of arguments all premised on the proposition that Congress may not extend an existing copyright

---

[11] (n16) ... The House and Senate Reports accompanying the CTEA reflect no purpose to make copyright a forever thing. Notably, the Senate Report expressly acknowledged that the Constitution "clearly precludes Congress from granting unlimited protection for copyrighted works," and disclaimed any intent to contravene that prohibition. Members of Congress instrumental in the CTEA's passage spoke to similar effect.

JUSTICE BREYER nevertheless insists that the "economic effect" of the CTEA is to make the copyright term "virtually perpetual." Relying on formulas and assumptions provided in an *amicus* brief supporting petitioners, he stresses that the CTEA creates a copyright term worth 99.8% of the value of a perpetual copyright. If JUSTICE BREYER's calculations were a basis for holding the CTEA unconstitutional, then the 1976 Act would surely fall as well, for — under the same assumptions he indulges — the term set by that Act secures 99.4% of the value of a perpetual term. Indeed, on that analysis even the "limited" character of the 1909 (97.7%) and 1831 (94.1%) Acts might be suspect. JUSTICE BREYER several times places the Founding Fathers on his side. It is doubtful, however, that those architects of our Nation, in framing the "limited Times" prescription, thought in terms of the calculator rather than the calendar.

absent new consideration from the author. They pursue this main theme under three headings. Petitioners contend that the CTEA's extension of existing copyrights (1) overlooks the requirement of "originality," (2) fails to "promote the Progress of Science," and (3) ignores copyright's *quid pro quo.*

Petitioners'"originality" argument draws on *Feist Publications, Inc. v. Rural Telephone Service Co.,* 499 U.S. 340 (1991). In *Feist*, we observed that "the *sine qua non* of copyright is originality," and held that copyright protection is unavailable to "a narrow category of works in which the creative spark is utterly lacking or so trivial as to be virtually nonexistent." Relying on *Feist*, petitioners urge that even if a work is sufficiently "original" to qualify for copyright protection in the first instance, any extension of the copyright's duration is impermissible because, once published, a work is no longer original.

Feist, however, did not touch on the duration of copyright protection. Rather, the decision addressed the core question of copyrightability, *i.e.*, the "creative spark" a work must have to be eligible for copyright protection at all. Explaining the originality requirement, *Feist* trained on the Copyright Clause words "Authors" and "Writings." The decision did not construe the "limited Times" for which a work may be protected, and the originality requirement has no bearing on that prescription.

More forcibly, petitioners contend that the CTEA's extension of existing copyrights does not "promote the Progress of Science" as contemplated by the preambular language of the Copyright Clause. Art. I, § 8, cl. 8. To sustain this objection, petitioners do not argue that the Clause's preamble is an independently enforceable limit on Congress' power. Rather, they maintain that the preambular language identifies the sole end to which Congress may legislate; accordingly, they conclude, the meaning of "limited Times" must be "determined in light of that specified end." The CTEA's extension of existing copyrights categorically fails to "promote the Progress of Science," petitioners argue, because it does not stimulate the creation of new works but merely adds value to works already created.

As petitioners point out, we have described the Copyright Clause as "both a grant of power and a limitation," and have said that "the primary objective of copyright" is "to promote the Progress of Science," The "constitutional command," we have recognized, is that Congress, to the extent it enacts copyright laws at all, create a "system" that "promotes the Progress of Science."

We have also stressed, however, that it is generally for Congress, not the courts, to decide how best to pursue the Copyright Clause's objectives. The justifications we earlier set out for Congress' enactment of the CTEA, provide a rational basis for the conclusion that the CTEA "promotes the Progress of Science."

On the issue of copyright duration, Congress, from the start, has routinely applied new definitions or adjustments of the copyright term to both future works and existing works not yet in the public domain. Such consistent congressional practice is entitled to "very great weight, and when it is remembered that the rights thus established have not been disputed during a period of [over two] centuries, it is almost conclusive." Indeed, "this Court has repeatedly laid down the principle that a contemporaneous legislative exposition of the Constitution when the founders of our Government and framers of our Constitution were actively participating in public affairs, acquiesced in for a long term of years, fixes the construction to be given [the Constitution's] provisions." Congress' unbroken practice since the founding generation thus overwhelms petitioners' argument that the CTEA's extension of existing copyrights fails *per se* to "promote the Progress of Science."

Closely related to petitioners' preambular argument, or a variant of it, is their assertion that the Copyright Clause "imbeds a quid pro quo." They contend, in this regard, that Congress may grant to an "Author" an "exclusive Right" for a "limited Time," but only in exchange for a "Writing." Congress' power to confer copyright protection, petitioners argue, is thus contingent upon an exchange: The author of an original work receives an "exclusive Right" for a "limited Time" in exchange for a dedication to the public thereafter. Extending an existing copyright without demanding additional consideration, petitioners maintain, bestows an unpaid-for benefit on copyright holders and their heirs, in violation of the *quid pro quo* requirement.

We can demur to petitioners' description of the Copyright Clause as a grant of legislative authority empowering Congress "to secure a bargain — this for that." But the legislative evolution earlier recalled demonstrates what the bargain entails. Given the consistent placement of existing copyright holders in parity with future holders, the author of a work created in the last 170 years would reasonably comprehend, as the "this" offered her, a copyright not only for the time in place when protection is gained, but also for any renewal or extension legislated during that time. Congress could rationally seek to "promote ... Progress" by including in every copyright statute an express guarantee that authors would receive the benefit of any later legislative extension of the copyright term. Nothing in the Copyright Clause bars Congress from creating the same incentive by adopting the same position as a matter of unbroken practice.

As an alternative to their various arguments that extending existing copyrights violates the Copyright Clause *per se*, petitioners urge heightened judicial review of such extensions to ensure that they appropriately pursue the purposes of the Clause. Specifically, petitioners ask us to apply the "congruence and proportionality" standard described in cases evaluating exercises of Congress' power under § 5 of the Four-teenth Amendment. But we have never applied that standard outside the § 5 context; it does not hold sway for judicial review of legislation enacted, as copyright laws are, pursuant to Article I authorization.

It would be no more appropriate for us to subject the CTEA to "con-gruence and proportionality" review under the Copyright Clause than it would be for us to hold the Act unconstitutional *per se.*

For the several reasons stated, we find no Copyright Clause impedi-ment to the CTEA's extension of existing copyrights.

III

Petitioners separately argue that the CTEA is a content-neutral reg-ulation of speech that fails heightened judicial review under the First Amendment. We reject petitioners' plea for imposition of uncommonly strict scrutiny on a copyright scheme that incorporates its own speech-protective purposes and safeguards. The Copyright Clause and First Amendment were adopted close in time. This proximity indicates that, in the Framers' view, copyright's limited monopolies are compatible with free speech principles. Indeed, copyright's purpose is to *promote* the creation and publication of free expression. As *Harper & Row [, Inc. v. Nation Enterprises]*, 471 U.S. 539 (1985), observed: "The Framers intended copyright itself to be the engine of free expression. By establishing a marketable right to the use of one's expression, copy-right supplies the economic incentive to create and disseminate ideas."

In addition to spurring the creation and publication of new expres-sion, copyright law contains built-in First Amendment accommoda-tions. First, it distinguishes between ideas and expression and makes only the latter eligible for copyright protection. As we said in *Harper & Row*, this "idea/expression dichotomy strikes a definitional balance between the First Amendment and the Copyright Act by permitting free communication of facts while still protecting an author's expression." Due to this distinction, every idea, theory, and fact in a copyrighted work becomes instantly available for public exploitation at the moment of publication.

Second, the "fair use" defense allows the public to use not only facts and ideas contained in a copyrighted work, but also expression itself in certain circumstances.

. . . .

. . . We recognize that the D.C. Circuit spoke too broadly when it declared copyrights "categorically immune from challenges underthe First Amendment." But when, as in this case, Congress has not altered the traditional contours of copyright protection, further First Amen-dment scrutiny is unnecessary.

IV

As we read the Framers' instruction, the Copyright Clause empowers Congress to determine the intellectual property regimes that, overall, in that body's judgment, will serve the ends of the Clause. Beneath the facade of their inventive constitutional interpretation, petitioners forcefully urge that Congress pursued very bad policy in prescribing the CTEA's long terms. The wisdom of Congress' action, however, is not within our province to second guess. Satisfied that the legislation before us remains inside the domain the Constitution assigns to the First Branch, we affirm the judgment of the Court of Appeals.

It is so ordered.

The majority opinion in *Eldred* was quite clear in its rejection of the challenge to the CTEA. The decision did not really silence the critics, however. Especially among high-tech circles and the many followers of Lawrence Lessig's free content philosophy, this decision is still loudly criticized, albeit on dogmatic rather than legal grounds.

Perhaps the reason the critics of the CTEA were not satisfied with the *Eldred* decision was not just because they lost, but also because the things they were most intense about were not the same issues which were relevant to the Court. Critics, for instance, often find the amounts of money contributed to help pass the CTEA by interested parties such as Disney to be indicative of brutal injustice in the legislative system and proof that Congress will bow to the whims of the content owners at every turn. They also wax poetic about the need for a robust public domain and the greed and bad intent of anyone seeking to profit by enforcing, or seeking to extend the term of, a copyright.[12] Unfortunately for them, none of that was particularly relevant to the legal issues in front of the Supreme Court. The Court did not address these policy arguments except in passing. The compelling issues for the public domain advocates were not so much that the CTEA violates the Constitution, but that it was a bad idea and should not have been passed. Legislative decisions are property left to the legislature, and the more compelling arguments on the free content side are really legislative policy. As Justice Ginsburg made clear, the time and the place for that argument is not the Court, but the Congress. The basic legal issue was whether the CTEA was unconstitutional, and the Court was able to rule easily that it was not. So although the legal issues of *Eldred* are now well settled, the larger issue and the ongoing criticism of the copyright system in general and term extensions in particular is in no way resolved. The battle was lost, but they are still geared up for war.

---

[12] Virtually any of the materials on www.lessig.org or www.eff.org will provide voluminous examples of these arguments.

2. *The Mechanics*

A. *Duration of Copyright*

i. *Duration of Copyright — 1976 Act*

Copyright terms under the 1976 Act are simple. Any work created after January 1, 1978,[13] is covered by the terms of the 1976 Act. Works created before that date are still covered by the old 1909 Act rules; existing copyrights were not transferred from the old system to the new one, but as discussed below, the old rules were amended several times.

Basic Duration: After the Sonny Bono Copyright Extension Act (CTEA), individually authored works will have a copyright lasting 70 years after the death of the Author. In the case of joint authors, the copyright will last 70 years after the death of the last surviving author.

Anonymous Works, Pseudonymous Works and Works Made for Hire. Since none of these works have an identifiable and human author whose life can be used as a measure of the copyright term, the term for these works falls back on the 1909 Act Publication Date standard. Anonymous Works, Pseudonymous Works and Works Made for Hire have a basic term of 95 years from publication or 120 years from creation, whichever is shorter.[14]

Resurrection. One point to keep in mind is that, like term extensions before it, the CTEA does not resurrect any dead copyrights. If a work has fallen into the public domain, it will not be pulled back out and given longer protection.

Of course there is an exception to that rule. Under Section 104A, implemented and amended to conform to varying requirements of a series of treaty and other international obligations, certain works may indeed be pulled out of the public domain and be covered anew by an enforceable U.S. copyright. Prof. Nimmer suggests that the vector of restoration may expand in the future,[15] but for now, with limited exceptions, once a copyright is dead, it is dead for good.[16]

ii. *Duration of Copyright — 1909 Act*

For works created before January 1, 1978, the 1909 Act rules, as amended, still control. The 1909 Act was much more complex than the 1976 Act, so although you need to be familiar with the ins and outs of the 1909 Act, you should remember to be grateful that the majority of

---

[13] The effective date of the 1976 Act.

[14] 17 U.S.C. 302(c).

[15] 3-9A Nimmer on Copyright § 9A.05.

[16] Copyright in this instance can be likened to a fatal disease. A cure discovered the day after you die of the dread disease does not benefit you at all; similarly, an extension of copyright term does not benefit an author whose copyright expired before the extension was granted.

works you will run across in your practice (although not, perhaps, in your exams) will be subject to the 1976 Act's much easier rules.

For 1909 Act works, copyright attached upon publication not creation, so the starting date for a copyright was the date of first publication. What constituted "publication" under the 1909 Act was subject to some uncertainty and much litigation.[17] Not only did copyright term begin with publication, but if a work were published without exact compliance with the formalities required under the 1909 Act, the work would fall into the public domain. As a result, many authors inadvertently lost their copyrights by casually sharing their work in a way that later was deemed to amount to publication.

Instead of a single term like the "life plus 70" term of the 1976 Act, under the 1909 Act, works had two potential copyright terms. Originally, both terms were 28 years, but with the enactment of the 1976 Act and related Congressional acts, the second, or "renewal," term was extended to 47 years, an additional 19 years of copyright. Then in 1998, any 1909 Act works still covered by a valid copyright were granted a second extension. The Sonny Bono Copyright Term Extension Act added 20 years to the already expanded second term.[18] This brought the total years of the 1909 Act second term to 67 years and the total term to 95 years.

The expansion of the terms only applied to the renewal term, and a renewal term would be granted only if the author applied for renewal during the final year of the first term.[19] The second term was a "new estate" in the copyright, which means that any rights transferred away by the author during the first term of the copyright were automatically restored to the author or author's heirs at the beginning of the second term. This was a purely paternalistic measure intended to protect artists and their heirs from the traditional story of the starving artist signing away all rights to a valuable work for a pittance.[20] Another effect of the "new estate" characteristic of the second term was that transferees began including clauses in the contracts which bound the author to retransfer all the rights on the same terms at the beginning of the second

---

[17] *See, e.g, King v. Mister Maestro, Inc.*, 224 F. Supp. 101 (S.D.N.Y. 1963); *Estate of Martin Luther King, Jr., Inc. v. CBS, Inc.*, 194 F.3d 1211 (11th Cir. 1999).

[18] 17 USC 304(b).

[19] Congress amended Section 304 in 1992 to eliminate the requirement that an author file for renewal in order to enjoy protection in a second term. From that point through 2005 (the point where all 1909 Act works were already in a second term), copyrights for 1909 Act works renewed automatically.

[20] Of course, it is difficult to determine how often authors really made such tragically bad deals, but anecdotal evidence abounds. One such story is Maria Von Trapp, the author (and subject) of the Sound of Music. Although she was invited to the Broadway show opening night, she had signed away all rights to a German film maker years earlier, so she did not receive a large share of the tremendous profits generated by her work and the derivative musical and movie. She also lacked the creative control to keep her husband from being portrayed as a harsh uncaring father, but copyright law does not even attempt to provide a protection against a lack of creative control on derivatives. *See generally* Maria Von Trapp, *Maria, My Own Story* (Creation House, 1972), http://www.trappfamily.com/story.

term.[21] Over time, this practice and supportive case law undermined the paternalistic intent of the statute.[22]

The purpose of the two term system may have been to protect the perhaps apocryphal widows and orphans (and the unwary authors themselves) from unwise deals, but the effect of the two term system was that at least 85% of works fell into the public domain after the first term.[23] If an author failed to file for renewal in a timely fashion, the work fell into the public domain after the first term. Although keeping track of the renewal deadline and filing accordingly was arguably not difficult for authors who wrote a couple of novels, keeping track of renewal dates was difficult at best for authors with many smaller works such as poems or photographs. Further complicating the process was the fact that under the 1909 Act, a work's copyright began on the actual date of publication and ended on the exact anniversary, so authors needed to track exact dates, not just years.[24]

In 1992, Congress changed the requirement for renewal filing by enacting the Copyright Renewal Act.[25] Under this new law, all works still in their first copyright term under the 1909 Act (i.e., any work copyrighted in 1964 or later) would automatically renew into their second term without any required filing; however, certain statutory benefits were provided for authors who completed the newly permissive renewal filing, including (a) the right to nullify first term grants of derivative works[26] and (b) prima facie proof of validity of the information in the certificate.[27]

iii.   Duration of Copyright — Gap Works

The 1976 Act applies to works created after January 1, 1978; the 1909 Act applies to works published before that date. This leaves a gap. Works created but not published and not copyrighted before January 1, 1978, do not fall under either set of rules and are referred to as Gap Works. These works are subject to special provisions under Section 303 of the 1976 Act. Under this section, Gap Works were all initially expressly brought within the rules of the 1976 Act and given

---

[21] These contracts were generally drafted by the lawyers of the very transferees against whom the two term system sought to protect the authors. The enforceability of the clauses was in question until *Fred Fisher Music Co. v. M. Witmark & Sons*, 318 U.S. 643 (1943). in which the Supreme Court chose to enforce notions of free alienability rather than statutory protection of artists.

[22] *Miller Music Corp. v. Charles N. Daniels, Inc.*, 362 U.S. 373 (1963); *Fred Fisher Music Co. v. M. Witmark & Sons*, 318 U.S. 643 (1943); *see also* Marshall A. Leaffler, *Understanding Copyright Law* (LexisNexis 2010).

[23] This statistic is commonly used to support two completely different points: 1. Authors didn't care about longer terms (used to argue against extending copyright terms each time it comes up in Congress) 2. The renewal process was so complicated that most authors couldn't successfully navigate it (used to support the 1976 Act single term and the 1992 auto-renewal provision).

[24] Under the 1976 Act, all terms expire on December 31 of the relevant year.

[25] 17 U.S.C. 304(a).

[26] 17 U.S.C. 304(a)(4)(A).

[27] 17 U.S.C. 304(a)(4)(B).

the applicable term thereunder. However, because some of these Gap Works could be quite old and written by a long dead author, they were also given a minimum term of protection of twenty five years. If the work remained unpublished as of January 1, 2003, the copyright expired and the work became public domain. If, however, the work was published before 2003, the term of the copyright was extended to Life of the Author Plus 70 or until December 31, 2047, whichever was later.[28]

Gap Works can be any copyrightable work, but they are generally thought of as diaries and personal letters, often stashed in a romantically old fashioned chest in a dusty attic. No one knows how many of these potential literary treasures exist, but if they remained unpublished, they all fell into the public domain on January 1, 2003.

B. *Termination of Transfers*

Although the 1976 Act abandoned the bifurcated copyright term system of the 1909 Act in favor of the simpler single term, it sought to retain the paternalistic concern of the 1909 Act by preserving a version of the "new estate" aspect of the second term. Section 203 provides authors of 1976 Act works the chance to recapture value they transferred away at a certain point within the single copyright term. The other Termination of Transfers provision in the 1976 Act, Section 304, serves the purpose of allowing authors to recapture rights, but it applies only to 1909 Act works and transfers made before 1978. Rather than protecting the authors against improvident deals, this section makes sure that authors rather than transferees enjoy the benefits of the two extensions to the 1909 Act second term.

i. *Section 203*

Section 203 applies to transfers made after January 1, 1978. It is the basic termination of transfers provision for modern works and is the section intended to replace the concept of the "new estate" in the second term. Unlike the second term new estate, an author must take affirmative action to take advantage of 203 and reclaim the rights that he or she transferred away in the past. There are detailed requirements set forth in the statute on how to effect the recapture of the rights and who may do so, but the basic requirement is that the author send written notice of the intent to terminate the transfer. This notice must comply with the statutory requirements and must be sent between the 35th and 40th year after the transfer that is being terminated. The timing is important and rather unusual. The window to make the termination is based not on the copyright or publication, but is counted from the date the rights were transferred. If the right that was transferred is the right of publication, then rather than the window beginning 35 years after

---

[28] 17 U.S.C. 303(a).

the grant, it will be the earlier of 35 years after publication or 40 years after the grant.[29]

Congress learned from the perceived failure of the 1909 Act to protect against contractual end runs around the intended protections for authors, and Section 203 expressly provides that no agreement to the contrary will remove or restrict the author's right to a Section 203 termination of transfer.[30]

ii.   Section 304

Section 304 is different in effect and intent than Section 203. Section 304 applies to 1909 Act works and transfers made before 1978. Rather than a replacement for the second term new estate, this section redistributes the benefits of the windfalls to 1909 Act rights holders granted by the initial extension of the second term by the 1976 Act and the second extension granted by the CTEA. If a 1909 Act author transferred away second term rights prior to 1978, he or she did so under the expectation that the second term would be shorter than it ultimately turned out to be. The original text of the 1976 Act added a "windfall" of 19 years to all 1909 Act works still covered by copyright as of January 1, 1978. The CTEA then added another twenty years to those works still under valid copyright in 1998. As a result, if an author still held the rights to the work, the author benefitted from the extension, as Congress intended. If, however, the author had already transferred away some or all of the rights, then the transferee would be the beneficiary of these windfall years and would enjoy the extension of rights without having paid anything more to the author. To avoid such a transferee from in effect getting more value than he or she had paid for, Section 304 allows an author to reclaim any transferred rights during these windfall years.

As with Section 203, the process of how to terminate the transfer of rights and who may do so is complex. In this case, along with specific requirements for the written notice of intent to terminate, the author must give this written notice within one of two windows. If the author recaptured the transferred rights in the first window of opportunity, the author may not do so again in the second window. The windfall is preserved for the author, but it is preserved only once, even though there were two separate extensions and two separate sets of windfall years.

The first window in which an author can make a section 304 termination is a five year period beginning at the later of (a) 56 years after the date of the copyright or (b) January 1, 1978.[31] This allows the author to recapture the windfall years given by the 19 year extension from the 1976 Act.

---

[29] 17 U.S.C. 203(a)(3).
[30] 17 U.S.C. 203(a)(5) ("Termination of the grant may be effected notwithstanding any agreement to the contrary, including an agreement to make a will or to make any future grant.").
[31] 17 U.S.C. 304(c)(3).

If the author does not file at that point, he or she has a second opportunity to terminate any pre-1978 transfers and capture the windfall from the CTEA 20 year extension. This second window of opportunity is a five year period beginning at the end of the extended second term, *i.e.,* 75 years after the date of the copyright.[32] An author may take advantage of one, but not both windows. Termination under Section 304 can only be effected once.

iii. *Derivative Works and Termination of Transfers*

Under both Acts, the issue of termination of transfers is more complicated when derivative works are involved. It is rather simple to put an end to permission to copy or perform a work, but if the author can end the grant of the right to make a derivative work, then the derivative works created under that grant might also need to be abandoned because they are now infringing works.

Under the 1909 Act, there was uncertainty as to how to decide this issue. The situation often arose in this fashion: an author grants the right to make a screenplay out of her novel during the first term of its copyright and then dies before the second term. Although the contract drafted by the movie studio clearly required the author to reassign these rights in the second term, the contract was not binding on the author's heir who was not a party to the original contract and now chooses not to reassign the rights in the renewal term. The movie is instantly transformed into an infringing work and cannot be distributed or shown in any fashion, thus causing the movie studio much financial woe. Whether such a forfeiture would result in all cases remained unclear until the 1990 Supreme Court decision of *Stewart v. Abend*,[33] which resolved a split amongst the circuits[34] by holding that, indeed, the derivative rights holder could not exploit the derivative work although it had been created under a valid grant. Faced with the possibility of having to renegotiate with an unknown and potentially difficult or greedy party in the future just to be able to continue to distribute a lawfully created derivative movie or musical or other such commercially significant work, movie studios and other common derivative creators would rationally avoid any 1909 Act work still in its first term. This likely had the effect of significantly decreasing the commercial value of many works, potentially harming author and heir alike.

The 1976 Act approached the issue differently. Sections 203(b)(1) and 304(c)(6)(A) provide that a derivative work prepared under a valid

---

[32]   17 U.S.C. 304(d)(2).
[33]   495 U.S. 207 (1990).
[34]   *See* 1-3 Nimmer on Copyright § 3.07.

grant may continue to be exploited by the grantee even after any termination of the grant, but upon such termination, no new derivatives may be prepared by that grantee without new permission. This removed the uncertainty which controlled the 1909 Act works with respect to this issue and avoided any chilling effect on the derivative market which followed the *Stewart v. Abend* approach.

3. ***Summary of the 1909 Act Rules:***

- *Beginning of Copyright:* Date of Publication

- *First term:* 28 years. Filing for second term must be done in the last year of the first term — failure to timely file for renewal results in the copyright ending at the end of the first term, unless the first term ended after 1992 when the Automatic Renewal provisions came into effect.

- *Second Term:* Originally a symmetric 28 years. The 1976 Act added 19 years and extended the second term to 47 years effective 1/1/78. The CTEA (1998) added another 20 years and extended the second term to its current length of 67 years. None of these extensions revived dead copyrights — extensions apply ONLY to works under valid copyright when the extension is granted.

- *Termination of Transfers:* Section 304. Pre-1978 transfers only. An 1909 Act author may terminate the transfer of rights once — either during the five year period beginning 56 years after the date of the copyright or during the five year period beginning 76 years after the date of the copyright. These two windows relate to the two term extensions granted to subsisting 1909 Act copyrights.

4. ***Summary of the 1976 Act Rules:***

- *Beginning of Copyright:* Date of fixation in a tangible media.

- *Term:* One term — extends 70 years after the death of the Author. Originally the term was Life of the Author Plus 50 years until it was extended by the CTEA to the current duration of Life of the Author Plus 70.

- *Termination of Transfers.* Section 203. This section provides 1976 Act authors with an equivalent to the 1909 Act "new estate" in the second term. A 1976 Act author may terminate any transfers of rights during the five year period beginning 35 years after the date of the transfer grant.

5. *Important Dates:*

January 1, 1978. Effective date of 1976 Act

October 27, 1998. Effective date of CTEA.

December 31, 2002. Gap Works (works created but not published or copyrighted before 1978) which are not published by this date fall into the public domain.

2013. First year in which Section 203 Terminations will occur (35 years after grants made in 1978).

December 31, 2047. Gap Works published by 12/31/02 enjoy a copyright of Life of the Author Plus 70 or extending until December 31 2047, whichever is longer.

EXERCISE

TOPIC: Copyright

    i.   Term

    ii. Termination of Transfers

SKILLS:

    i.   Application of statutory rules

ESTIMATED TIME FOR COMPLETING THIS EXERCISE:

Approximately one hour.

ESTIMATED LEVEL OF DIFFICULTY (1–5): 3—Straightforward.

This exercise is in the on-line materials — it is a self guided quiz covering elements of duration and termination of transfers. You may want to have the code on hand to help you through the quiz, or if you are using it as an exam prep, try it completely closed book.

The answers are available on-line, as well, and are incorporated into the quiz rather than presented in the Student Self Assessment Tool with the other chapters.

Chapter 4

MY SWEET LORD — COPYRIGHT INFRINGEMENT

OVERVIEW: INFRINGEMENT

1. Elements of Infringement

An analysis of copyright infringement starts with Section 106 of the 76 Act.[1] Section 106 lists the exclusive rights which are granted to the owner of a copyright. Normally infringement cases focus on 106(1) — the right to copy, but infringement actions will lie for a violation of any of the exclusive rights:

Sec. 106 Exclusive Rights in Copyrighted Works

Subject to sections 107 through 122, the owner of copyright under this title has the exclusive rights to do and to authorize any of the following:

(1) to reproduce the copyrighted work in copies or phonorecords;

(2) to prepare derivative works based upon the copyrighted work;

(3) to distribute copies or phonorecords of the copyrighted work to the public by sale or other transfer of ownership, or by rental, lease, or lending;

(4) in the case of literary, musical, dramatic, and choreographic works, pantomimes, and motion pictures and other audiovisual works, to perform the copyrighted work publicly;

(5) in the case of literary, musical, dramatic, and choreographic works, pantomimes, and pictorial, graphic, or sculptural works, including the individual images of a motion picture or other audiovisual work, to display the copyrighted work publicly; and

(6) in the case of sound recordings, to perform the copyrighted work publicly by means of a digital audio transmission.

With respect to infringement of the reproduction right, there is very seldom direct evidence of wholesale, verbatim copying, so a wealth of case law has developed to help judges determine the boundaries of the right.

---

[1]   17 U.S.C. 106.

On a basic level there are three elements to an infringement[2] case.

1.   Valid copyright owned by the plaintiff;

2.   Copying of the work by defendant;

3.   The copying amounts to improper appropriation.

The first element is an absolute requirement for any infringement action, but it is generally a fairly straightforward matter of proof. It is also another reason that it is best practice to always complete a copyright registration for works even though it is no longer technically required under the Act.

The second element, copying, is where the deeper analysis begins and where the terminology can become confusing. Different courts sometimes use a contradictory mishmash of terms like substantial similarity, striking similarity, probative similarity and copying to refer to an array of related concepts. Courts will sometimes refer to both levels of copying as substantial similarity. More correctly, and more clearly, the first level is probative similarity. The second level is substantial similarity. What follows is a (mostly) straightforward approach to analyzing the second and third elements of infringement, but it is not the only way to do so. It can be a useful framework to utilize, but a smart lawyer will always tailor his or her argument to match the judge or jurisdiction, much like a smart law student will tailor an exam answer to match the professor's analytical preference.

A. Copying — Probative Similarity

This prong of infringement is focused purely on whether copying occurred. It does not yet take into account whether too much was taken, or whether what was taken was protected or public domain material. This is purely an attempt to decide if the alleged infringer did indeed copy the author's work. Rarely will there be a reliable witness who is able to say "Yes, I saw the defendant copying straight out of plaintiff's book into his own." Accordingly, courts look to indirect or circumstantial evidence to determine whether copying occurred.

Judge Frank sets out the elements of proof of copying as either, (a) admission or (b) access plus similarity.[3] Unlike Patent protection, copyright only protects against copying; if a subsequent author creates even an identical work independently, there is no infringement. Therefore it follows, that if there were no way that the alleged infringer could have been exposed to the first work, then there could not have been copying. On the other hand, as long as there is no evidence that the defendant could not possibly have seen plaintiff's work, most courts will hold copying has occurred at the probative similarity level without

---

[2]   Although as mentioned above, "infringement" refers to a violation of any of the 106 exclusive rights, this section is focusing exclusively on the reproduction right.

[3]   *Arnstein v. Porter*, 154 F.2d 464 (2d Cir. 1946), *cert denied,* 330 U.S. 851 (1947).

evidence of access if the similarities are "so striking as to preclude the possibility that plaintiff and defendant independently arrived at the same result."[4] Also, at this first level of analysis, it is appropriate to engage in detailed dissection of the works and to admit expert testimony as to the similarity.[5] This is where to really dig into the details of the works and figure out if the works are similar enough that copying can be inferred.

B. Illicit Copying — Substantial Similarity

At the second level, the court will look to whether the copying was illicit. Now the target is the lay audience, and Judge Frank suggests that experts have no place at this level. Of course as litigation has expanded over the years, experts have found their way into this layer as well under the guise of helping the lay hearer understand what is being heard.[6]

In determining substantial similarity, the analysis focuses both on what was taken and on whether too much was taken. Is the similar material in the second work taken from protected elements of the first? Or are the similarities grounded in public domain sources from which both works drew and which the second work may freely appropriate?

Judge Hand presents an "abstractions test" to help distinguish wheat from chaff at this level:

> Upon any work, and especially upon a play, a great number of patterns of increasing generality will fit equally well, as more and more of the incident is left out. The last may perhaps be no more than the most general statement of what the play is about, and at times might consist only of its title; but there is a point in this series of abstractions where they are no longer protected, since otherwise the playwright could prevent the use of his "ideas," to which, apart from their expression, his property is never extended. Nobody has ever been able to fix that boundary, and nobody ever can.[7]

In theory, under this test, by contemplating the level of abstraction, one is better able to distinguish between idea and expression, and one will also be able to determine how much is too much for the defendant to have taken from the original work.

---

[4] *Id.*

[5] *Id.*

[6] Judge Learned Hand also takes a dim view of the over-use of experts in infringement cases, which was apparent even in his day: "We cannot approve the length of the record, which was due chiefly to the use of expert witnesses. Argument is argument whether in the box or at the bar, and its proper place is the last. The testimony of an expert upon such issues, especially his cross-examination, greatly extends the trial and contributes nothing which cannot be better heard after the evidence is all submitted." *Nichols v. Universal Pictures Corp.*, 45 F.2d 119, 123 (2d Cir. 1930).

[7] *Id.* at 121 (citations omitted).

The *Altai* court suggests a "filtration test" to add to Judge Hand's Abstraction test as an analysis for substantial similarity of software.[8] The Filtration approach has since been applied beyond software.

> Once the program's abstraction levels have been discovered, the substantial similarity inquiry moves from the conceptual to the concrete. Professor Nimmer suggests, and we endorse, a "successive filtering method" for separating protectable expression from non-protectable material. *See generally* 3 Nimmer § 13.03[F]. This process entails examining the structural components at each level of abstraction to determine whether their particular inclusion at that level was "idea" or was dictated by considerations of efficiency, so as to be necessarily incidental to that idea; required by factors external to the program itself; or taken from the public domain and hence is nonprotectable expression. *See also* Kretschmer, at 844–45 (arguing that program features dictated by market externalities or efficiency concerns are unprotectable). The structure of any given program may reflect some, all, or none of these considerations. Each case requires its own fact specific investigation.

> Strictly speaking, this filtration serves "the purpose of defining the scope of plaintiff's copyright."[9]

After analyzing the level of abstraction, one filters out all non-protected elements, including both those that are drawn from the public domain and those that are more properly part of the idea than the expression of the work. Such elements include, for instance, facts, ideas, "scenes a faire" and in the case of computer programs, any elements which are included out of efficiency. The final step in the *Altai* approach is comparing the remaining protected bits of each work for similarity.

There is a quantitative element as well. How much is too much? When Vanilla Ice "forgot" to credit Queen and David Bowie in his blatant sample of their song "Under Pressure" in his own "Ice Ice Baby," although it was only seven or eight notes, it seems clear that the repeating motif and distinctive sound would easily clear both levels of copying inquiry. Including a poster of a copyrighted quilt in the background of a television set could be infringement and not excusable as *de minimus* in spite of the fact that the poster was visible for less than two minutes during the program.[10]

Do concepts like filtration and abstraction really help make a determination of whether the copying was indeed illicit? Perhaps they provide a mental framework for discerning if what was taken was indeed "too much," but it seems that the esoteric thought processes expressed by the judges leaves the lines still ill-defined. Some thirty years after his

[8] *Computer Assocs. Int'l v. Altai*, 982 F.2d 693, 707 (2d Cir 1992).
[9] *Id.*
[10] *Ringgold v. Black Entertainment Television, Inc.*, 126 F.3d. 70 (2d Cir. 1997).

description of the "Abstractions Test," Judge Hand famously wrote that, "The test for infringement of a copyright is of necessity vague.... Decisions must therefore inevitably be ad hoc."[11] If Judge Learned Hand, one of the most respected legal minds in the history of American Jurisprudence, finds the tests slippery, it is hard to imagine mere mortals will fare much better.

On a doctrinal level, it is easy to express the three requirements: existence of a valid copyright, proof of copying or probative similarity and illicit copying or substantial similarity. Although often expressed imprecisely, the distinction between the two levels of copying is fairly clear as well. First one determines if there was any copying. Then one decides if what was taken was too much. Applying those concepts to two actual works, however, becomes murkier. Perhaps in this area, a persuasive and creative litigator can often tip the scales.

2. Independent Creation

The probative similarity analysis of infringement touches on the concept of independent creation. Independent creation is a straightforward notion and is grounded in the very basis of copyright protection. Copyright law in the United States is not based on a natural law theory. Although the area of law is called Intellectual Property, natural law notions of property are not relevant to copyright. The Constitution provides the basis for copyright law in the United States and authorizes Congress "To promote the Progress of Science and the useful Arts, by securing for limited Times, to Authors and Inventors, the exclusive Right to their respective Writings and Discoveries."[12] Copyright law, therefore, exists only to encourage creation by awarding a monopoly to an author for a limited period of time. Only the rights conveyed by Congress are enjoyed by authors; the law does not recognize a natural law "ownership" of the fruits of one's efforts in the realm of copyright.

---

[11] *Peter Pan Fabrics, Inc. v. Martin Weiner Corp.*, 274 F.2d 487, 489 (2d Cir. 1960). The rest of this often quoted passage reads as follows:

> The test for infringement of a copyright is of necessity vague. In the case of verbal "works" it is well settled that although the "proprietor's" monopoly extends beyond an exact reproduction of the words, there can be no copyright in the 'ideas' disclosed but only in their "expression." Obviously, no principle can be stated as to when an imitator has gone beyond copying the "idea," and has borrowed its "expression." Decisions must therefore inevitably be ad hoc. In the case of designs, which are addressed to the aesthetic sensibilities of an observer, the test is, if possible, even more intangible. No one disputes that the copyright extends beyond a photographic reproduction of the design, but one cannot say how far an imitator must depart from an undeviating reproduction to escape infringement. In deciding that question one should consider the uses for which the design is intended, especially the scrutiny that observers will give to it as used. In the case at bar we must try to estimate how far its overall appearance will determine its aesthetic appeal when the cloth is made into a garment. Both designs have the same general color, and the arches, scrolls, rows of symbols, etc. on one resemble those on the other though they are not identical. Moreover, the patterns in which these figures are distributed to make up the design as a whole are not identical. However, the ordinary observer, unless he set out to detect the disparities, would be disposed to overlook them, and regard their aesthetic appeal as the same. That is enough; and indeed it is all that can be said, unless protection against infringement is to be denied because of variants irrelevant to the purpose for which the design is intended.

[12] U.S. Constitution, Article I, Section 8, Clause 8.

The exclusive rights granted in Section 106, therefore, define the scope of an author's rights, and nothing in Section 106 prevents an individual from creating and exploiting his or her own work, so long as the creation lies solely with that individual. Suppose some unfortunate soul, shipwrecked alone on a deserted isle for decades had passed the time writing music to lighten the weight of isolation. Upon his return to civilization after an appropriately dramatic rescue, he may find that not only do record companies no longer exist in the form he remembers, but that they are not interested in any of his most catchy compositions: "The Macarena," "Living La Vida Loca," "Who Let the Dogs Out" and "I Love You, You Love Me (the Barney Song)." With his obvious musical talent, he will likely find both success and a comfortable livelihood writing jingles that lodge permanently in the mind of unsuspecting listeners, and he can be content with the knowledge that his island compositions in no way infringe any existing copyrights. Patent law grants the inventor the right to foreclose anyone from using her invention, regardless of whether the infringer copies her invention or discovers it independently. Copyright law, under the terms of the Constitution and the 1976 Act, does not reach that far.

EXERCISE

TOPIC: Copyright

    i.   Infringement

    ii. Independent Creation

    iii. Subconscious Infringement

SKILLS:

    i.   Drafting

    ii. Critical Reasoning

    iii. Analysis

ESTIMATED TIME FOR COMPLETING THIS EXERCISE:

Approximately three hours.

ESTIMATED LEVEL OF DIFFICULTY (1-5): 3—Creative/ Moderate.

Congratulations! You have just been appointed to the 2d Circuit Court of Appeals! Being a Circuit Court Judge is an unattainable dream for many aspiring jurists, and you have made it!

The first case before you is an appeal from an infringement case. *Bright Tunes Music Corp. v. Harrisongs Music, Ltd.,* 420 F. Supp. 177 (S.D.N.Y. 1976), was a rather infamous case in which former Beatle and respected musician George Harrison was found to have subconsciously infringed the Chiffons' bubble gum pop hit "He's So Fine." You haven't had time to hire your clerks yet, so it looks like you will be researching, deciding and drafting all on your own for this one.

After the initial decision, a remarkable number of appeals developed, focusing mainly on a rather ugly dispute over who all got to get a share of the damages award. The long and winding trial of *Bright Tunes v. Harrisongs* seemed to have come to an end in 1991, with *ABKCO Music, Inc. v. Harrisongs Music, Ltd.,* 944 F.2d 971 (2d Cir. 1991). Recently, however, an intrepid young litigator hired by the estate of George Harrison has found unanticipated grounds for appeal from the original district court holding. You will want to skim briefly over the intervening opinions just to get a feel for how tortured the full record truly is, but the matter before you is the original question of copyright infringement.

You will, of course want to review the original District Court holding closely, since it is the one on appeal before you. As you read and consider your opinion, think about the impact your holding will have on the doctrine of independent creation. Are you willing to gut it by replacing it with the notion of "subconscious infringement" — even in the face of direct evidence of independent creation?[13] After the District Court opinion, can there be independent creation if the first work is famous? Is that a good policy choice?

Do you rely more on experts or on your own ears? Do the songs really sound alike? Does it make a difference that George Harrison went on to have a successful career as a respected musician in his own right — not just as one of the Beatles?

Additional materials and links can be found on the LexisNexis webcourse.

You will want to review the two songs of course. You can find them here:

http://cip.law.ucla.edu/cases/case_brightharrisongs.html

It seems a bit beneath a Judge's dignity to stoop to Wikipedia, but this case probably happened before your time, and you would like to familiarize yourself with some of the issues surrounding the musicians, so you may want to peek at: http://en.wikipedia.org/wiki/My_Sweet_Lord and http://en.wikipedia.org/wiki/He%27s_So_Fine But please, never cite Wikipedia. It's like the World Book Encyclopedia loved and cited for decades by elementary school children, but without the editorial staff. It's fine for what it is — but not for dedicated legal research.

You may also find these clips interesting or helpful

http://www.youtube.com/watch?v=azAk9rCJ7fg&feature=related

http://www.youtube.com/watch?v=bsUkACDSIZY&feature=related

http://www.youtube.com/watch?v=CmyoQSoKWRs&feature=related

Draft an opinion for the court affirming or reversing the original district court holding on infringement. Once you have completed the opinion, review the Self-Assessment materials on the LexisNexis webcourse.

---

[13] Billy Preston, who was with George Harrison and helped him compose *My Sweet Lord*, was a very well-respected musician and gave direct testimony about sitting with Mr. Harrison as the two of them developed the ultimately fateful riffs.

Chapter 5

TRASH, TREASURE AND TACKY — USEFUL ITEMS AND COPYRIGHT

OVERVIEW: PICTORIAL, GRAPHIC AND SCULPTURAL WORKS

In any copyright analysis, the first inquiry is whether the work at issue falls within the statutory subject matter of copyright. Often this is an easy question, but as any law student would expect, there are some grey areas. One of these is the issue of whether a useful article will be deemed within the subject matter of copyright or whether it will be excluded. Copyright is not intended to cover functional aspects of works. The Act expressly excludes a fairly comprehensive list of "practical" things: "idea, procedure, process, system, method of operation, concept, principle or discovery."[1] On a very basic level, this can be summed up as follows: practical and science stuff is patentable; pretty and artsy stuff is copyrightable. But what happens when your practical stuff is also pretty? Patents take a very long time, have very high standards and can be prohibitively expensive. Copyright is sometimes much more attractive than patent to inventors on a practical level due to the procedural burden of the patent process, even though the protection offered by patent is so much more comprehensive. As suggested by the exclusion of the practical and "idea, procedure ..." list, copyright protects only expression. It does not protect an underlying idea, and it does not protect "science-y" practical and functional things. To determine whether something tainted with a useful purpose will qualify for copyright coverage, the first step is looking to the statutorily defined boundaries.

Section 102 of the 1976 Act tells us that "pictorial, graphic, and sculptural works" are among the categories of expressly copyrightable works. Section 101 defines those terms as follows:

> "Pictorial, graphic, and sculptural works" include two-dimensional and three-dimensional works of fine, graphic, and applied art, photographs, prints and art reproductions, maps, globes, charts, diagrams, models, and technical drawings, including architectural plans. Such works shall include works of artistic craftsmanship insofar as their form but not their mechanical or utilitarian aspects are concerned; the design of a useful article, as defined in this section, shall be considered a pictorial, graphic, or sculptural work only if, and only to the extent that, such design incorporates pictorial,

---

[1] 17 U.S.C. 102(b).

graphic, or sculptural features that can be identified separately from, and are capable of existing independently of, the utilitarian aspects of the article.

....

A "useful article" is an article having an intrinsic utilitarian function that is not merely to portray the appearance of the article or to convey information. An article that is normally a part of a useful article is considered a "useful article".[2]

So although a useful article, like a chair or a lamp, is potentially copyrightable, protection will only extend to the non-utilitarian elements of the article. The determination hinges on whether the useful article is just a nice looking practical item or really a piece of art. In order to be deemed to be copyrightable, as set forth in the code section quoted above, the work must have artistic or aesthetic elements that exist independently or can be separated from the utilitarian function. This is expressed as the concept of separability and originated under the 1909 Act, so some of the older cases are still relevant and helpful in trying to figure out how to delineate between form and function.

When the overall form of a useful item is generally aesthetically pleasing rather than having specific elements of artistic appeal, even if the item was specifically designed for that pleasing impact rather than just for the practical or efficient considerations, the article will generally not be protected.[3] In *Esquire, Inc. v. Ringer*, copyright protection was not extended to a street light even though its design was artistic and visually pleasing.[4] Overall design is not separable from the basic form, so a pretty street lamp is apparently just a street lamp and not protectable under copyright law.

Mazer v. Stein[5] is the classic case of utility and separability. The case addressed the copyrightability of a table lamp with a base in the shape of a Balinese dancer. The Court found that the dancer part of the lamp was "separable" and therefore protectable, but the issue of separability was far from settled. In the following years, many related tests, but no real consensus, developed. Prof. Nimmer offers a very detailed analysis of the development and varying approaches to this issue[6] that a thorough lawyer will have in his or her arsenal when arguing a utility issue.

The basic concept is still separability, and arguably the most straightforward version is *physical separability*. If the item is such that

---

[2]   17 U.S.C. 101.
[3]   *See Esquire, Inc. v. Ringer,* 591 F.2d 796 (D.C. Cir. 1978).
[4]   *Id.*
[5]   347 U.S. 201 (1954).
[6]   1 – 2 NIMMER ON COPYRIGHT § 2.08[B][3] Works of Applied Art (2010). Another excellent treatment of this topic is Robert C. Denicola, *Applied Art and Industrial Design: A Suggested Approach to Copyright in Useful Articles,* 67 MINN. L. REV. 707 (April 1983).

the artistic or aesthetic element can be physically separated from the utilitarian aspects of the item, then it will be copyrightable. The classic example from Prof. Nimmer is the iconic hood ornament on a Jaguar sports car.[7] The little statuette of a wild cat is easily separated from the car — as many Jag owners have learned much to their chagrin. Of course judges do not actually come at potentially copyrightable works with saws and chisels; even physical separability is a mental exercise.

The next approach is *conceptual separability*. Conceptual separability makes sense as an alternative to pure physical separability; even if the aesthetic elements cannot be neatly broken off like the metal feline off the hood of a car,[8] there needs to be a more flexible test to extend coverage to artistic items in spite of a practical purpose. Under Conceptual Separability, if the reviewer can intellectually delineate between the aesthetic and function elements, then these parts will be protectable.[9] In *Kieselstein-Cord v. Accessories By Pearl*,[10] the court found that the highly ornamented surface of a belt buckle was conceptually separable, because the decoration was unrelated to the function and the belt buckle would function perfectly well were it altogether plain. This case also added an extra justification which has been adopted by other courts when it noted that the ornamental impact of the buckles was reinforced by the fact that people had been wearing the buckles as jewelry, not just around their waists. If the item would be marketable as a purely aesthetic item, without regard to its function, then its aesthetic features would be deemed conceptually separable and the article would be protectable.[11]

Another approach, suggested by Judge Newman in the dissent in *Carol Barnhardt, Inc. v. Economy Cover Corp.*,[12] is the "temporal displacement" test:

> A chair may be so artistically designed as to merit display in a museum, but that fact alone cannot satisfy the test of "conceptual separateness." The viewer in the museum sees and apprehends a well-designed chair, not a work of art with a design that is conceptually separate from the functional purposes of an object on which people sit.
>
> How, then, is "conceptual separateness" to be determined? In my view, the answer derives from the word "conceptual." For the design features to be "conceptually separate" from the utilitarian aspects of the useful

---

[7] 1 – 2 Nimmer on Copyright § 2.08[B][3] Works of Applied Art (2010).

[8] *Id.*

[9] Note, however, that even when the aesthetic elements are protectable, copyright will not extend to the functional parts of the article.

[10] 632 F.2d 989 (2d Cir. 1980).

[11] *Id. See also Poe v. Missing Persons*, 745 F.2d 1238 (9th Cir. 1984).

[12] 773 F.2d 411 (2d Cir. 1985).

article that embodies the design, the article must stimulate in the mind of the beholder a concept that is separate from the concept evoked by its utilitarian function.
The test turns on what may reasonably be understood to
be occurring in the mind of the beholder or, as some
might say, in the "mind's eye" of the beholder. ... I think
the requisite "separateness" exists whenever the design
creates in the mind of the ordinary observer two different concepts that are not inevitably entertained simultaneously. Again, the example of the artistically designed
chair displayed in a museum may be helpful. The ordinary observer can be expected to apprehend the design
of a chair whenever the object is viewed. He may, in
addition, entertain the concept of a work of art, but, if
this second concept is engendered in the observer's mind
simultaneously with the concept of the article's utilitarian function, the requisite "separateness" does not exist.
The test is not whether the observer fails to recognize
the object as a chair but only whether the concept of the
utilitarian function can be displaced in the mind by some
other concept. That does not occur, at least for the ordinary observer, when viewing even the most artistically
designed chair. It may occur, however, when viewing
some other object if the utilitarian function of the object
is not perceived at all; it may also occur, even when the
utilitarian function is perceived by observation, perhaps
aided by explanation, if the concept of the utilitarian
function can be displaced in the observer's mind while
he entertains the separate concept of some non-
utilitarian function. The separate concept will normally
be that of a work of art.[13]

Judge Newman makes a valiant attempt to describe a meaningful way
of separating form from function. It is still not a bright line test; it is
subjective at best, but it does provide an expansion on the basic separability language. So if the ordinary observer would see art rather than a
belt buckle, bike rack or bread box, then copyright would apply under
the temporal displacement test. If, on the other hand, the same observer
would merely think "Oh! Pretty Chair!" then it is just a place to sit and
is not deserving of copyright.

    None of these options is a magic bullet solution to a useful item
determination, but some combination or selection of the more dominant approaches will support a reasoned determination in the face of
any factual circumstance.

---

[13] *Id.* at 422–23.

EXERCISE

TOPIC: Copyright

    i.   Useful Items

    ii.   Copyrightability – Subject Matter of Copyright

SKILLS:

    i.   Critical Reasoning

    ii.   Analysis

ESTIMATED TIME FOR COMPLETING THIS EXERCISE:

Approximately one hour.

ESTIMATED LEVEL OF DIFFICULTY (1-5): 1—Straightforward.

This is an on-line exercise. In the on-line materials, you will find a series of images of various useful articles. Your job is to analyze each article and determine not only whether it is copyrightable, but how you will support your decision.

When you have completed your analysis, review the Self-Assessment.

- The relatedness of the goods or services as described in an application or registration or in connection with which a prior mark is in use.
- The similarity or dissimilarity of established, likely-to-continue trade channels.
- The conditions under which and buyers to whom sales are made, i.e., "impulse" vs. careful, sophisticated purchasing.
- The number and nature of similar marks in use on similar goods.
- A valid consent agreement between the applicant and the owner of the previously registered mark.

The Court of Appeals for the Federal Circuit has provided the following guidance with regard to determining and articulating likelihood of confusion:

> The basic principle in determining confusion between marks is that marks must be compared in their entireties and must be considered in connection with the particular goods or services for which they are used (citations omitted). It follows from that principle that likelihood of confusion cannot be predicated on dissection of a mark, that is, on only part of a mark (footnote omitted). On the other hand, in articulating reasons for reaching a conclusion on the issue of confusion, there is nothing improper in stating that, for rational reasons, more or less weight has been given to a particular feature of a mark, provided the ultimate conclusion rests on consideration of the marks in their entireties (footnote omitted). Indeed, this type of analysis appears to be unavoidable.

In re National Data Corp., 753 F.2d 1056, 1058, 224 USPQ 749, 750–51 (Fed. Cir. 1985).

There is no mechanical test for determining likelihood of confusion. The issue is not whether the actual goods are likely to be confused but, rather, whether there is a likelihood of confusion as to the *source* of the goods. *In re Shell Oil Co.*, 992 F.2d 1204, 1208, 26 USPQ2d 1687, 1690 (Fed. Cir. 1993), and cases cited therein. Each case must be decided on its own facts.

The determination of likelihood of confusion under § 2(d) in an intent-to-use application under § 1(b) of the Trademark Act does not differ from the determination in any other type of application.

1207.01(a) Relatedness of the Goods or Services

If the marks of the respective parties are identical, the relationship between the goods or services need not be as close to support a finding of likelihood of confusion as would be required in a case where there are differences between the marks. *Amcor, Inc. v. Amcor Industries, Inc.*, 210 USPQ 70, 78 (TTAB 1981).

In some instances, because of established marketing practices, the use of identical marks on seemingly unrelated goods and services could result in a likelihood of confusion. *See In re Phillips-Van Heusen Corp.*, 228 USPQ 949, 951 (TTAB 1986) ("The licensing of commercial trademarks for use on 'collateral' products (such as clothing, glassware, linens, etc.), that are unrelated in nature to those goods or services on which the marks are normally used, has become a common practice in recent years.")

1207.01(a)(i) Goods or Services Need Not Be Identical

The goods or services do not have to be identical or even competitive in order to determine that there is a likelihood of confusion. The inquiry is whether the goods are related, not identical. The issue is not whether the goods will be confused with each other, but rather whether the public will be confused about their source. (citation omitted)

1207.01(a)(ii) Goods May Be Related to Services

It is well recognized that confusion is likely to occur from the use of the same or similar marks for goods, on the one hand, and for services involving those goods, on the other. (citation omitted)

. . . .

1207.01(a)(iii) Reliance on Identification of Goods/Services in Registration and Application

The nature and scope of a party's goods or services must be determined on the basis of the goods or services recited in the application or registration. (citation omitted)

If the cited registration describes goods or services broadly, and there is no limitation as to the nature, type, channels of trade, or class of purchasers, it is presumed that the registration encompasses all goods or services of the type described, that they move in all normal channels of trade, and that they are available to all classes of purchasers.

. . . .

1207.01(a)(iv) No "Per Se" Rule

The facts in each case vary and the weight to be given each factor may be different in light of the varying circumstances; therefore, there can be no rule that certain goods or services are *per se* related, such that there must be a likelihood of confusion from the use of similar marks in relation thereto. (citation omitted)

1207.01(a)(v) Expansion of Trade Doctrine

The examining attorney must consider any goods or services in the registrant's normal fields of expansion to determine whether the registrant's goods or services are related to the applicant's identified goods or services under § 2(d). *In re General Motors Corp.*, 196 USPQ 574 (TTAB 1977). A trademark owner is entitled to protection against the registration of a similar mark on products that might reasonably be expected to be produced by him in the normal expansion of his business. The test is whether purchasers would believe the product or service is within the registrant's logical zone of expansion. *In re 1st USA Realty Professionals, Inc.*, 84 USPQ2d 1581 (TTAB 2007); *CPG Products Corp. v. Perceptual Play, Inc.*, 221 USPQ 88 (TTAB 1983).

....

1207.01(b) Similarity of the Marks

If it appears that confusion may be likely as a result of the contemporaneous use of similar marks by the registrant and the applicant with the identified goods or services, the next step is to evaluate the marks themselves, in relation to the goods and services. Under *In re E. I. du Pont de Nemours & Co.*, 476 F.2d 1357, 1361, 177 USPQ 563, 567 (C.C.P.A. 1973), the first factor requires examination of "the similarity or dissimilarity of the marks in their entireties as to appearance, sound, connotation and commercial impression." The test of likelihood of confusion is not whether the marks can be distinguished when subjected to a side-by-side comparison, but whether the marks are sufficiently similar that there is a likelihood of confusion as to the source of the goods or services. When considering the similarity of the marks, "[a]ll relevant facts pertaining to appearance, sound, and connotation must be considered before similarity as to one or more of those factors may be sufficient to support a finding that the marks are similar or dissimilar." *Recot, Inc. v. M.C. Becton*, 214 F.3d 1322, 1329, 54 USPQ2d 1894, 1899 (Fed. Cir. 2000). In evaluating the similarities between marks, the emphasis must be on the recollection of the average purchaser who normally retains a general, rather than specific, impression of trademarks. *Sealed Air Corp. v. Scott Paper Co.*, 190 USPQ 106, 108 (TTAB 1975).

Where the goods are identical, "the degree of similarity [between the marks] necessary to support a conclusion of likely confusion declines." (citation omitted)

1207.01(b)(i) Word Marks

The points of comparison for a word mark are appearance, sound, meaning, and commercial impression. (citation omitted) Similarity of the marks in one respect — sight, sound, or meaning — will not automatically result in a finding of likelihood of confusion even if the goods are identical or closely related. Rather, the rule is that taking into account all of the relevant facts of a particular case, similarity as to one factor alone *may* be sufficient to support a holding that the marks are confusingly similar. *In re Lamson Oil Co.*, 6 USPQ2d 1041, 1043 (TTAB 1987).

1207.01(b)(ii) Similarity In Appearance

Similarity in appearance is one factor in determining whether there is a likelihood of confusion between marks. Marks may be confusingly similar in appearance despite the addition, deletion, or substitution of letters or words. (citation omitted)

. . . .

1207.01(b)(iv) Similarity in Sound – Phonetic Equivalents

Similarity in sound is one factor in determining whether there is a likelihood of confusion between marks. There is no "correct" pronunciation of a trademark because it is impossible to predict how the public will pronounce a particular mark. Therefore, "correct" pronunciation cannot be relied on to avoid a likelihood of confusion. (citation omitted)

1207.01(b)(v) Similarity in Meaning

Similarity in meaning or connotation is another factor in determining whether there is a likelihood of confusion between marks. The focus is on the recollection of the average purchaser who normally retains a general, rather than specific, impression of trademarks. (citation omitted)

The meaning or connotation of a mark must be determined in relation to the named goods or services. Even marks that are identical in sound and/or appearance may create sufficiently different commercial impressions when applied to the respective parties' goods or services so that there is no likelihood of confusion.

. . . .

1207.01(b)(vii) Transposition of Terms

Where the primary difference between marks is the transposition of the elements that compose the marks, and where this transposition does not change the overall commercial impression, there may be a likelihood of confusion.

. . . .

1207.01(b)(viii) Marks Consisting of Multiple Words

When assessing the likelihood of confusion between compound word marks, one must determine whether a portion of the word mark is dominant in terms of creating the commercial impression. Although there is no mechanical test to select a "dominant" element of a compound word mark, consumers would be more likely to perceive a fanciful or arbitrary term, rather than a descriptive or generic term, as the source-indicating feature of the mark. Accordingly, if two marks for related goods or services share the same dominant feature and the marks, when viewed in their entireties, create similar overall commercial impressions, then confusion is likely.

. . . .

1207.01(b)(ix) Weak or Descriptive Marks

The Trademark Trial and Appeal Board and the courts have recognized that merely descriptive and weak designations may be entitled to a narrower scope of protection than an entirely arbitrary or coined word. (citation omitted)

In *In re Hunke & Jochheim*, 185 USPQ 188, 189 (TTAB 1975), the Board stated:

> [R]egistration on the Supplemental Register may be considered to establish prima facie that, at least at the time of registration, the registered mark possessed a merely descriptive significance. (citation omitted.) This is significant because it is well established that the scope of protection afforded a merely descriptive or even a highly suggestive term is less than that accorded an arbitrary or coined mark. That is, terms falling within the former category have been generally categorized as "weak" marks, and the scope of protection extended to these marks has been limited to the substantially identical notation and/or to the subsequent use and registration thereof for substantially similar goods.

However, even marks that are registered on the Supplemental Register may be cited under § 2(d). *In re Clorox Co.*, 578 F.2d 305, 198 USPQ 337 (C.C.P.A. 1978).

1207.01(b)(x) Parody Marks

Parody is not a defense to a likelihood of confusion refusal. There are confusing parodies and non-confusing parodies. *See* J. Thomas McCarthy, *McCarthy on Trademarks and Unfair Competition*, § 31.153 (4th ed. 2006). A true parody actually decreases the likelihood of confusion because the effect of the parody is to create a distinction in the viewer's mind between the actual product and the joke. While a parody must call to mind the actual product to be successful, the same success also necessarily distinguishes the parody from the actual product.

. . . .

1207.01(c)(ii) Composite Marks Consisting of Both Words and Designs

Often, the examining attorney must determine whether a likelihood of confusion exists between composite marks that consist of a design element as well as words and/or letters. Frequently, the marks at issue are similar in only one element. Although it is not proper to dissect a mark, if one feature of a mark is more significant than another feature, greater weight may be given to the dominant feature for purposes of determining likelihood of confusion.

. . . .

1207.01(d) Miscellaneous Considerations

1207.01(d)(i) Doubt Resolved in Favor of Registrant

If there is any doubt as to whether there is a likelihood of confusion, that doubt must be resolved in favor of the prior registrant. (citation omitted)

1207.01(d)(ii) Absence of Actual Confusion

It is well settled that the relevant test is *likelihood of confusion*, not actual confusion. It is unnecessary to show actual confusion to establish likelihood of confusion. (citation omitted)

. . . .

1207.01(d)(vii) Sophisticated Purchasers

The fact that purchasers are sophisticated or knowledgeable in a particular field does not necessarily mean that they are immune from source confusion. *See In re Decombe*, 9 USPQ2d 1812 (TTAB 1988); *In re Pellerin Milnor Corp.*, 221 USPQ 558 (TTAB 1983). However, circumstances suggesting care in purchasing may tend to minimize likelihood of confusion.

. . . .

1207.01(d)(ix) Fame of Mark

The fame of a registered mark is a factor to be considered in determining likelihood of confusion. *In re E.I. du Pont de Nemours & Co.*, 476 F.2d 1357, 1361, 177 USPQ 563, 567 (C.C.P.A. 1973). Famous marks enjoy a wide latitude of legal protection because they are more likely to be remembered and associated in the public mind than a weaker mark. (citation omitted)

[A] mark with extensive public recognition and renown deserves and receives more legal protection than an obscure or weak mark.

> Achieving fame for a mark in a marketplace where countless symbols clamor for public attention often requires a very distinct mark, enormous advertising investments, and a product of lasting value. After earning fame, a mark benefits not only its owner, but the consumers who rely on the symbols to identify the source of a desired product. Both the mark's fame and the consumer's trust in that symbol, however, are subject to exploitation by free riders.

Kenner Parker Toys, 963 F.2d at 353, 22 USPQ2d at 1456.

When present, the fame of the mark is "a dominant factor in the likelihood of confusion analysis for a famous mark, independent of the consideration of the relatedness of the goods."

. . . .

1207.02 Marks That Are Likely to Deceive

In addition to referring to a mark that so resembles another mark as to be likely to cause confusion or mistake, § 2(d) refers to a mark being likely "to deceive." As a practical matter, this provision is rarely applied in examination, because deceptiveness involves intent and would be difficult to prove in an ex parte proceeding.

EXERCISE

TOPIC: Trademark

    i.   Infringement

    ii.   Comparative Strength of Marks

    iii. Likelihood of Confusion

SKILLS:

    i.   Application of Standards

    ii.   Critical Reasoning

    iii. Analysis

ESTIMATED TIME FOR COMPLETING THIS EXERCISE:

Less than one hour.

ESTIMATED LEVEL OF DIFFICULTY (1-5): 1—Straightforward.

    This is an on-line exercise. In the on line materials you will find a series of names, logos and/or descriptions of marks involved in infringement actions. Your job is to analyze each potential infringement and see how well you can predict what the judges held in each case. There is no separate student assessment tool for this exercise since the answers are incorporated into the on-line exercise.

Chapter 7

WAYA SOAP — TRADEMARK REGISTRATION

OVERVIEW: TRADEMARK REGISTRATION STANDARDS

1. Strength of a Proposed Mark

The first phase in this process is assessing the strength of the mark. A mark will only be accepted for registration if it is sufficiently distinctive. Under the well established framework set forth by Judge Friendly in *Abercrombie & Fitch Co. v. Hunting World, Inc.*, 537 F.2d 4 (2d Cir. 1976), a mark is analyzed and placed within one of four categories: 1) arbitrary or fanciful, 2) suggestive, 3) descriptive and 4) generic. This is sometimes referred to as a spectrum of distinctiveness, with arbitrary marks being the most distinctive and therefore most strongly protected and with generic marks being the least distinctive and not eligible for federal protection at all. The lines between the different categories are not always easily distinguished, although on a black letter level, they are easily described.

A. Generic Marks

A generic mark is one in which the good or service is directly named. The Green Chair Company would not be able to register its name as a trademark, assuming it did in fact make chairs. Biscuits LLC for a bakery featuring biscuits would similarly be generic and therefore unprotectable. The basic policy reason behind denying any protection to these unimaginative names is that no producer should be foreclosed from being able to say what he or she actually makes. The inclusion of a generic word within a mark does not preclude registration entirely, but the generic term will be "disclaimed" meaning it is not considered part of the protectable mark. Old Crow Whiskey would be a protectable mark, but the company would only receive protection for *Old Crow*; it would not have any exclusive rights to use the name *Whiskey* for the distilled beverage.

B. Descriptive Marks

Descriptive marks are one step removed from generic marks. Rather than being the actual name of the product, they are descriptive of its attributes or characteristics. *Golden* for a pineapple or *Tough* for children's clothing all would be descriptive. *Tender Vittles* is a descriptive mark. Surnames are also deemed descriptive. A descriptive mark, often referred to as "merely" descriptive, is not registerable as a federal trademark unless it has been used so widely as to have acquired secondary meaning in the marketplace.

C. Suggestive Marks

A suggestive mark is one which is only indirectly descriptive. Generally you would not be able to distinguish what the related good is from the name, but once you know the good, the connection is clear. Or at least sort of clear. Some marks which have been held "suggestive" take great stretches of the imagination to relate to their goods. Samsonite for luggage can be classified as suggestive; Samson was strong, as are the bags in question. 7-11 for a convenience store open from 7am to 11pm is likely suggestive. Suggestive marks are fully registerable without any proof of secondary meaning; thus the distinction between merely descriptive and suggestive is often an important, if sometimes obscure, one.

D. Arbitrary, Fanciful and Coined Marks

These are the marks which in no way relate to the underlying good. A coined mark is one which is a completely made up word. Examples of coined marks include Xerox, Exxon, Kleenex and Google. These words had no meaning before they were used as a mark. A fanciful mark is similar, but it may bear slight relation to another word or may be an obsolete word, such as *Fab*. An arbitrary mark, on the other hand, is one that is in the dictionary, but is not related to the underlying good or service. Apple is an example of an arbitrary mark when used for computers or for a record company. Note, however, that Apple would *not* be arbitrary if it were used for a produce company. In that case it would be descriptive or generic; a trademark can never be analyzed without respect to the particular goods or services to which it relates. Arbitrary, Fanciful and Coined marks are readily registerable and receive the highest level of protection due to their distinctiveness.

2. Doctrine of Foreign Equivalents

If a mark includes a foreign word, under the Doctrine of Foreign Equivalents, it is also analyzed with the translated meaning of the word. Accordingly, *Handtasche* for pocketbooks would be generic; it is the German word for purse or handbag.

A fantastic source for information about Trademarks and the registration process is the Trademark Manual of Examining Procedure (TMEP). It contains the guidelines used by Trademark Examiners in the USPTO and is available in its entirety on line at: http://tess2.uspto.gov/tmdb/tmep/.

The TMEP provides the following (slightly edited) information about applying the Doctrine of Foreign Equivalents:

Trademark Manual of Examining Procedure (TMEP) — 6th Edition Rev. 2

1207.01(b)(vi) Doctrine of Foreign Equivalents

Under the doctrine of foreign equivalents, a foreign word (from a language familiar to an appreciable segment of

American consumers) and the English equivalent may be held to be confusingly similar. *See, e.g., Continental Nut Co. v. Cordon Bleu, Ltee*, 494 F.2d 1397, 181 USPQ 647 (C.C.P.A. 1974); *In re Thomas*, 79 USPQ2d 1021 (TTAB 2006) (MARCHE NOIR for jewelry held likely to be confused with BLACK MARKET MINERALS for retail jewelry store services); *In re American Safety Razor Co.*, 2 USPQ2d 1459 (TTAB 1987) (BUENOS DIAS for soap held likely to be confused with GOOD MORNING and design for latherless shaving cream); *In re Hub Distributing, Inc.*, 218 USPQ 284 (TTAB 1983) (EL SOL for clothing and footwear held likely to be confused with SUN and design for footwear).

Whether an examining attorney should apply the doctrine of foreign equivalents turns upon the significance of the foreign mark to the relevant purchasers, which is based on an analysis of the evidence of record, including, for example, dictionary, Internet, and LexisNexis® evidence. If the evidence shows that the relevant English translation is literal and direct, and no contradictory evidence of shades of meaning or other relevant meanings exists, the doctrine generally should be applied by the examining attorney. *See, e.g., In re Ithaca Indus., Inc.*, 230 USPQ 702 (TTAB 1986) (holding the Italian language mark LUPO for men's and boys' underwear, which translates to mean "wolf," likely to be confused with WOLF and design for various clothing items, because LUPO had a literal and direct English translation such that the doctrine was applied).

If an examining attorney determines that the doctrine is applicable, the examining attorney must also apply the relevant *du Pont* factors to assess whether there is a likelihood of confusion between the marks. *See In re E.I. du Pont de Nemours & Co.*, 476 F.2d 1357, 1361, 177 USPQ 563, 567 (C.C.P.A. 1973); *In re L'Oreal S.A.*, 222 USPQ 925, 926 (TTAB 1984) (noting that "similarity in connotation [of the marks] must be viewed as but a single factor in the overall evaluation of likelihood of confusion").

1207.01(b)(vi)(A) Background

With respect to likelihood of confusion, "[i]t is well established that foreign words or terms are not entitled to be registered if the English language equivalent has been previously used on or registered for products which might reasonably be assumed to come from the same source." *Mary Kay Cosmetics, Inc. v. Dorian Fragrances, Ltd.*, 180 USPQ 406, 407 (TTAB 1973).

Although words from modern languages are generally translated into English, the doctrine of foreign equivalents has evolved into a guideline, not an absolute rule, and is applied only when the "ordinary American purchaser" would "stop and translate" the foreign wording in a mark. *Palm Bay Imports, Inc. v. Veuve Clicquot Ponsardin Maison Fondee en 1772*, 396 F.3d 1369, 1377, 73 USPQ2d 1689, 1696 (Fed. Cir. 2005) (reversing finding of likelihood of confusion between VEUVE ROYALE — the French equivalent of "Royal Widow" — and THE WIDOW, both for sparkling wine, deeming it improbable that American purchasers would be aware that "Veuve" means "widow"). The "ordinary American purchaser" includes "all American purchasers, including those proficient in a non-English language who would ordinarily be expected to translate words into English." *In re Spirits Int'l, N.V.*, 563 F.3d 1347, 1352, 90 USPQ2d 1489, 1492 (Fed. Cir. 2009).

. . . .

1207.01(b)(vi)(B) When an Ordinary American Purchaser Would "Stop and Translate"

Issues regarding the doctrine of foreign equivalents arise early in examination, that is, at the time of conducting a search for confusingly similar marks. The search of foreign words in an applied-for mark must include a search of their English translation to ensure that all possible conflicting registrations and prior-filed applications have been identified in the event that the doctrine applies. *See* TMEP §§ 809 *et seq.* for information regarding how to ascertain the meaning of non-English wording in a mark.

After conducting a complete search, an examining attorney must then assess whether a refusal under § 2(d) may be warranted. If so, the examining attorney should research the English translation further using available resources, such as dictionaries, the Internet, and LexisNexis®, to ascertain whether there is sufficient evidence to support applying the doctrine.

. . . .

Common, Modern Foreign Languages

The doctrine applies to words or terms from common, modern languages, which encompasses all but dead, obscure, or unusual languages. An applicant may respond to the application of the doctrine by arguing that the foreign language is obscure, or not commonly spoken in the United States, and thus the doctrine is inapplicable. If this or a similar argument is set forth, or if the foreign language appears to be obscure or unusual, an examining attorney should provide evidence to show that the foreign language is a common, modern language. The type of evidence will vary depending on the particular facts of the case but, if available, the examining attorney should provide evidence of the percentage or number of United States consumers who speak the language in question. For example:

- Census evidence provided by applicant to show that only 0.6% of the population speak French "very well" or "well" was used by the Board against the applicant to show that, of the foreign languages with the greatest number of speakers in the United States, French was second only to Spanish. *Thomas*, 79 USPQ2d at 1024.

- Evidence showing that 706,000 Russian-speakers live in the United States was persuasive evidence to establish that a "significant portion of consumers" would understand the English meaning of the Russian mark for Russian vodka. *In re Joint Stock Co. "Baik,"* 80 USPQ2d 1305, 1310 (TTAB 2006).

Census evidence identifying the number of people who speak various foreign languages in the United States can be found at http://www.census.gov/population/cen 2000/phc-t20/tab05.pdf.

. . . .

Common, modern languages have been found to include Spanish, French, Italian, German, Chinese, Japanese, Russian, Polish, Hungarian, Serbian, and Yiddish. *(citations omitted)*

If evidence shows that the language at issue is highly obscure or a dead language, the doctrine will generally not be applied. *See Enrique Bernat F. S.A. v. Guadalajara Inc.*, 210 F.3d 439, 54 USPQ2d 1497 (5th Cir. 2000), *reh'g denied* 218 F.3d 745 (2000). The determination of whether a language is "dead" must be made on a case-by-case basis, based upon the meaning the word or term would have to the relevant purchasing public. For example, Latin is generally considered a dead language. However, if evidence shows that a Latin term is still in use by the relevant purchasing public (i.e., if the term appears in current dictionaries or news articles), then this Latin term would not be considered dead. The same analysis is applied to other words or terms from uncommon or obscure languages.

....

1207.01(b)(vi)(C) Likelihood of Confusion Factors Still Apply When Assessing Whether Marks are Confusingly Similar

If the examining attorney has sufficient evidence to show that the foreign wording has a relevant, literal, and direct English translation such that the foreign wording has an English language equivalent, then the doctrine generally should be applied to the foreign wording in a mark or marks. However, applying the doctrine is only part of the process of determining whether the marks being compared are confusingly similar. Appearance, sound, meaning, and commercial impression are also factors to be considered when comparing marks. *See Palm Bay*, 396 F.3d at 1371, 73 USPQ2d at 1691 (citing *E.I. du Pont*, 476 F.2d at 1361, 177 USPQ at 567).

Similarity of the marks in one respect — sight, sound, or meaning — does not automatically result in a finding of likelihood of confusion even if the goods are identical or closely related. Rather, the rule is that, taking into account all of the relevant facts of a particular case, similarity as to one factor alone may be sufficient to support a holding that the marks are confusingly similar. *In re Lamson Oil Co.*, 6 USPQ2d 1041, 1043 (TTAB 1987); TMEP § 1207.01(b)(i).

....

See also TMEP §§1209.03(g), 1210.05(b), 1210.10 and 1211.01(a)(vii) regarding the doctrine of foreign equivalents.

3. *Filing A Trademark Application*

Assuming you find your mark to be either suggestive or arbitrary and therefore eligible for registration, the next step is to make sure the mark is available. The USPTO has an easily searchable database of all registered trademarks, live and dead. This is a great resource not only for the basic information of whether there is a prior use of the proposed mark, but it also can provide examples of applications which were accepted together with examples of some of the underlying correspondence relating to registration.

In addition to searching for a previously registered mark, you will need to try to assess whether the proposed mark, or something like it, has been used by anyone else in commerce albeit without federal registration. Common Law does provide rights to anyone using a trademark even if it is not federally registered. These rights are limited by geographic scope, but it is never fun to have to admit to your client that the newly registered trademark, on which a huge marketing budget has already been lavishly spent, is actually one that the client is not going to be able to use in Northern Virginia due to the existence of a local mom-n-pop that has used the same name for decades but flew beneath the federal radar. Although it is not, of course, completely determinative, a thorough web search often helps find such prior use conflicts BEFORE it is too late.

The registration process itself is now completed almost exclusively online. Paper forms are still accepted, but the USPTO *strongly* encourages the use of the on-line TEAS registration form which is found at the USPTO website. The details of the process change from time to time as the website is updated, but the basics are fairly consistent. First, you complete the application, including attaching a jpeg of the mark itself and a second jpeg showing an example or "specimen" of how the mark is actually used in commerce. The submission is complete when you sign (e-sign) the application and pay the application fee. At that point, the application will be assigned to a USPTO staff attorney who will generally be responsible for the application for the duration of the process. The attorney will review the application for technical compliance and for substantive merit. The reviewing attorney will analyze the mark and complete a basic search for conflicting marks. Often the reviewing attorney will send a letter (an "office action") asking for some changes to the application. It may be a clarification of the description of the goods or service, a request for a different specimen, a correction to the description of the logo or something else. The applicant has six months from the date of the office action to respond, either accepting the suggested amendments, or trying to convince the examining attorney that the changes are not really necessary. The latter is seldom completely successful.

4. Opposition Proceedings

Once the application has been fully cleared by the USPTO attorney, the mark is published for opposition, meaning it is published by the USPTO in its *Official Gazette* so that outside parties can review all the proposed marks and object to a registration if they believe they would be harmed by the registration of the proposed mark. If an opposition is filed, a process equivalent to a federal trial will take place in front of the Trademark Trial and Appeal Board (TTAB). If no opposition is filed, the mark moves forward and is formally registered.[1]

It is not uncommon for some well-financed companies to use the opposition process strategically to protect their marks. More than

---

[1]   More detailed information about the application process is available on the USPTO website. A good overview of the registration process in particular may be found at: http://www.uspto.gov/faq/trademarks. jsp#Patent002 and http://www.uspto.gov/trademarks/process/afterapp.jsp.

one poorly funded start up company has been in effect forced to abandon its mark in the face of the legal fees associated with the opposition process even though the opposition filed was substantively weak.

In analyzing whether a mark too closely resembles another, the standard is the familiar "likelihood of confusion," i.e., whether consumers are likely to be confused between the two marks. Since the standard is likelihood of confusion with respect to the *consumer*, in practice, companies involved in a trademark dispute often commission consumer surveys to be used as evidence of confusion, or lack thereof, in the market.

Additionally, a number of factual considerations are relevant in analyzing likelihood of confusion between two marks, including the following: (i) how similar the underlying goods are, (ii) the sophistication of the typical consumer of the underlying good, (iii) the price of the good, (iv) where it is sold, (v) how it is sold, and (vi) the amount of care which is generally used in making the p urchase. For instance, in a dispute between two similarly named salty snack chips, confusion is more likely because (1) the goods are similar, (2) they are inexpensive and consumers do not take great care in making the purchase and (3) they would often be sold in a supermarket aisle potentially side by side or in a check-out lane as an impulse item.

The similarity or dissimilarity of the underlying goods is of prime importance. The closer the goods, the more likely consumers will be confused as to the source of the goods. Similarly, if the goods are within a family of related goods, then consumers are also more likely to think they are from the same source. Reasonable consumers expect a single company to produce related goods, like milk and yogurt or winter coats and gloves.

There are also a wide variety of elements that should be compared between the two marks, including the following: how the marks sound, the number of syllables, the number of letters, the number of identical letters, the meaning, the similarity in appearance of the words, and the similarity in appearance of the marks.

All of these aspects are compared and balanced to determine whether the two marks are likely to cause consumers to be confused as to the source of the relevant goods or services.

EXERCISE

TOPIC:

    i.   Trademark Registration Process

    ii.   Standards for Registration

    iii. Strength of Marks

    iv. Likelihood of Confusion

SKILLS:

    i.   Research (on-line – general and USPTO website and processes)

    ii.   Critical Reasoning

    iii. Analysis

ESTIMATED TIME FOR COMPLETING THIS EXERCISE:

Part I: Less than one hour.
Part II: One and a half hours.
Part III: One hour.

ESTIMATED LEVEL OF DIFFICULTY (1-5): 3—Moderate.

Waya Soap: Part One

You represent Waya Soap, Inc., a small, start-up company that makes fabulous, all natural soaps. "Waya" is the Cherokee word for wolf. Happily, the soap is not in fact made from wild dogs, but the label features a picture of one of the owner's pet wolves, and a portion of the profits will be donated to wolf conservation causes.

The owner of Waya is Lynne Jeffry. She is ambitious but is not an experienced entrepreneur and has no legal background beyond a penchant for *Law and Order* and old reruns of *Matlock*.

Her current products are all traditional bar soaps which are appropriate for facial or all-over use, but she may in the future want to expand to a liquid soap or special purpose soap. It is possible she will want to develop a full line of shampoos and conditioners and other related products as well, but for now Ms. Jeffry and Waya are focusing on the base product.

Waya soap is currently sold in several small independent gift shops throughout the southeast. Ms. Jeffry's first sale was at the Yellow Daisy Festival in Stone Mountain Georgia on March 21, 2007, and she has been expanding ever since. She is hoping to place her product with Target, but a friend told her she should look into registering the trademark before she even started talking to a major retailer like that.

Accordingly, she has come to you for advice on registering a trademark for her soap. She is very cost conscious and does not want to spend more money than she has to in order to protect her name. For now, she only wants to register the soap; she is not concerned with protecting the company name *per se*, so it is not necessary to address a registration for Waya Soap, Inc. There are a number of varieties of the soap, including violet, lavender, oatmeal, espresso, baby, earth and patchouli. The client does not want to register any of the specific types at this point, just the basic brand name unless you advise her that she must make separate registrations for each type. The company will own all of the intellectual property related to the soap or other operations.

Here is the logo your client has been using:

Your first task is to analyze the strength of the name as a trademark. Prepare a short memo answering the following: Is it registerable? Is it a strong mark? What about registering each type of the soap?

Would that increase the cost of the filing? (Just address the cost of filing with the USPTO, we will leave calculating the legal billing to the assigning partner.) Is it necessary that each type have a separate registration?

When completed, compare your conclusions to the LexisNexis web-course.

Waya Soap: Part Two

1. Having completed your assessment of the Waya mark, your next step is to do some background research and analysis on the name. You need to know if anyone else is using the name in way likely to cause confusion with your client. Although in the past this involved hiring a search firm in Washington DC, now all the information you need is at your fingertips online. You will want to perform a basic on-line search to see if you find any other uses of the name.

2. After completing the basic web search, it is time to look to a more specific trademark search. You need to determine if there is a registered trademark that would conflict with the Waya mark. Go to www.uspto.gov. Under Trademarks, you may first want to click on "Where Do I Start" and look around the site a bit to familiarize yourself with the variety of resources available there. To do an actual search, go to "Search TESS database" and follow the instructions. It is a very user friendly Boolean search engine for the entire U.S. Trademark Database.

3. Finally, it is time to complete an online registration for the mark. Again your starting point is www.USPTO.gov. This time after clicking on Trademarks, you will click on "4. File online forms (TEAS)" on the left hand box. Once in the Trademark Electronic Application System (TEAS) you may find it helpful to scroll to the bottom of the page and avail yourself of the "other resources" offered there. You will find a comprehensive tutorial for completing a filing and navigating the TEAS system. Your application can be completed based on the above information and the following:

    a. You have not been provided with anything to be a "specimen" as required by the USPTO. You may skip this step in the Application; however, you should determine what you would be able to use. The requirements for the specimen are provided on the USPTO website and in help sections attached to the TEAS form. Be sure you know what would be an acceptable specimen for this product and what the format requirements are. You would need to be able to tell your client both things in order to get a specimen from her that complies with the USPTO requirements.

b. Waya's address is 3298 Centerville Plaza, Atlanta Ga 30307. *ljeff@waya.com* Phone: 404-555-9899 Fax: 404-555-9890. You are to serve as the attorney of record.

c. As part of the registration process, you will be asked to choose in which International Class the goods will categorized. A list of the classes (as well as a lot of other very useful information about the registration process) is available in the FAQs at http://www.uspto.gov/faq/trademarks.jsp.

d. As you fill out the registration form, you may find that you need other information. Make a note of what else you would need to ask the client and what information you would need in order to make the filing. For purposes of this exercise, after noting what else you needed to know, make it up and complete the filing (noting what decisions you made and what you made up). Include this when you turn in the Application to your Professor.

e. Of course please do NOT actually submit your form to the USPTO!! Just work through the form and save a copy. To save the application form: You are given four options after you attach your signature. Do not worry about signing the document; it is not actually filed until you provide a credit card number. In the top of the "Validation" page is a window with a green border. Please click on "text form" and save a copy of that. Then at the bottom of the page select the "Download Portable Data" button and turn in both files via email to your Professor. You will probably not be able to open the .obj file that you get when you click on "Download Portable Data," it is intended for use in the TEAS system and Microsoft does not usually have an app to handle it. Don't worry about that and just hand in both files.

When completed, review the Self-Assessment on the LexisNexis webcourse.

Waya Soap: Part Three

Eight months after you submitted the application for Waya Soap (and after your successful completion of the inevitable Office Action requesting a few amendments to your filing), you are surprised to receive a Notice of Opposition by Naya Water. Before you call Ms. Jeffry and give her the bad news, you need to figure out just how likely this Opposition is to succeed. You should also craft a feasible argument to support Waya's right to the mark, including a frank analysis of the weakness of your argument.

To analyze the strength of Naya's claim, try to think of the best argument and justifications their counsel would be able to craft. What is the legal standard? What other factors relevant to these particular products are relevant?

For your review, attached is the Notice of Opposition filed by Naya Water Corp.

Here is an example of the Naya logo. You may see more complete examples of Naya's logo and trade dress at www.naya.com.

Once you have drafted your argument, review the Self-Assessment on the LexisNexis webcourse.

In the United States Patent and Trademark Office

Before the Trademark Trial and Appeal Board

In the matter of Application Serial No. _____999999999_____

Filed On _____April 22, 2009_____

For the Mark _____Waya Soap_____

Published in the *Official Gazette (Trademarks)* on __Sept 16, 2009__

Naya Water	)	
Corporation,	)	
Opposer.	)	
v.	)	Cancellation No. [*To be inserted by the*
Waya Soap, Inc.,	)	*Patent and Trademark Office*]
Applicant.	)	
	)	

Commissioner for Trademarks

P.O. Box 1451 Alexandria, Virginia 22313-1451

Notice of Opposition

Dear Commissioner:

Naya Water Corporation, a Colorado corporation with its principal address at 345 Spring Water Rd., Colorado Springs, CO, Opposer.

The above-identified opposer believes that it will be damaged by registration of the mark shown in the above-identified application, and hereby opposes the same.

The grounds for opposition are as follows: False suggestion of a connection. Applicant's mark, when used on or in connection with the identified goods, so closely resembles the mark in Opposer's U.S. Registration No. 999999 as to be likely to cause confusion, to cause mistake or to deceive.

The examining attorney must look at the marks themselves for similarities in appearance, sounds, connotation and commercial impression. *In re E.I. DuPont de Nemours & Co.,* 476 F.2d 1357, 177 USPQ 563 (CCPA 1973). Second, the examining attorney must compare the goods or services to determine if they are related or if the activities surrounding their marketing are such that confusion as to origin is likely. *In re August Storck KG,* 218 USPQ 823 (TTAB 1983); *In re International Telephone and Telegraph Corp.* 197 USPQ 910 (TTAB 1978); *Guardian Products Co. v. Scott Paper Co.,* 200 USPQ 738 (TTAB 1978).

The marks are confusingly similar. Applicant's mark varies from Opposer's only by one letter. The two names sound and look similar. Similarity in sound alone is enough to find a likelihood of confusion. *Molenaar, Inc. v. Hapy Toys, Inc.*, 188 USPQ 469 (TTAB 1975). When the Applicant's mark is compared to Opposer's mark, "the points of similarity are of greater importance than the points of difference." *Esso Standard Oil Co. v. Sun Oil Co.*, 229 F.2d 37, 108 USPQ 161 (D.C. Cir), *cert. denied,* 351 U.S. 973 109 USPQ 517 (1956).

The goods represented by Opposer's mark and applicant's mark are closely related enough to falsely suggest a connection. The examining attorney must consider any goods or services in the normal fields of expansion to determine whether the applicant's goods or services are related to the Opposer's identified goods or services under Section 2(d). *In re General Motors Corp.*, 196 USPQ 574 (TTAB 1977). Soap and water are inevitably linked in the general consumer's mind and are closely enough related to suggest a false connection.

The applicant's mark is confusingly similar to Opposer's mark, and Opposer therefore opposes the registration of the Applicant's mark, "Waya Soap" and requests that Applicant's application for registration be rejected.

By _____Nadia Linksey_____

/s/

Attorney of Record for Opposer.

Chapter 8

BY ANY OTHER NAME — DOMAIN NAME AND TRADEMARK INFRINGEMENT

OVERVIEW: DOMAIN NAME DISPUTES

Trademark disputes and less formal conflicts involving celebrity names are by no measure a new phenomenon; a very young David Bowie began his recording career under his original name, Davey Jones but then reluctantly gave that name up due to the much greater fame of the Monkees front man. Instead, he chose to name himself after the famous wild-west knives and ended up greatly outlasting the *other* Davey Jones in the spotlight. With the advent of the internet, new realms of trademark conflict arose. Some clever early-adopters reserved domain names either with an eye to use them or in hopes of profiting when the slower mark holders finally clued in to the value of trademarks in domain names. Some people bought up celebrity domain names so they could set up fan pages, others bought them up so they could turn around and sell them to the celebrities down the road when everyone wanted his or her own eponymous domain. Bruce Springsteen, Julia Roberts, Dan Marino, Madonna and Sting are just a few of the famous people who ended up fighting, with varying results, to claim the domain bearing their names.[1] There were also honest uses of particular domains that frustrated a more famous user. One perfectly legitimate example is www.Delta.com. For years, this URL led users to the corporate website for Delta Faucets. Delta Air Lines was left with the rather unwieldy www.delta-airlines.com. At some point, the two corporations came to an understanding; Delta Faucets is now at www.deltafaucets.com and Delta Air Lines has the much easier www.delta.com. Delta Faucets' use, however, was completely legitimate. Delta Air Lines had no legitimate legal

---

[1] WIPO Arbitration and Mediation Center, Administrative Panel Decision, *Bruce Springsteen v. Jeff Burgar and Bruce Springsteen Club*, Case No. D2000-1532 http://www.wipo.int/amc/en/domains/decisions/html/2000/d2000-1532.html; WIPO Arbitration and Mediation Center, Administrative Panel Decision, Julia Fiona Roberts v. Russell Boyd, Case No. D2000-0210 http://www.wipo.int/amc/en/domains/decisions/html/2000/d2000-0210.html; WIPO Arbitration and Mediation Center, Administrative Panel Decision, *Daniel C. Marino, Jr. v. Video Images Productions, et al.*, Case No. D2000-0598, http://www.wipo.int/amc/en/domains/decisions/html/2000/d2000-0598.html; WIPO Arbitration and Mediation Center, Administrative Panel Decision, *Madonna Ciccone, p/k/a Madonna v. Dan Parisi and "Madonna.com,"* Case No. D2000-0847, http://www.wipo.int/amc/en/domains/decisions/html/2000/d2000-0847.html; WIPO Arbitration and Mediation Center, Administrative Panel Decision, *Gordon Sumner, p/k/a Sting v. Michael Urvan*, Case No. D2000-0596, http://www.wipo.int/amc/en/domains/decisions/html/2000/d2000-0596.html. *See also* Kieren McCarthy, *Madonna wins her domain namesake, WIPO — friend to rich people everywhere*, The Register, 17 October 2000, http://www.theregister.co.uk/2000/10/17/madonna_wins_her_domain_namesake/. Kieren McCarthy, *It's a cybersquatting extravaganza! Microsoft, Reuters happy; Sting stung*, THE REGISTER, 28 July 2000, http://www.theregister.co.uk/2000/07/28/its_a_cybersquatting_extravaganza/.

grounds to object, although the company has been very vigilant in protecting its corporate name and domain name against infringing uses.[2]

As more unscrupulous entrepreneurs began to appreciate the potential value of famous name domains, the era of the cybersquatter began. At first, without any specific prohibitions of the practice, the quick thinking "domain pirates" held names hostage until the rightful owners paid ransom to free the targeted URL for use in commerce. Eventually, rights holders were able to secure some legal protection. In 1999, ICANN, the overseeing registrar of domain name registrations adopted the Uniform Domain Name Dispute Resolution Policy (UDRP) setting forth the conditions under which ICANN would reassign a domain name based on a cybersquatting claim. In the same year, Congress passed the Anticybersquatting Consumer Protection Act (ACPA)[3] as Section 43(d) of the Lanham Act in an effort to provide meaningful remedies to the victims of cybersquatting.

1. *Primary Source — UDRP*

Uniform Domain-Name Dispute-Resolution Policy[4]

General Information

All registrars must follow the the Uniform Domain-Name Dispute-Resolution Policy (often referred to as the "UDRP"). Under the policy, most types of trademark-based domain-name disputes must be resolved by agreement, court action, or arbitration before a registrar will cancel, suspend, or transfer a domain name. Disputes alleged to arise from abusive registrations of domain names (for example, cybersquatting) may be addressed by expedited administrative proceedings that the holder of trademark rights initiates by filing a complaint with an approved dispute-resolution service provider.

To invoke the policy, a trademark owner should either (a) file a complaint in a court of proper jurisdiction against the domain-name holder (or where appropriate an in-rem action concerning the domain name) or (b) in cases of abusive registration submit a complaint to an approved dispute-resolution service provider (see below for a list and links).

[2] *See, e.g.*, WIPO Arbitration and Mediation Center, Administrative Panel Decision, *Delta Air Lines, Inc. v. CCDP Consulting*, Case No. D2010-0997, at www.wipo.int/amc/en/domains/search/text.jsp?case=D2010-0997; WIPO Arbitration and Mediation Center, Administrative Panel Decision, *Delta Air Lines, Inc. v. Ruslan Moussaev*, Case No. D2009-0718 at http://www.wipo.int/amc/en/domains/decisions/html/2009/d2009-0718.html
[3] 15 U.S.C. 1125(d).
[4] www.icann.org/en/udrp/udrp.htm

Uniform Domain Name Dispute Resolution Policy[5]
(As Approved by ICANN on October 24, 1999)

1. **Purpose.** This Uniform Domain Name Dispute Resolution Policy (the "Policy") has been adopted by the Internet Corporation for Assigned Names and Numbers ("ICANN"), is incorporated by reference into your Registration Agreement, and sets forth the terms and conditions in connection with a dispute between you and any party other than us (the registrar) over the registration and use of an Internet domain name registered by you. Proceedings under Paragraph 4 of this Policy will be conducted according to the Rules for Uniform Domain Name Dispute Resolution Policy (the "Rules of Procedure"), which are available at http://www.icann.org/en/dndr/udrp/uniform-rules.htm, and the selected administrative-dispute-resolution service provider's supplemental rules.

2. **Your Representations.** By applying to register a domain name, or by asking us to maintain or renew a domain name registration, you hereby represent and warrant to us that (a) the statements that you made in your Registration Agreement are complete and accurate; (b) to your knowledge, the registration of the domain name will not infringe upon or otherwise violate the rights of any third party; (c) you are not registering the domain name for an unlawful purpose; and (d) you will not knowingly use the domain name in violation of any applicable laws or regulations. It is your responsibility to determine whether your domain name registration infringes or violates someone else's rights.

3. **Cancellations, Transfers, and Changes.** We will cancel, transfer or otherwise make changes to domain name registrations under the following circumstances:

   a. subject to the provisions of Paragraph 8, our receipt of written or appropriate electronic instructions from you or your authorized agent to take such action;

   b. our receipt of an order from a court or arbitral tribunal, in each case of competent jurisdiction, requiring such action; and/or

   c. our receipt of a decision of an Administrative Panel requiring such action in any administrative proceeding to which you were a party and which was conducted under this Policy or a later version of this Policy adopted by ICANN. (See Paragraph 4(i) and (k) below.)

We may also cancel, transfer or otherwise make changes to a domain name registration in accordance with the terms of your Registration Agreement or other legal requirements.

4. **<u>Mandatory Administrative Proceeding</u>.** This Paragraph sets forth the type of disputes for which you are required to submit to a mandatory administrative proceeding. These proceedings will be conducted before one of the administrative-dispute-resolution service providers listed at www.icann .org/udrp/approved-providers.htm (each, a "Provider").

   a. **Applicable Disputes.** You are required to submit to a mandatory administrative proceeding in the event that a third party (a "complainant") asserts to the applicable Provider, in compliance with the Rules of Procedure, that

      (i) your domain name is identical or confusingly similar to a trademark or service mark in which the complainant has rights; and

      (ii) you have no rights or legitimate interests in respect of the domain name; and

      (iii) your domain name has been registered and is being used in bad faith.

      In the administrative proceeding, the complainant must prove that each of these three elements are present.

   b. **Evidence of Registration and Use in Bad Faith.** For the purposes of Paragraph 4(a)(iii), the following circumstances, in particular but without limitation, if found by the Panel to be present, shall be evidence of the registration and use of a domain name in bad faith:

      (i) circumstances indicating that you have registered or you have acquired the domain name primarily for the purpose of selling, renting, or otherwise transferring the domain name registration to the complainant who is the owner of the trademark or service mark or to a competitor of that complainant, for valuable consideration in excess of your documented out-of-pocket costs directly related to the domain name; or

      (ii) you have registered the domain name in order to prevent the owner of the trademark or service mark from reflecting the mark in a corresponding domain name, provided that you have engaged in a pattern of such conduct; or

      (iii) you have registered the domain name primarily for the purpose of disrupting the business of a competitor; or

      (iv) by using the domain name, you have intentionally attempted to attract, for commercial gain, Internet users to your web site or other on-line location, by creating a likelihood of confusion with the complainant's mark as to the source, sponsorship, affiliation, or endorsement of your web site or location or of a product or service on your web site or location.

c. **How to Demonstrate Your Rights to and Legitimate Interests in the Domain Name in Responding to a Complaint.** When you receive a complaint, you should refer to Paragraph 5 of the Rules of Procedure in determining how your response should be prepared. Any of the following circumstances, in particular but without limitation, if found by the Panel to be proved based on its evaluation of all evidence presented, shall demonstrate your rights or legitimate interests to the domain name for purposes of Paragraph 4(a)(ii):

(i)   before any notice to you of the dispute, your use of, or demonstrable preparations to use, the domain name or a name corresponding to the domain name in connection with a bona fide offering of goods or services; or

(ii) you (as an individual, business, or other organization) have been commonly known by the domain name, even if you have acquired no trademark or service mark rights; or

(iii) you are making a legitimate noncommercial or fair use of the domain name, without intent for commercial gain to misleadingly divert consumers or to tarnish the trademark or service mark at issue.

2. *Primary Source — ACPA/Lanham Act*

Anticybersquatting Consumer Protection Act (ACPA)[6]

(d) Cyberpiracy prevention.

(1) (A) A person shall be liable in a civil action by the owner of a mark, including a personal name which is protected as a mark under this section, if, without regard to the goods or services of the parties, that person —

(i)   has a bad faith intent to profit from that mark, including a personal name which is protected as a mark under this section; and

(ii) registers, traffics in, or uses a domain name that —

(I) in the case of a mark that is distinctive at the time of registration of the domain name, is identical or confusingly similar to that mark;

---

[6] 15 U.S.C. 1125(d).

(II)   in the case of a famous mark that is famous at the time of registration of the domain name, is identical or confusingly similar to or dilutive of that mark; or

(III)   is a trademark, word, or name protected by reason of section 706 of title 18, United States Code, or section 220506 of title 36, United States Code.

(B) (i) In determining whether a person has a bad faith intent described under subparagraph (A), a court may consider factors such as, but not limited to —

(I)   the trademark or other intellectual property rights of the person, if any, in the domain name;

(II)   the extent to which the domain name consists of the legal name of the person or a name that is otherwise commonly used to identify that person;

(III)   the person's prior use, if any, of the domain name in connection with the bona fide offering of any goods or services;

(IV)   the person's bona fide noncommercial or fair use of the mark in a site accessible under the domain name;

(V)   the person's intent to divert consumers from the mark owner's online location to a site accessible under the domain name that could harm the goodwill represented by the mark, either for commercial gain or with the intent to tarnish or disparage the mark, by creating a likelihood of confusion as to the source, sponsorship, affiliation, or endorsement of the site;

(VI)   the person's offer to transfer, sell, or otherwise assign the domain name to the mark owner or any third party for financial gain without having used, or having an intent to use, the domain name in the bona fide offering of any goods or services, or the person's prior conduct indicating a pattern of such conduct;

(VII)   the person's provision of material and misleading false contact information when applying for the registration of the domain name, the person's intentional failure to maintain accurate contact information, or the person's prior conduct indicating a pattern of such conduct;

(VIII) the person's registration or acquisition of multiple domain names which the person knows are identical or confusingly similar to marks of others that are distinctive at the time of registration of such domain names, or dilutive of famous marks of others that are famous at the time of registration of such domain names, without regard to the goods or services of the parties; and

(IX) the extent to which the mark incorporated in the person's domain name registration is or is not distinctive and famous within the meaning of subsection (c).

(ii) Bad faith intent described under subparagraph (A) shall not be found in any case in which the court determines that the person believed and had reasonable grounds to believe that the use of the domain name was a fair use or otherwise lawful.

(C) In any civil action involving the registration, trafficking, or use of a domain name under this paragraph, a court may order the forfeiture or cancellation of the domain name or the transfer of the domain name to the owner of the mark.

(D) A person shall be liable for using a domain name under subparagraph (A) only if that person is the domain name registrant or that registrant's authorized licensee.

(E) As used in this paragraph, the term "traffics in" refers to transactions that include, but are not limited to, sales, purchases, loans, pledges, licenses, exchanges of currency, and any other transfer for consideration or receipt in exchange for consideration.

(2) (A) The owner of a mark may file an in rem civil action against a domain name in the judicial district in which the domain name registrar, domain name registry, or other domain name authority that registered or assigned the domain name is located if —

(i) the domain name violates any right of the owner of a mark registered in the Patent and Trademark Office, or protected under subsection (a) or (c); and

(ii) the court finds that the owner —

(I) is not able to obtain in personam jurisdiction over a person who would have been a defendant in a civil action under paragraph (1); or

(II) through due diligence was not able to find a person who would have been a defendant in a civil action under paragraph (1) by —

        (aa) sending a notice of the alleged violation and intent to proceed under this paragraph to the registrant of the domain name at the postal and e-mail address provided by the registrant to the registrar; and

        (bb) publishing notice of the action as the court may direct promptly after filing the action.

(B) The actions under subparagraph (A)(ii) shall constitute service of process.

(C) In an in rem action under this paragraph, a domain name shall be deemed to have its situs in the judicial district in which —

    (i) the domain name registrar, registry, or other domain name authority that registered or assigned the domain name is located; or

    (ii) documents sufficient to establish control and authority regarding the disposition of the registration and use of the domain name are deposited with the court.

(D) (i) The remedies in an in rem action under this paragraph shall be limited to a court order for the forfeiture or cancellation of the domain name or the transfer of the domain name to the owner of the mark. Upon receipt of written notification of a filed, stamped copy of a complaint filed by the owner of a mark in a United States district court under this paragraph, the domain name registrar, domain name registry, or other domain name authority shall —

    (I) expeditiously deposit with the court documents sufficient to establish the court's control and authority regarding the disposition of the registration and use of the domain name to the court; and

    (II) not transfer, suspend, or otherwise modify the domain name during the pendency of the action, except upon order of the court.

    (ii) The domain name registrar or registry or other domain name authority shall not be liable for injunctive or monetary relief under this paragraph except in the case of bad faith or reckless disregard, which includes a willful failure to comply with any such court order.

(3) The civil action established under paragraph (1) and the in rem action established under paragraph (2), and any remedy available under either such action, shall be in addition to any other civil action or remedy otherwise applicable.

(4) The in rem jurisdiction established under paragraph (2) shall be in addition to any other jurisdiction that otherwise exists, whether in rem or in personam.

3. *Recent Developments*

As rightsholders gained tools like the UDRP and UCPA to combat cybersquatters, new abuses and strategies began to appear. One such development is Reverse Domain Name Hijacking in which the anticybersquatting provisions are used offensively, usually by a well-financed or famous mark holder to intimidate or force a smaller, but innocent, player to surrender a key domain name. The World Intellectual Property Organization (WIPO) has addressed this issue and recognizes actions based on this legal theory: "Paragraph 1 of the Rules defines reverse domain name hijacking as "using the Policy in bad faith to attempt to deprive a registered domain name holder of a domain name". To prevail on such a claim, a respondent must show that the complainant knew of the respondent's strong rights or legitimate interests in the disputed domain name or the clear lack of bad faith registration and use, and nevertheless brought the complaint in bad faith."[7]

Relief for victims of Reverse Domain Name Hijacking under the UDRP and UCPA focus on the bad faith aspects of the activity. The UDRP defines Reverse Domain Name Hijacking as " using the Policy in bad faith to attempt to deprive a Registrant of a Domain Name"[8] and provides:

> Panel decisions shall normally comply with the guidelines as to length set forth in the Provider's Supplemental Rules. If the Panel concludes that the dispute is not within the scope of Paragraph 4(a) of the Policy, it shall so state. If after considering the submissions the Panel finds that the complaint was brought in bad faith, for example in an attempt at Reverse Domain Name Hijacking or was brought primarily to harass the domain-name holder, the Panel shall declare in its decision that the complaint was brought in bad faith and constitutes an abuse of the administrative proceeding.[9]

Proving bad faith can be a challenge in some situations, but the panels and boards overseeing these procedures are aware of the tactic and take what actions they can to remedy it.

---

[7] WIPO Arbitration and Mediation Center, Administrative Panel Decision, *Jay Leno v. Guadalupe Zambrano*, Case No. D2009-0570, at www.wipo.int/amc/en/domains/decisions/html/2009/d2009-0570.html.

[8] Domain Name Dispute Resolution Policies, Charter Eligibility Dispute Resolution Policy Rules, Paragraph 1 "Definitions," at www.icann.org/en/udrp/cedrp-rules.html.

[9] *Id*. at Paragraph 15(4).

EXERCISE

TOPIC: Trademark

    i.   Domain Name Disputes

    ii. CyberSquatting

    iii. Reverse Domain Name Hijacking

SKILLS:

    i.   Critical Reasoning

    ii. Analysis

ESTIMATED TIME FOR COMPLETING THIS EXERCISE:

Approximately two hours.

ESTIMATED LEVEL OF DIFFICULTY (1–5): 3—Moderate/ Creative.

In undergrad, one of your friends was a charmingly naïve and well intentioned Renaissance Literature major who dreamed of joining the Peace Corps. When he learned that the Peace Corps require relevant skills and living in unpleasant locations, he redirected his enthusiasm to non-profit companies in comfortable cities. In 2004, when you were a junior associate, you donated ten hours of legal services as part of a "tool box" award for a contest award for one of his projects. The company that won you was a small non-profit focused on electrification of impoverished rural areas both domestically and abroad. This company, "Kindle" needed your help with some basic formation issues and has called you from time to time with random questions since then, and although they exhausted the "tool box" award some time ago, you are still in the habit of answering their questions for free.

Today you have a rather frantic sounding voice mail from Ian Fiskle, the CEO of Kindle, ranting about intimidation and oppression by corporate giants. Fortunately he also emailed you a copy the following letter that triggered his phone call. Review the letter and conduct any relevant research necessary to educate yourself about the issues and possible strategies to suggest to your rather panicky client. You will need to be able to accurately summarize the relevant law and possible outcomes. Keeping in mind that his company is chronically underfunded, you know he will be concerned with the costs associated with any dispute or action, so be sure to be able to address this issue with your client when you talk.

Prepare a written summary of the legal implications of this situation, the options available to your client, and what you would advise him (and why). When completed, review the Self-Assessment on the LexisNexis webcourse.

Frankler, Chatham & Rowe, *attorneys*

Mr. Ian Fiskle
Kindle, LLC
1819 Monticello Cir
Charlottesville VA 22904

Re: CEASE AND DESIST LETTER

Dear Mr. Fiskle:

I represent the Amazon.com family of companies, and I am writing this letter to inform you that your use of www.kindle.org is in direct violation of my client's *KINDLE* trademark. Accordingly, I must demand that you immediately cease and desist all use of the infringing domain name.

If you immediately take down the infringing website, cease all use of the domain name www.kindle.org and agree to a formal transfer of ownership of the domain and all related rights, my client has agreed to let the matter drop and not pursue further, more formal, legal proceedings and monetary awards.

Please respond to this letter within fifteen (15) days to avoid the commencement of formal legal action in Federal Court for violation of The Anticybersquatting Consumer Protection Act (Lanham Act Section 43(d), or under the auspices of the ICANN Uniform Domain-Name Dispute-Resolution Policy.

Very Truly Yours,

Throckmorton Chatham, esq.

17 Corporate Plaza
Seattle, WA 98109

PHONE   (326) 555-0125
FAX   (326) 555-0126
E-MAIL   attorney@FRCLaw.com
WEB SITE http://www.FRCLaw.com

PART III

APPLIED INTELLECTUAL PROPERTY: LICENSING AND SOFTWARE PROTECTIONS

Chapter 9

COPYLEFT AND LICENSING

OVERVIEW: APPROACHES TO LICENSING

1. *The Creative Commons*

The Creative Commons is a nonprofit organization founded in large part by Prof. Lawrence Lessig to promote the free circulation and sharing of information and creative works. The theory espoused by this group is basically that U.S. Copyright law is too inflexible and unwieldy to allow authors to distribute their works most efficiently. The group has a strong bias towards the public domain; in fact, most of Prof. Lessig's books are released both in trade paperback and free online. He and many other authors make the argument that authors actually profit *more* when their works are freely available than when they are tightly protected under the traditional system. They posit that the current copyright laws are so focused on protecting authors in a strict and outdated way that a more flexible alternative is needed.

The main Creative Commons philosophy is that many, if not most, authors do not need or want the full bundle of rights reserved under the Copyright Act. Accordingly, Creative Commons has developed a flexible, user friendly license, which can be easily attached to any work when it is released, so that the author can choose the rights to be reserved as well as those to be shared. Authors only protect the rights they value, and on the terms they chose. This allows them to participate in the modern, digital community which values sharing and the ability to remix and alter existing works in the creation of new ones. This also serves the purpose of injecting life into the public domain which, in the CC view, has been squeezed beyond reason as the Act has expanded well beyond what is reasonable to incentivize authors as authorized by the Constitutional grant of authority.

The Creative Commons group is also a very active advocacy group. They are very vocal in copyright reform and were involved in trying to overturn the Sonny Bono Copyright Term Extension Act of 1998 (the "CTEA"). The Creative Commons organization helped rally public opinion against the CTEA, and Prof. Lessig was deeply involved in the lawsuit *Eldred v. Ashcroft*, 537 U.S. 186 (2003), which unsuccessfully attempted to overturn the 20-year copyright term extension in the CTEA. Prof Lessig devoted a large chunk of his next book, *Free Culture*, to expressing regrets and second guessing the strategic decisions made by the Eldred legal team.[1]

---

[1] LAWRENCE LESSIG, FREE CULTURE (2004).

The Creative Commons license is intended to be used by artists, musicians and authors without the need to hire a lawyer. They have tried to explain the different license options and level of restrictiveness in plain English so people can understand which license best suits their needs even if they cannot really parse the actual contract language. There are six main options provided in the free downloadable licenses: (a) Attribution Only (the most permissive of the options, which only requires that people copying or modifying the work give credit to the original author); (b) Attribution Share Alike (this requires not only attribution, but also that any derivative work be distributed under an equivalent CC license; this concept is central in the GNU licenses discussed *infra*); (c) Attribution, No Derivatives (as the name suggests, credit must be given to the original author, but no adaptation of the work is allowed); (d) Attribution, Non-Commercial (attribution is required, use and adaptation are allowed, but all use of the work must be non-commercial in nature); (e) Attribution, Non-Commercial, Share Alike (attribution is required, all derivative or other use must be non-commercial and also released under an identical license); (f) Attribution, Non-Commercial, No Derivatives (This is the most restrictive license available from the Creative Commons. Attribution is required, all use must be noncommercial, and no adaptation is allowed.)

On the Creative Commons website, the licenses and the options are explained in a variety of ways. The basic distinctions are put forth in language that is fairly easy to understand, although of course the nuances of the law are left out. They even have a set of symbols to help people see which license does which, and these symbols are sometimes used on the licensed works in place of a traditional copyright notice.

Here is the way the Creative Commons presents the license options, followed by the full text of the most restrictive license:

A. *Creative Commons Materials — "About Licenses."*

About
Licenses

The following describes each of the six main licenses offered when you choose to publish your work with a Creative Commons license. We have listed them starting with the most accommodating license type you can choose and ending with the most restrictive license type you can choose.

License Conditions

Creators choose a set of conditions they wish to apply to their work.

Attribution by	Share Alike sa	Non-Commercial nc	No Derivative Works nd
You let others copy, distribute, display, and perform your copyrighted work — and derivative works based upon it — but only if they give credit the way you request.	You allow others to distribute derivative works only under a license identical to the license that governs your work.	You let others copy, distribute, display, and perform your work — and derivative works based upon it — but for non-commercial purposes only.	You let others copy, distribute, display, and perform only verbatim copies of your work, not derivative works based upon it.

The Licenses

Attribution
cc by

This license lets others distribute, remix, tweak, and build upon your work, even commercially, as long as they credit you for the original creation. This is the most accommodating of licenses offered, in terms of what others can do with your works licensed under Attribution.

Attribution Share Alike
cc by-sa

This license lets others remix, tweak, and build upon your work even for commercial reasons, as long as they credit you and license their new creations under the identical terms. This license is often compared to open source software licenses. All new works based on yours will carry the same license, so any derivatives will also allow commercial use.

Attribution No Derivatives
cc by-nd
This license allows for redistribution, commercial and non-commercial, as long as it is passed along unchanged and in whole, with credit to you.

Attribution Non-Commercial
cc by-nc
This license lets others remix, tweak, and build upon your work non-commercially, and although their new works must also acknowledge you and be non-commercial, they don't have to license their derivative works on the same terms.

Attribution Non-Commercial Share Alike
cc by-nc-sa
This license lets others remix, tweak, and build upon your work non-commercially, as long as they credit you and license their new creations under the identical terms. Others can download and redistribute your work just like the by-nc-nd license, but they can also translate, make remixes, and produce new stories based on your work. All new work based on yours will carry the same license, so any derivatives will also be non-commercial in nature.

Attribution Non-Commercial No Derivatives
cc by-nc-nd
This license is the most restrictive of our six main licenses, allowing redistribution. This license is often called the "free advertising" license because it allows others to download your works and share them with others as long as they mention you and link back to you, but they can't change them in any way or use them commercially.

B. The "Legal Deed"

Because the Creative Commons team realizes that even a straightforward and fairly short license like this is beyond the ability (or attention span) of most laymen to understand, they include a short summary, or as they explain it: "This is a human-readable summary of the Legal Code (the full license)."

Creative Commons License Deed

Attribution-NonCommercial-NoDerivs 3.0 Unported

You are free:

- **to Share** — to copy, distribute and transmit the work

Under the following conditions:

- **Attribution** — You must attribute the work in the manner specified by the author or licensor (but not in any way that suggests that they endorse you or your use of the work).
- **Noncommercial** — You may not use this work for commercial purposes.
- **No Derivative Works** — You may not alter, transform, or build upon this work.

With the understanding that:

- **Waiver** — Any of the above conditions can be waived if you get permission from the copyright holder.
- **Public Domain** — Where the work or any of its elements is in the public domain under applicable law, that status is in no way affected by the license.
- **Other Rights** — In no way are any of the following rights affected by the license:
  - Your fair dealing or fair use rights, or other applicable copyright exceptions and limitations;
  - The author's moral rights;
  - Rights other persons may have either in the work itself or in how the work is used, such as publicity or privacy rights.

Notice — For any reuse or distribution, you must make clear to others the license terms of this work. The best way to do this is with a link to this web page.

Learn More —

What does "conditions can be waived" mean?

CC licenses anticipate that a licensor may want to waive compliance with a specific condition, such as attribution.

What does "Public Domain" mean?

A work is in the public domain when it is free for use by anyone for any purpose without restriction under copyright.

What does "Fair use" mean?

All jurisdictions allow some limited uses of copyrighted material without permission. CC licenses do not affect the rights of users under those copyright limitations and exceptions, such as fair use and fair dealing where applicable.

What are "Moral Rights"?

In addition to the right of licensors to request removal of their name from the work when used in a derivative or collective they don't like, copyright laws in most jurisdictions around the world (with the notable exception of the US except in very limited circumstances) grant creators "moral rights" which may provide some redress if a derivative work represents a "derogatory treatment" of the licensor's work.

What are "Publicity Rights"?

Publicity rights allow individuals to control how their voice, image or likeness is used for commercial purposes in public. If a CC-licensed work includes the voice or image of anyone other than the licensor, a user of the work may need to get permission from those individuals before using the work for commercial purposes.

Disclaimer

The Commons Deed is not a license. It is simply a handy reference for understanding the Legal Code (the full license) — it is a human-readable expression of some of its key terms. Think of it as the user-friendly interface to the Legal Code beneath. This Deed itself has no legal value, and its contents do not appear in the actual license.

Creative Commons is not a law firm and does not provide legal services. Distributing of, displaying of, or linking to this Commons Deed does not create an attorney-client relationship.

C. License Agreement

Following is the current version of the most restrictive CC license. You can view all of the licenses at the Creative Commons website, www. creativecommons.org.

Attribution-NonCommercial-NoDerivs 3.0 Unported

License

THE WORK (AS DEFINED BELOW) IS PROVIDED UNDER THE TERMS OF THIS CREATIVE COMMONS PUBLIC LICENSE ("CCPL" OR "LICENSE"). THE WORK IS PROTECTED BY COPYRIGHT AND/OR OTHER APPLICABLE LAW. ANY USE OF THE WORK OTHER THAN AS AUTHORIZED UNDER THIS LICENSE OR COPYRIGHT LAW IS PROHIBITED.

BY EXERCISING ANY RIGHTS TO THE WORK PROVIDED HERE, YOU ACCEPT AND AGREE TO BE BOUND BY THE TERMS OF THIS LICENSE. TO THE EXTENT THIS LICENSE MAY BE CONSIDERED TO BE A CONTRACT, THE LICENSOR GRANTS YOU THE RIGHTS CONTAINED HERE IN CONSIDERATION OF YOUR ACCEPTANCE OF SUCH TERMS AND CONDITIONS.

1. Definitions

a. **"Adaptation"** means a work based upon the Work, or upon the Work and other pre-existing works, such as a translation, adaptation, derivative work, arrangement of music or other alterations of a literary or artistic work, or phonogram or performance and includes cinematographic adaptations or any other form in which the Work may be recast, transformed, or adapted including in any form recognizably derived from the original, except that a work that constitutes a Collection will not be considered an Adaptation for the purpose of this License. For the avoidance of doubt, where the Work is a musical work, performance or phonogram, the synchronization of the Work in timed-relation with a moving image ("synching") will be considered an Adaptation for the purpose of this License.

b. **"Collection"** means a collection of literary or artistic works, such as encyclopedias and anthologies, or performances, phonograms or broadcasts, or other works or subject matter other than works listed in Section 1(f) below, which, by reason of the selection and arrangement of their contents, constitute intellectual creations, in which the Work is included in its entirety in unmodified form along with one or more other contributions, each constituting separate and independent works in themselves, which together are assembled into a collective whole. A work that constitutes a Collection will not be considered an Adaptation (as defined above) for the purposes of this License.

c. **"Distribute"** means to make available to the public the original and copies of the Work through sale or other transfer of ownership.

d. **"Licensor"** means the individual, individuals, entity or entities that offer(s) the Work under the terms of this License.

e. **"Original Author"** means, in the case of a literary or artistic work, the individual, individuals, entity or entities who created the Work or if no individual or entity can be identified, the publisher; and in addition (i) in the case of a performance the actors, singers, musicians, dancers, and other persons who act, sing, deliver, declaim, play in, interpret or otherwise perform literary or artistic works or expressions of folklore; (ii) in the case of a phonogram the producer being the person or legal entity who first fixes the sounds of a performance or other sounds; and (iii) in the case of broadcasts, the organization that transmits the broadcast.

f. **"Work"** means the literary and/or artistic work offered under the terms of this License including without limitation any production in the literary, scientific and artistic domain, whatever may be the mode or form of its expression including digital form, such as a book, pamphlet and other writing; a lecture, address, sermon or other work of the same nature; a dramatic or dramatico-musical work; a choreographic work or entertainment in dumb show; a musical composition with or without words; a cinematographic work to which are assimilated works expressed by a process analogous to cinematography; a work of drawing, painting, architecture, sculpture, engraving or lithography; a photographic work to which are assimilated works expressed by a process analogous to photography; a work of applied art; an illustration, map, plan, sketch or three-dimensional work relative to geography, topography, architecture or science; a performance; a broadcast; a phonogram; a compilation of data to the extent it is protected as a copyrightable work; or a work performed by a variety or circus performer to the extent it is not otherwise considered a literary or artistic work.

g. **"You"** means an individual or entity exercising rights under this License who has not previously violated the terms of this License with respect to the Work, or who has received express permission from the Licensor to exercise rights under this License despite a previous violation.

h. **"Publicly Perform"** means to perform public recitations of the Work and to communicate to the public those public recitations, by any means or process, including by wire or wireless means or public digital performances; to make available to the public Works in such a way that members of the public may access these Works from a place and at a place individually chosen by them; to perform the Work to the public by any means or process and the communication to the public of the performances of the Work, including by public digital performance; to broadcast and rebroadcast the Work by any means including signs, sounds or images.

i. **"Reproduce"** means to make copies of the Work by any means including without limitation by sound or visual recordings and the right of fixation and reproducing fixations of the Work, including storage of a protected performance or phonogram in digital form or other electronic medium.

2. Fair Dealing Rights. Nothing in this License is intended to reduce, limit, or restrict any uses free from copyright or rights arising from limitations or exceptions that are provided for in connection with the copyright protection under copyright law or other applicable laws.

3. License Grant. Subject to the terms and conditions of this License, Licensor hereby grants You a worldwide, royalty-free, non-exclusive, perpetual (for the duration of the applicable copyright) license to exercise the rights in the Work as stated below:

a. to Reproduce the Work, to incorporate the Work into one or more Collections, and to Reproduce the Work as incorporated in the Collections; and,

b. to Distribute and Publicly Perform the Work including as incorporated in Collections.

The above rights may be exercised in all media and formats whether now known or hereafter devised. The above rights include the right to make such modifications as are technically necessary to exercise the rights in other media and formats, but otherwise you have no rights to make Adaptations. Subject to 8(f) [should be 8(e) — Ed.], all rights not expressly granted by Licensor are hereby reserved, including but not limited to the rights set forth in Section 4(d).

4. Restrictions. The license granted in Section 3 above is expressly made subject to and limited by the following restrictions:

a. You may Distribute or Publicly Perform the Work only under the terms of this License. You must include a copy of, or the Uniform Resource Identifier (URI) for, this License with every copy of the Work You Distribute or Publicly Perform. You may not offer or impose any terms on the Work that restrict the terms of this License or the ability of the recipient of the Work to exercise the rights granted to that recipient under the terms of the License. You may not sublicense the Work. You must keep intact all notices that refer to this License and to the disclaimer of warranties with every copy of the Work You Distribute or Publicly Perform. When You Distribute or Publicly Perform the Work, You may not impose any effective technological measures on the Work that restrict the ability of a recipient of the Work from You to exercise the rights granted to that recipient under the terms of the License. This Section 4(a) applies to the Work as incorporated in a Collection, but this does not require the Collection apart from the Work itself to be made subject to the terms of this License. If You create a Collection, upon notice from any Licensor You must, to the extent practicable, remove from the Collection any credit as required by Section 4(c), as requested.

b. You may not exercise any of the rights granted to You in Section 3 above in any manner that is primarily intended for or directed toward commercial advantage or private monetary compensation. The exchange of the Work for other copyrighted works by means of digital file-sharing or otherwise shall not be considered to be intended for or directed toward commercial advantage or private monetary compensation, provided there is no payment of any monetary compensation in connection with the exchange of copyrighted works.

c. If You Distribute, or Publicly Perform the Work or Collections, You must, unless a request has been made pursuant to Section 4(a), keep intact all copyright notices for the Work and provide, reasonable to the medium or means You are utilizing: (i) the name of the Original Author (or pseudonym, if applicable) if supplied, and/or if the Original Author and/or Licensor designate another party or parties (e.g., a sponsor institute, publishing entity, journal) for attribution ("Attribution Parties") in Licensor's copyright notice, terms of service or by other reasonable means, the name of such party or parties; (ii) the title of the Work if supplied; (iii) to the extent reasonably practicable, the URI, if any, that Licensor specifies to be associated with the Work, unless such URI does not refer to the copyright notice or licensing information for the Work. The credit required by this Section 4(c) may be implemented in any reasonable manner; provided, however, that in the case of a Collection, at a minimum such credit will appear, if a credit for all contributing authors of Collection appears, then as part of these credits and in a manner at least as prominent as the credits for the other contributing authors. For the avoidance of doubt, You may only use the credit required by this Section for the purpose of attribution in the manner set out above and, by exercising Your rights under this License, You may not implicitly or explicitly assert or imply any connection with, sponsorship or endorsement by the Original Author, Licensor and/or Attribution Parties, as appropriate, of You or Your use of the Work, without the separate, express prior written permission of the Original Author, Licensor and/or Attribution Parties.

d. For the avoidance of doubt:

    i. **Non-waivable Compulsory License Schemes**. In those jurisdictions in which the right to collect royalties through any statutory or compulsory licensing scheme cannot be waived, the Licensor reserves the exclusive right to collect such royalties for any exercise by You of the rights granted under this License;

    ii. **Waivable Compulsory License Schemes**. In those jurisdictions in which the right to collect royalties through any statutory or compulsory licensing scheme can be waived, the Licensor reserves the exclusive right to collect such royalties for any exercise by You of the rights granted under this License if Your exercise of such rights is for a purpose or use which is otherwise than noncommercial as permitted under Section 4(b) and otherwise waives the right to collect royalties through any statutory or compulsory licensing scheme; and,

    iii. **Voluntary License Schemes**. The Licensor reserves the right to collect royalties, whether individually or, in the event that the Licensor is a member of a collecting society that administers voluntary licensing schemes, via that society, from any exercise by You of the rights granted under this License that is for a purpose or use which is otherwise than noncommercial as permitted under Section 4(b).

e. Except as otherwise agreed in writing by the Licensor or as may be otherwise permitted by applicable law, if You Reproduce, Distribute or Publicly Perform the Work either by itself or as part of any Collections, You must not distort, mutilate, modify or take other derogatory action in relation to the Work which would be prejudicial to the Original Author's honor or reputation.

5. Representations, Warranties and Disclaimer

UNLESS OTHERWISE MUTUALLY AGREED BY THE PARTIES IN WRITING, LICENSOR OFFERS THE WORK AS-IS AND MAKES NO REPRESENTATIONS OR WARRANTIES OF ANY KIND CONCERNING THE WORK, EXPRESS, IMPLIED, STATUTORY OR OTHERWISE, INCLUDING, WITHOUT LIMITATION, WARRANTIES OF TITLE, MERCHANTIBILITY, FITNESS FOR A PARTICULAR PURPOSE, NONINFRINGEMENT, OR THE ABSENCE OF LATENT OR OTHER DEFECTS, ACCURACY, OR THE PRESENCE OF ABSENCE OF ERRORS, WHETHER OR NOT DISCOVERABLE. SOME JURISDICTIONS DO NOT ALLOW THE EXCLUSION OF IMPLIED WARRANTIES, SO SUCH EXCLUSION MAY NOT APPLY TO YOU.

6. Limitation on Liability. EXCEPT TO THE EXTENT REQUIRED BY APPLICABLE LAW, IN NO EVENT WILL LICENSOR BE LIABLE TO YOU ON ANY LEGAL THEORY FOR ANY SPECIAL, INCIDENTAL, CONSEQUENTIAL, PUNITIVE OR EXEMPLARY DAMAGES ARISING OUT OF THIS LICENSE OR THE USE OF THE WORK, EVEN IF LICENSOR HAS BEEN ADVISED OF THE POSSIBILITY OF SUCH DAMAGES.

7. Termination

a. This License and the rights granted hereunder will terminate automatically upon any breach by You of the terms of this License. Individuals or entities who have received Collections from You under this License, however, will not have their licenses terminated provided such individuals or entities remain in full compliance with those licenses. Sections 1, 2, 5, 6, 7, and 8 will survive any termination of this License.

b. Subject to the above terms and conditions, the license granted here is perpetual (for the duration of the applicable copyright in the Work). Notwithstanding the above, Licensor reserves the right to release the Work under different license terms or to stop distributing the Work at any time; provided, however that any such election will not serve to withdraw this License (or any other license that has been, or is required to be, granted under the terms of this License), and this License will continue in full force and effect unless terminated as stated above.

8. Miscellaneous

a. Each time You Distribute or Publicly Perform the Work or a Collection, the Licensor offers to the recipient a license to the Work on the same terms and conditions as the license granted to You under this License.

b. If any provision of this License is invalid or unenforceable under applicable law, it shall not affect the validity or enforceability of the remainder of the terms of this License, and without further action by the parties to this agreement, such provision shall be reformed to the minimum extent necessary to make such provision valid and enforceable.

c. No term or provision of this License shall be deemed waived and no breach consented to unless such waiver or consent shall be in writing and signed by the party to be charged with such waiver or consent.

d. This License constitutes the entire agreement between the parties with respect to the Work licensed here. There are no understandings, agreements or representations with respect to the Work not specified here. Licensor shall not be bound by any additional provisions that may appear in any communication from You. This License may not be modified without the mutual written agreement of the Licensor and You.

e. The rights granted under, and the subject matter referenced, in this License were drafted utilizing the terminology of the Berne Convention for the Protection of Literary and Artistic Works (as amended on September 28, 1979), the Rome Convention of 1961, the WIPO Copyright Treaty of 1996, the WIPO Performances and Phonograms Treaty of 1996 and the Universal Copyright Convention (as revised on July 24, 1971). These rights and subject matter take effect in the relevant jurisdiction in which the License terms are sought to be enforced according to the corresponding provisions of the implementation of those treaty provisions in the applicable national law. If the standard suite of rights granted under applicable copyright law includes additional rights not granted under this License, such additional rights are deemed to be included in the License; this License is not intended to restrict the license of any rights under applicable law.

D. *Conclusion*

Perhaps because of the heavy involvement of academics as well as lawyers, the "human readable" text is fairly accurate, yet quite accessible. Most advocacy groups with legal contracts for their members to use have products of a much lower quality. The Creative Commons project and related organizations are rather unique in that instead of just lobbying and agitating for changes to the relevant laws, they have created a framework within the existing legal environment to enable their members and adherents to accomplish the free exchange of ideas and creative materials that they desire. Grass roots legal reform is not common. It can also be viewed as somewhat of a force of anarchy amongst those who have a more traditional view of intellectual property rights, but this movement is surprisingly well grounded and is wildly popular with a wide variety of musicians, artists, authors and others.[2]

Beatnik Turtle is one example of an up and coming band which owes its burgeoning success to free sharing on the web under a Creative Commons license.[3] In the current music industry, it is nearly impossible for a band to land a professional recording deal without a significant web following. Rather than fan clubs being the result of mainstream fame, today the web-based fan club, whether represented on a band's website or on a social networking site like Facebook or My Space, can drive a band's success. Some bands are even finding that in an age of MP3 files and accessible high quality recording equipment, there is less need of a traditional "record deal" than in the past. Major stardom and celebrity still only happens through the traditional channels, but moderate commercial success is already happening for many bands and musicians outside the bounds of the traditional music industry. It is not hard to imagine even top level commercial success evolving into a more grass roots and less industry controlled system. It is already happening.

The publishing industry is also being impacted by the free sharing movement. Of course, a frightening number of minimally talented would-be authors have long used "web publishing" as the modern (and much more affordable) version of the print vanity press. Instead of paying for physical print runs, these individuals can post their works on their own website and share their talents (such as they are) with the masses for very little capital outlay. However, even successful

---

[2] The Creative Commons website highlights some of their well known users: Al Jazeera, Flickr, Google, Nine Inch Nails, MIT Open CourseWare, Public Library of Science, Wikipedia and the Obama White House. *See http://creativecommons.org/about/who-uses-cc/.* Although on first glance it seems odd to list Al Jazeera first, and the U.S. President last, after a moment, it is clear that the list is alphabetical, not, one hopes, prioritized.

[3] www.beatnikturtle.com. Some of their material is also available in the Web Course Materials.

authors with real publishing deals are finding the free sharing move-ment to be a helpful vehicle for their careers and their sales numbers. Cory Doctorow, for instance, is a successful and commercially pub-lished author who is an advocate of the Creative Commons style free sharing model.[4] He not only makes his non-fiction articles available on-line, but also releases his novels for free on-line and releases his works under a CC license. This practice is far from industry standard in the commercial publishing world, but Doctorow and others have found that free on-line releases increase rather than harm bottomline profits from book sales. Baen Books is among the traditional publish-ers with an on line free library.[5] Eric Flint, a popular Sci Fi author and "First Librarian" at Baen, walks through the Creative Commons sort of arguments about sharing and the public domain in his on-line introduction to the Baen Free Library, but he steps back and admits that the real reason Baen is promoting the free on-line distribution is that it increases the publisher's profits.[6] If it didn't work, they wouldn't do it. It is counterintuitive, but this belief that free sharing can be profitable and practical rather than just a utopian fantasy is gaining momentum. If you represent clients who are involved in the creative arts, you can expect this to be part of their understanding. Do not, however, overestimate their full understanding of the actual law and even the impact of the CC licenses. Even amongst well-informed advo-cates, much of the actual law and the specific effects of the CC license are widely misunderstood by the enthusiastic users.

2. *GNU General Public License*

The GNU project carries with it much of the same dogma as the Creative Commons, but the GNU General Public License (GPL) is intended for use exclusively with software. Users sometimes confuse the two licenses, but the differences are significant. In addition to being drafted with the sole intention of application to software, the GNU GPL has a much stricter set of requirements. While the Creative Commons license offers a variety of options to be more or less restrictive according to the author's preferences, the GNU GPL has a strict "share alike" requirement. As a result, any time a programmer uses a piece of code that is released under a GNU GPL, the new program which incorporates the GNU GPL code (whether altered or not) will also be covered by the terms of the GNU GPL. There are a number of

---

[4]   *See, e.g.,* Cory Doctorow, *Content Selected Essays on Technology, Creativity, Copyright and the Future of the Future* (2008); http://craphound.com/content/Cory_Doctorow_-_Content.html.

[5]   Baen Books is a legitimate and traditional publishing house focusing on mainly Sci-Fi and Fantasy genre books. www.baen.com.

[6]   Eric Flint, *Introducing the Baen Free Library*, www.baen.com/library/.

other built-in restrictions on the author's rights, such as: adaptations and modifications are always allowed, commercial and non-commercial use is permitted, a copy of the source code must be provided with (or available) for each piece of GNU GPL code as well as any work which contains even a small piece of GNU GPL code. This last piece is quite significant; retaining the source (machine readable) code is a very practical way of keeping users from making modifications to the program. The requirement to provide source code along with the object (human readable) code keeps the express permission to adapt and modify from becoming toothless.

The GNU copyleft version of a license is intended to allow programmers to share code without worrying that someone downstream will use their freely shared code in a proprietary and profit-generating piece of commercial software. There is no restriction against commercial activity per se, so long as the four freedoms of the GNU Public License (GPL) are preserved. These Four Freedoms are the fundamental purpose of the GPL. The GNU site describes the four freedoms[7] as

"Free software" is a matter of liberty, not price. To understand the concept, you should think of "free" as in "free speech," not as in "free beer."

Free software is a matter of the users' freedom to run, copy, distribute, study, change and improve the software. More precisely, it means that the program's users have the four essential freedoms:

- The freedom to run the program, for any purpose (freedom 0).
- The freedom to study how the program works, and change it to make it do what you wish (freedom 1). Access to the source code is a precondition for this.
- The freedom to redistribute copies so you can help your neighbor (freedom 2).
- The freedom to distribute copies of your modified versions to others (freedom 3). By doing this you can give the whole community a chance to benefit from your changes. Access to the source code is a precondition for this.

The GNU website, like the Creative Commons site, is intended to be user friendly for non- lawyers. It does not, however have the variety of options and associated cute symbols, although like Creative Commons, it provides a specific notice in the form of a recognizable logo to be used to identify the code as covered by the GNU GPL terms.

[7] You will notice the Four Freedoms are numbered 0–3 not 1–4. This has to do with how programmers number things and is related somehow to why some people argued that the 21st Century began in 2001 not 2000, the way the rest of the world counted it. This definition is found at www.gnu.org/philosophy/free-sw.html and is reprinted without any particular express permission, because it is free text.

As you read through the attached GNU materials, you will no doubt be struck by the rather evangelical language in the description of the license. In spite of the fervor with which they push their free software dogma, the license itself is well-drafted and legally sound.

If you prefer, you may read these materials on line at the Free Software Foundation's website: www.gnu.org/licenses/gpl-3.0.txt. The main page (with a lot of interesting links) is: www.gnu.org and their main license page is: www.gnu.org/licenses/licenses.html.

A. GNU in a Nutshell

A Quick Guide to GPLv3[8]

Brett Smith

Free Software Foundation, Inc.

licensing@fsf.org

---

[8]   This document is available at: www.gnu.org/licenses/quick-guide-gplv3.pdf. It may not be evident in print, but the fonts used in this document are not normal word processing fonts. The cover page reproduced here is in "CMR10" and is reproduced in that original font as is the rest of this FSF document. These are free software fonts and are used throughout the FSF universe.

Introduction

After a year and a half of public consultation, thousands of comments, and four drafts, version 3 of the GNU General Public License (GPLv3) was finally published on June 29. While there's been a lot of discussion about the license since the first draft appeared, not many people have talked about the benefits that it provides developers. We've published this guide to fill that gap. We'll start with a brief refresher on free software, copyleft, and the goals of the GPL. We'll then review the major changes in the license to see how they advance those goals and benefit developers.

The Foundations of the GPL

Nobody should be restricted by the software they use. There are four freedoms that every user should have:

- the freedom to use the software for any purpose,
- the freedom to share the software with your friends and neighbors,
- the freedom to change the software to suit your needs, and
- the freedom to share the changes you make.

When a program offers users all of these freedoms, we call it free software.

Developers who write software can release it under the terms of the GNU GPL. When they do, it will be free software and stay free software, no matter who changes or distributes the program. We call this copyleft: the software is copyrighted, but instead of using those rights to restrict users like proprietary software does, we use them to ensure that every user has freedom.

We update the GPL to protect its copyleft from being undermined by legal or technological developments.

The most recent version protects users from three recent threats:

- Tivoization: Some companies have created various different kinds of devices that run GPLed software, and then rigged the hardware so that they can change the software that's running, but you cannot. If a device can run arbitrary software, it's a general-purpose computer, and its owner should control what it does. When a device thwarts you from doing that, we call that tivoization.
- Laws prohibiting free software: Legislation like the Digital Millennium Copyright Act and the European Union Copyright Directive make it a crime to write or share software that can break DRM. These laws should not interfere with the rights the GPL grants you.

- Discriminatory patent deals: Microsoft has recently started telling people that they will not sue free software users for patent infringement—as long as you get the software from a vendor that's paying Microsoft for the privilege. Ultimately, Microsoft is trying to collect royalties for the use of free software, which interferes with users' freedom. No company should be able to do this. Version 3 also has a number of improvements to make the license easier for everyone to use and understand. But even with all these changes, GPLv3 isn't a radical new license; instead it's an evolution of the previous version. Though a lot of text has changed, much of it simply clarifies what GPLv2 said. With that in mind, let's review the major changes in GPLv3, and talk about how they improve the license for users and developers.

Neutralizing Laws That Prohibit Free Software — But Not Forbidding DRM

You're probably familiar with the Digital Restrictions Management (DRM) on DVDs and other media. You're probably also familiar with the laws that make it illegal to write your own tools to bypass those 2 restrictions, like the Digital Millennium Copyright Act and the European Union Copyright Directive. Nobody should be able to stop you from writing any code that you want, and GPLv3 protects this right for you.

It's always possible to use GPLed code to write software that implements DRM. However, if someone does that with code protected by GPLv3, section 3 says that the system will not count as an effective technological "protection" measure. This means that if you break the DRM, you'll be free to distribute your own software that does that, and you won't be threatened by the DMCA or similar laws.

As usual, the GNU GPL does not restrict what people do in software; it just stops them from restricting others.

Protecting Your Right to Tinker

Tivoization is a dangerous attempt to curtail users' freedom: the right to modify your software will become meaningless if none of your computers let you do it. GPLv3 stops tivoization by requiring the distributor to provide you with whatever information or data is necessary to install modified software on the device. This may be as simple as a set of instructions, or it may include special data such as cryptographic keys or information about how to bypass an integrity check in the hardware. It will depend on how the hardware was designed—but no matter what information you need, you must be able to get it.

This requirement is limited in scope. Distributors are still allowed to use cryptographic keys for any purpose, and they'll only be required to disclose a key if you need it to modify GPLed software on the device they gave you. The GNU Project itself uses GnuPG to prove the integrity of all the software on its FTP site, and measures like that are beneficial to users. GPLv3 does not stop people from using cryptography; we wouldn't want it to. It only stops people from taking away the rights that the license provides you—whether through patent law, technology, or any other means.

Stronger Protection Against Patent Threats

In the 17 years since GPLv2 was published, the software patent landscape has changed considerably, and free software licenses have developed new strategies to address them. GPLv3 reflects these changes too. Whenever someone conveys software covered by GPLv3 that they've written or modified, they must provide every recipient with any patent licenses necessary to exercise the rights that the GPL gives them. In addition to that, if any licensee tries to use a patent suit to stop another user from exercising those rights, their license will be terminated.

What this means for users and developers is that they'll be able to work with GPLv3-covered software without worrying that a desperate contributor will try to sue them for patent infringement later. With these changes, GPLv3 affords its users more defenses against patent aggression than any other free software license.

Clarifying License Compatibility

If you found some code and wanted to incorporate it into a GPLed project, GPLv2 said that the license on the other code was not allowed to have any restrictions that were not already in GPLv2. As long as that was the case, we said the license was GPL-compatible.

However, some licenses had requirements that weren't really restrictive, because they were so easy to comply with. For example, some licenses say that they don't give you permission to use certain trademarks. That's not really an additional restriction: if that clause wasn't there, you still wouldn't have permission to use the trademark. We always said those licenses were compatible with GPLv2, too. Now, GPLv3 explicitly gives everyone permission to use code that has requirements like this. These new terms should help clear up misunderstandings about which licenses are GPL-compatible, why that is, and what you can do with GPL-compatible code.

New Compatible Licenses

In addition to clarifying the rules about licenses that are already GPL-compatible, GPLv3 is also newly compatible with a few other licenses. The Apache License 2.0 is a prime example. Lots of great free software is available under this license, with strong communities surrounding it. We hope that this change in GPLv3 will foster more cooperation and sharing within the free software community. The chart below helps illustrate some common compatibility relationships between different free software licenses:

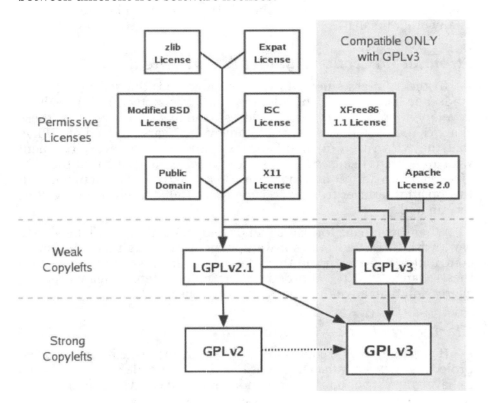

Arrows pointing from one license to another indicate that the first license is compatible with the second. This is true even if you follow multiple arrows to get from one license to the other; so, for example, the ISC license is compatible with GPLv3. GPLv2 is compatible with GPLv3 if the program allows you to choose "any later version" of the GPL, which is the case for most software released under this license. This diagram is not comprehensive (see our licenses page for a more complete list of licenses compatible with GPLv2 and GPLv3), but plainly illustrates that GPLv3 is compatible with just about everything GPLv2 is, and then some.

The GNU Affero GPL version 3 has also been brought into the fold. The original Affero GPL was designed to ensure that all users of a web application would be able to receive its source. The GNU Affero GPL version 3 broadens this goal: it is applicable to all network-interactive software, so it will also work well for programs like game servers. The additional provision is also more flexible, so that if someone uses

AGPLed source in an application without a network interface, they'll only have to provide source in the same sort of way the GPL has always required. By making these two licenses compatible, developers of network-interactive software will be able to strengthen their copyleft while still building on top of the mature body of GPLed code available to them.

More Ways for Developers to Provide Source

One of the fundamental requirements of the GPL is that when you distribute object code to users, you must also provide them with a way to get the source. GPLv2 gave you a few ways to do this, and GPLv3 keeps those intact with some clarification. It also offers you new ways to provide source when you convey object code over a network. For instance, when you host object code on a web or FTP server, you can simply provide instructions that tell visitors how to get the source from a third-party server. Thanks to this new option, fulfilling this require-ment should be easier for many small distributors who only make a few changes to large bodies of source.

The new license also makes it much easier to convey object code via BitTorrent. First, people who are merely downloading or seeding the torrent are exempt from the license's requirements for conveying the software. Then, whoever starts the torrent can provide source by simply telling other torrent users where it is available on a public network server.

These new options help keep the GPL in line with community standards for offering source, without making it harder for users to get.

Less Source to Distribute: New System Libraries Exception

Both versions of the GPL require you to provide all the source nec-essary to build the software, including supporting libraries, compila-tion scripts, and so on. They also draw the line at System Libraries: you're not required to provide the source for certain core components of the operating system, such as the C library.

GPLv3 has adjusted the definition of System Library to include software that may not come directly with the operating system, but that all users of the software can reasonably be expected to have. For example, it now also includes the standard libraries of common programming languages such as Python and Ruby.

The new definition also makes it clear that you can combine GPLed software with GPL-incompatible System Libraries, such as Open-Solaris' C library, and distribute them both together. These changes will make life easier for free software distributors who want to provide these combinations to their users.

A Global License

GPLv2 talks about "distribution" a lot—when you share the program with someone else, you're distributing it. The license never says what distribution is, because the term was borrowed from United States copyright law. We expected that judges would look there for the definition. However, we later found out that copyright laws in other countries use the same word, but give it different meanings. Because of this, a judge in such a country might analyze GPLv2 differently than a judge in the United States.

GPLv3 uses a new term, "convey," and provides a definition for that term. "Convey" has the same meaning we intended for "distribute," but now that this is explained directly in the license, it should be easy for people everywhere to understand what we meant. There are other minor changes throughout the license that will also help ensure it is applied consistently worldwide.

When the Rules Are Broken: A Smooth Path to Compliance

Under GPLv2, if you violated the license in any way, your rights were automatically and permanently lost. The only way to get them back was to petition the copyright holder. While a strong defense against violations is valuable, this policy could cause a lot of headache when someone accidentally ran afoul of the rules. Asking all the copyright holders for a formal restoration of the license could be burdensome and costly: a typical GNU/Linux distribution draws upon the work of thousands.

GPLv3 offers a reprieve for good behavior: if you violate the license, you'll get your rights back once you stop the violation, unless a copyright holder contacts you within 60 days. After you receive such a notice, you can have your rights fully restored if you're a first-time violator and correct the violation within 30 days. Otherwise, you can work out the issue on a case-by-case basis with the copyright holders who contacted you, and your rights will be restored afterward.

Compliance with the GPL has always been the top priority of the FSF Compliance Lab and other groups enforcing the license worldwide. These changes ensure that compliance remains the top priority for enforcers, and gives violators incentive to comply.

The Latest and Greatest

Some of these changes probably seem less important to you than others. That's okay. Every project is different, and needs different things from its license. But odds are that a number of these improvements will help you and your work.

And taken as a whole, all these upgrades represent something more: we made a better copyleft. It does more to protect users' freedom, but it also enables more cooperation in the free software community. But updating the license is only part of the job: in order for people to get the benefits it offers, developers need to use GPLv3 for their projects, too. By releasing your own software under the new license, everyone who deals with it—users, other developers, distributors, even lawyers—will benefit. We hope you'll use GPLv3 for your next release.

If you'd like to learn more about upgrading your project to GPLv3, the FSF Compliance Lab would be happy to assist you. On our web site, you can find basic instructions for using the license, and an FAQ addressing common concerns that people have about it. If your situation is more complicated than that, please contact us and we'll do what we can to help you with your transition. Together, we can help protect freedom for all users.

B. *The Current Version (3.0) of the GNU GPL*

GNU GENERAL PUBLIC LICENSE
Version 3, 29 June 2007

Copyright (C) 2007 Free Software Foundation, Inc. <http://fsf.org/>
Everyone is permitted to copy and distribute verbatim copies
of this license document, but changing it is not allowed.

Preamble

 The GNU General Public License is a free, copyleft license for
software and other kinds of works.

 The licenses for most software and other practical works are designed
to take away your freedom to share and change the works. By contrast,
the GNU General Public License is intended to guarantee your freedom to
share and change all versions of a program — to make sure it remains free
software for all its users. We, the Free Software Foundation, use the
GNU General Public License for most of our software; it applies also to
any other work released this way by its authors. You can apply it to
your programs, too.

 When we speak of free software, we are referring to freedom, not
price. Our General Public Licenses are designed to make sure that you
have the freedom to distribute copies of free software (and charge for
them if you wish), that you receive source code or can get it if you
want it, that you can change the software or use pieces of it in new
free programs, and that you know you can do these things.

 To protect your rights, we need to prevent others from denying you
these rights or asking you to surrender the rights. Therefore, you have
certain responsibilities if you distribute copies of the software, or if
you modify it: responsibilities to respect the freedom of others.

 For example, if you distribute copies of such a program, whether
gratis or for a fee, you must pass on to the recipients the same
freedoms that you received. You must make sure that they, too, receive
or can get the source code. And you must show them these terms so they
know their rights.

 Developers that use the GNU GPL protect your rights with two steps:
(1) assert copyright on the software, and (2) offer you this License
giving you legal permission to copy, distribute and/or modify it.

 For the developers' and authors' protection, the GPL clearly explains
that there is no warranty for this free software. For both users' and
authors' sake, the GPL requires that modified versions be marked as
changed, so that their problems will not be attributed erroneously to
authors of previous versions.

 Some devices are designed to deny users access to install or run
modified versions of the software inside them, although the manufacturer
can do so. This is fundamentally incompatible with the aim of
protecting users' freedom to change the software. The systematic
pattern of such abuse occurs in the area of products for individuals to
use, which is precisely where it is most unacceptable. Therefore, we
have designed this version of the GPL to prohibit the practice for those
products. If such problems arise substantially in other domains, we

stand ready to extend this provision to those domains in future versions
of the GPL, as needed to protect the freedom of users.

Finally, every program is threatened constantly by software patents.
States should not allow patents to restrict development and use of
software on general-purpose computers, but in those that do, we wish to
avoid the special danger that patents applied to a free program could
make it effectively proprietary. To prevent this, the GPL assures that
patents cannot be used to render the program non-free.

The precise terms and conditions for copying, distribution and
modification follow.

                         TERMS AND CONDITIONS

  0. Definitions.

  "This License" refers to version 3 of the GNU General Public License.

  "Copyright" also means copyright-like laws that apply to other kinds of
works, such as semiconductor masks.

  "The Program" refers to any copyrightable work licensed under this
License. Each licensee is addressed as "you". "Licensees" and
"recipients" may be individuals or organizations.

  To "modify" a work means to copy from or adapt all or part of the work
in a fashion requiring copyright permission, other than the making of an
exact copy. The resulting work is called a "modified version" of the
earlier work or a work "based on" the earlier work.

  A "covered work" means either the unmodified Program or a work based
on the Program.

  To "propagate" a work means to do anything with it that, without
permission, would make you directly or secondarily liable for
infringement under applicable copyright law, except executing it on a
computer or modifying a private copy. Propagation includes copying,
distribution (with or without modification), making available to the
public, and in some countries other activities as well.

  To "convey" a work means any kind of propagation that enables other
parties to make or receive copies. Mere interaction with a user through
a computer network, with no transfer of a copy, is not conveying.

  An interactive user interface displays "Appropriate Legal Notices"
to the extent that it includes a convenient and prominently visible
feature that (1) displays an appropriate copyright notice, and (2)
tells the user that there is no warranty for the work (except to the
extent that warranties are provided), that licensees may convey the
work under this License, and how to view a copy of this License. If
the interface presents a list of user commands or options, such as a
menu, a prominent item in the list meets this criterion.

  1. Source Code.

  The "source code" for a work means the preferred form of the work for making modifications to it. "Object code" means any non-source form of a work.

A "Standard Interface" means an interface that either is an official standard defined by a recognized standards body, or, in the case of interfaces specified for a particular programming language, one that is widely used among developers working in that language.

The "System Libraries" of an executable work include anything, other than the work as a whole, that (a) is included in the normal form of packaging a Major Component, but which is not part of that Major Component, and (b) serves only to enable use of the work with that Major Component, or to implement a Standard Interface for which an implementation is available to the public in source code form. A "Major Component", in this context, means a major essential component (kernel, window system, and so on) of the specific operating system (if any) on which the executable work runs, or a compiler used to produce the work, or an object code interpreter used to run it.

The "Corresponding Source" for a work in object code form means all the source code needed to generate, install, and (for an executable work) run the object code and to modify the work, including scripts to control those activities. However, it does not include the work's System Libraries, or general-purpose tools or generally available free programs which are used unmodified in performing those activities but which are not part of the work. For example, Corresponding Source includes interface definition files associated with source files for the work, and the source code for shared libraries and dynamically linked subprograms that the work is specifically designed to require, such as by intimate data communication or control flow between those subprograms and other parts of the work.

The Corresponding Source need not include anything that users can regenerate automatically from other parts of the Corresponding Source.

The Corresponding Source for a work in source code form is that same work.

2. Basic Permissions.

All rights granted under this License are granted for the term of copyright on the Program, and are irrevocable provided the stated conditions are met. This License explicitly affirms your unlimited permission to run the unmodified Program. The output from running a covered work is covered by this License only if the output, given its content, constitutes a covered work. This License acknowledges your rights of fair use or other equivalent, as provided by copyright law.

You may make, run and propagate covered works that you do not convey, without conditions so long as your license otherwise remains in force. You may convey covered works to others for the sole purpose of having them make modifications exclusively for you, or provide you with facilities for running those works, provided that you comply with the terms of this License in conveying all material for which you do not control copyright. Those thus making or running the covered works for you must do so exclusively on your behalf, under your direction and control, on terms that prohibit them from making any copies of your copyrighted material outside their relationship with you.

Conveying under any other circumstances is permitted solely under the conditions stated below. Sublicensing is not allowed; section 10 makes it unnecessary.

3. Protecting Users' Legal Rights From Anti-Circumvention Law.

No covered work shall be deemed part of an effective technological measure under any applicable law fulfilling obligations under article 11 of the WIPO copyright treaty adopted on 20 December 1996, or similar laws prohibiting or restricting circumvention of such measures.

When you convey a covered work, you waive any legal power to forbid circumvention of technological measures to the extent such circumvention is effected by exercising rights under this License with respect to the covered work, and you disclaim any intention to limit operation or modification of the work as a means of enforcing, against the work's users, your or third parties' legal rights to forbid circumvention of technological measures.

4. Conveying Verbatim Copies.

You may convey verbatim copies of the Program's source code as you receive it, in any medium, provided that you conspicuously and appropriately publish on each copy an appropriate copyright notice; keep intact all notices stating that this License and any non-permissive terms added in accord with section 7 apply to the code; keep intact all notices of the absence of any warranty; and give all recipients a copy of this License along with the Program.

You may charge any price or no price for each copy that you convey, and you may offer support or warranty protection for a fee.

5. Conveying Modified Source Versions.

You may convey a work based on the Program, or the modifications to produce it from the Program, in the form of source code under the terms of section 4, provided that you also meet all of these conditions:

a) The work must carry prominent notices stating that you modified it, and giving a relevant date.

b) The work must carry prominent notices stating that it is released under this License and any conditions added under section 7. This requirement modifies the requirement in section 4 to "keep intact all notices".

c) You must license the entire work, as a whole, under this License to anyone who comes into possession of a copy. This License will therefore apply, along with any applicable section 7 additional terms, to the whole of the work, and all its parts, regardless of how they are packaged. This License gives no permission to license the work in any other way, but it does not invalidate such permission if you have separately received it.

d) If the work has interactive user interfaces, each must display Appropriate Legal Notices; however, if the Program has interactive interfaces that do not display Appropriate Legal Notices, your work need not make them do so.

A compilation of a covered work with other separate and independent works, which are not by their nature extensions of the covered work, and which are not combined with it such as to form a larger program, in or on a volume of a storage or distribution medium, is called an "aggregate" if the compilation and its resulting copyright are not used to limit the access or legal rights of the compilation's users beyond what the individual works permit. Inclusion of a covered work in an aggregate does not cause this License to apply to the other parts of the aggregate.

6. Conveying Non-Source Forms.

You may convey a covered work in object code form under the terms of sections 4 and 5, provided that you also convey the machine-readable Corresponding Source under the terms of this License, in one of these ways:

a) Convey the object code in, or embodied in, a physical product (including a physical distribution medium), accompanied by the Corresponding Source fixed on a durable physical medium customarily used for software interchange.

b) Convey the object code in, or embodied in, a physical product (including a physical distribution medium), accompanied by a written offer, valid for at least three years and valid for as long as you offer spare parts or customer support for that product model, to give anyone who possesses the object code either (1) a copy of the Corresponding Source for all the software in the product that is covered by this License, on a durable physical medium customarily used for software interchange, for a price no more than your reasonable cost of physically performing this conveying of source, or (2) access to copy the Corresponding Source from a network server at no charge.

c) Convey individual copies of the object code with a copy of the written offer to provide the Corresponding Source. This alternative is allowed only occasionally and noncommercially, and only if you received the object code with such an offer, in accord with subsection 6b.

d) Convey the object code by offering access from a designated place (gratis or for a charge), and offer equivalent access to the Corresponding Source in the same way through the same place at no further charge. You need not require recipients to copy the Corresponding Source along with the object code. If the place to copy the object code is a network server, the Corresponding Source may be on a different server (operated by you or a third party) that supports equivalent copying facilities, provided you maintain clear directions next to the object code saying where to find the Corresponding Source. Regardless of what server hosts the Corresponding Source, you remain obligated to ensure that it is available for as long as needed to satisfy these requirements.

e) Convey the object code using peer-to-peer transmission, provided you inform other peers where the object code and Corresponding Source of the work are being offered to the general public at no charge under subsection 6d.

A separable portion of the object code, whose source code is excluded from the Corresponding Source as a System Library, need not be included in conveying the object code work.

A "User Product" is either (1) a "consumer product", which means any tangible personal property which is normally used for personal, family, or household purposes, or (2) anything designed or sold for incorporation into a dwelling. In determining whether a product is a consumer product, doubtful cases shall be resolved in favor of coverage. For a particular product received by a particular user, "normally used" refers to a typical or common use of that class of product, regardless of the status of the particular user or of the way in which the particular user actually uses, or expects or is expected to use, the product. A product is a consumer product regardless of whether the product has substantial commercial, industrial or non-consumer uses, unless such uses represent the only significant mode of use of the product.

"Installation Information" for a User Product means any methods, procedures, authorization keys, or other information required to install and execute modified versions of a covered work in that User Product from a modified version of its Corresponding Source. The information must suffice to ensure that the continued functioning of the modified object code is in no case prevented or interfered with solely because modification has been made.

If you convey an object code work under this section in, or with, or specifically for use in, a User Product, and the conveying occurs as part of a transaction in which the right of possession and use of the User Product is transferred to the recipient in perpetuity or for a fixed term (regardless of how the transaction is characterized), the Corresponding Source conveyed under this section must be accompanied by the Installation Information. But this requirement does not apply if neither you nor any third party retains the ability to install modified object code on the User Product (for example, the work has been installed in ROM).

The requirement to provide Installation Information does not include a requirement to continue to provide support service, warranty, or updates for a work that has been modified or installed by the recipient, or for the User Product in which it has been modified or installed. Access to a network may be denied when the modification itself materially and adversely affects the operation of the network or violates the rules and protocols for communication across the network.

Corresponding Source conveyed, and Installation Information provided, in accord with this section must be in a format that is publicly documented (and with an implementation available to the public in source code form), and must require no special password or key for unpacking, reading or copying.

7. Additional Terms.

"Additional permissions" are terms that supplement the terms of this
License by making exceptions from one or more of its conditions.
Additional permissions that are applicable to the entire Program shall
be treated as though they were included in this License, to the extent
that they are valid under applicable law. If additional permissions
apply only to part of the Program, that part may be used separately
under those permissions, but the entire Program remains governed by
this License without regard to the additional permissions.

When you convey a copy of a covered work, you may at your option
remove any additional permissions from that copy, or from any part of
it. (Additional permissions may be written to require their own
removal in certain cases when you modify the work.) You may place
additional permissions on material, added by you to a covered work,
for which you have or can give appropriate copyright permission.

Notwithstanding any other provision of this License, for material you
add to a covered work, you may (if authorized by the copyright holders of
that material) supplement the terms of this License with terms:

   a) Disclaiming warranty or limiting liability differently from the
   terms of sections 15 and 16 of this License; or

   b) Requiring preservation of specified reasonable legal notices or
   author attributions in that material or in the Appropriate Legal
   Notices displayed by works containing it; or

   c) Prohibiting misrepresentation of the origin of that material, or
   requiring that modified versions of such material be marked in
   reasonable ways as different from the original version; or

   d) Limiting the use for publicity purposes of names of licensors or
   authors of the material; or

   e) Declining to grant rights under trademark law for use of some
   trade names, trademarks, or service marks; or

   f) Requiring indemnification of licensors and authors of that
   material by anyone who conveys the material (or modified versions of
   it) with contractual assumptions of liability to the recipient, for
   any liability that these contractual assumptions directly impose on
   those licensors and authors.

All other non-permissive additional terms are considered "further
restrictions" within the meaning of section 10. If the Program as you
received it, or any part of it, contains a notice stating that it is
governed by this License along with a term that is a further
restriction, you may remove that term. If a license document contains
a further restriction but permits relicensing or conveying under this
License, you may add to a covered work material governed by the terms
of that license document, provided that the further restriction does
not survive such relicensing or conveying.

If you add terms to a covered work in accord with this section, you
must place, in the relevant source files, a statement of the

additional terms that apply to those files, or a notice indicating
where to find the applicable terms.

  Additional terms, permissive or non-permissive, may be stated in the
form of a separately written license, or stated as exceptions;
the above requirements apply either way.

  8. Termination.

  You may not propagate or modify a covered work except as expressly
provided under this License. Any attempt otherwise to propagate or
modify it is void, and will automatically terminate your rights under
this License (including any patent licenses granted under the third
paragraph of section 11).

  However, if you cease all violation of this License, then your
license from a particular copyright holder is reinstated (a)
provisionally, unless and until the copyright holder explicitly and
finally terminates your license, and (b) permanently, if the copyright
holder fails to notify you of the violation by some reasonable means
prior to 60 days after the cessation.

  Moreover, your license from a particular copyright holder is
reinstated permanently if the copyright holder notifies you of the
violation by some reasonable means, this is the first time you have
received notice of violation of this License (for any work) from that
copyright holder, and you cure the violation prior to 30 days after
your receipt of the notice.

  Termination of your rights under this section does not terminate the
licenses of parties who have received copies or rights from you under
this License. If your rights have been terminated and not permanently
reinstated, you do not qualify to receive new licenses for the same
material under section 10.

  9. Acceptance Not Required for Having Copies.

  You are not required to accept this License in order to receive or
run a copy of the Program. Ancillary propagation of a covered work
occurring solely as a consequence of using peer-to-peer transmission
to receive a copy likewise does not require acceptance. However,
nothing other than this License grants you permission to propagate or
modify any covered work. These actions infringe copyright if you do
not accept this License. Therefore, by modifying or propagating a
covered work, you indicate your acceptance of this License to do so.

  10. Automatic Licensing of Downstream Recipients.

  Each time you convey a covered work, the recipient automatically
receives a license from the original licensors, to run, modify and
propagate that work, subject to this License. You are not responsible
for enforcing compliance by third parties with this License.

  An "entity transaction" is a transaction transferring control of an
organization, or substantially all assets of one, or subdividing an
organization, or merging organizations. If propagation of a covered
work results from an entity transaction, each party to that

transaction who receives a copy of the work also receives whatever licenses to the work the party's predecessor in interest had or could give under the previous paragraph, plus a right to possession of the Corresponding Source of the work from the predecessor in interest, if the predecessor has it or can get it with reasonable efforts.

You may not impose any further restrictions on the exercise of the rights granted or affirmed under this License. For example, you may not impose a license fee, royalty, or other charge for exercise of rights granted under this License, and you may not initiate litigation (including a cross-claim or counterclaim in a lawsuit) alleging that any patent claim is infringed by making, using, selling, offering for sale, or importing the Program or any portion of it.

11. Patents.

A "contributor" is a copyright holder who authorizes use under this License of the Program or a work on which the Program is based. The work thus licensed is called the contributor's "contributor version".

A contributor's "essential patent claims" are all patent claims owned or controlled by the contributor, whether already acquired or hereafter acquired, that would be infringed by some manner, permitted by this License, of making, using, or selling its contributor version, but do not include claims that would be infringed only as a consequence of further modification of the contributor version. For purposes of this definition, "control" includes the right to grant patent sublicenses in a manner consistent with the requirements of this License.

Each contributor grants you a non-exclusive, worldwide, royalty-free patent license under the contributor's essential patent claims, to make, use, sell, offer for sale, import and otherwise run, modify and propagate the contents of its contributor version.

In the following three paragraphs, a "patent license" is any express agreement or commitment, however denominated, not to enforce a patent (such as an express permission to practice a patent or covenant not to sue for patent infringement). To "grant" such a patent license to a party means to make such an agreement or commitment not to enforce a patent against the party.

If you convey a covered work, knowingly relying on a patent license, and the Corresponding Source of the work is not available for anyone to copy, free of charge and under the terms of this License, through a publicly available network server or other readily accessible means, then you must either (1) cause the Corresponding Source to be so available, or (2) arrange to deprive yourself of the benefit of the patent license for this particular work, or (3) arrange, in a manner consistent with the requirements of this License, to extend the patent license to downstream recipients. "Knowingly relying" means you have actual knowledge that, but for the patent license, your conveying the covered work in a country, or your recipient's use of the covered work in a country, would infringe one or more identifiable patents in that country that you have reason to believe are valid.

If, pursuant to or in connection with a single transaction or

arrangement, you convey, or propagate by procuring conveyance of, a
covered work, and grant a patent license to some of the parties
receiving the covered work authorizing them to use, propagate, modify
or convey a specific copy of the covered work, then the patent license
you grant is automatically extended to all recipients of the covered
work and works based on it.

A patent license is "discriminatory" if it does not include within
the scope of its coverage, prohibits the exercise of, or is
conditioned on the non-exercise of one or more of the rights that are
specifically granted under this License. You may not convey a covered
work if you are a party to an arrangement with a third party that is
in the business of distributing software, under which you make payment
to the third party based on the extent of your activity of conveying
the work, and under which the third party grants, to any of the
parties who would receive the covered work from you, a discriminatory
patent license (a) in connection with copies of the covered work
conveyed by you (or copies made from those copies), or (b) primarily
for and in connection with specific products or compilations that
contain the covered work, unless you entered into that arrangement,
or that patent license was granted, prior to 28 March 2007.

Nothing in this License shall be construed as excluding or limiting
any implied license or other defenses to infringement that may
otherwise be available to you under applicable patent law.

12. No Surrender of Others' Freedom.

If conditions are imposed on you (whether by court order, agreement or
otherwise) that contradict the conditions of this License, they do not
excuse you from the conditions of this License. If you cannot convey a
covered work so as to satisfy simultaneously your obligations under this
License and any other pertinent obligations, then as a consequence you may
not convey it at all. For example, if you agree to terms that obligate you
to collect a royalty for further conveying from those to whom you convey
the Program, the only way you could satisfy both those terms and this
License would be to refrain entirely from conveying the Program.

13. Use with the GNU Affero General Public License.

Notwithstanding any other provision of this License, you have
permission to link or combine any covered work with a work licensed
under version 3 of the GNU Affero General Public License into a single
combined work, and to convey the resulting work. The terms of this
License will continue to apply to the part which is the covered work,
but the special requirements of the GNU Affero General Public License,
section 13, concerning interaction through a network will apply to the
combination as such.

14. Revised Versions of this License.

The Free Software Foundation may publish revised and/or new versions of
the GNU General Public License from time to time. Such new versions will
be similar in spirit to the present version, but may differ in detail to
address new problems or concerns.

Each version is given a distinguishing version number. If the

Program specifies that a certain numbered version of the GNU General Public License "or any later version" applies to it, you have the option of following the terms and conditions either of that numbered version or of any later version published by the Free Software Foundation. If the Program does not specify a version number of the GNU General Public License, you may choose any version ever published by the Free Software Foundation.

   If the Program specifies that a proxy can decide which future versions of the GNU General Public License can be used, that proxy's public statement of acceptance of a version permanently authorizes you to choose that version for the Program.

   Later license versions may give you additional or different permissions. However, no additional obligations are imposed on any author or copyright holder as a result of your choosing to follow a later version.

   15. Disclaimer of Warranty.

   THERE IS NO WARRANTY FOR THE PROGRAM, TO THE EXTENT PERMITTED BY APPLICABLE LAW. EXCEPT WHEN OTHERWISE STATED IN WRITING THE COPYRIGHT HOLDERS AND/OR OTHER PARTIES PROVIDE THE PROGRAM "AS IS" WITHOUT WARRANTY OF ANY KIND, EITHER EXPRESSED OR IMPLIED, INCLUDING, BUT NOT LIMITED TO, THE IMPLIED WARRANTIES OF MERCHANTABILITY AND FITNESS FOR A PARTICULAR PURPOSE. THE ENTIRE RISK AS TO THE QUALITY AND PERFORMANCE OF THE PROGRAM IS WITH YOU. SHOULD THE PROGRAM PROVE DEFECTIVE, YOU ASSUME THE COST OF ALL NECESSARY SERVICING, REPAIR OR CORRECTION.

   16. Limitation of Liability.

   IN NO EVENT UNLESS REQUIRED BY APPLICABLE LAW OR AGREED TO IN WRITING WILL ANY COPYRIGHT HOLDER, OR ANY OTHER PARTY WHO MODIFIES AND/OR CONVEYS THE PROGRAM AS PERMITTED ABOVE, BE LIABLE TO YOU FOR DAMAGES, INCLUDING ANY GENERAL, SPECIAL, INCIDENTAL OR CONSEQUENTIAL DAMAGES ARISING OUT OF THE USE OR INABILITY TO USE THE PROGRAM (INCLUDING BUT NOT LIMITED TO LOSS OF DATA OR DATA BEING RENDERED INACCURATE OR LOSSES SUSTAINED BY YOU OR THIRD PARTIES OR A FAILURE OF THE PROGRAM TO OPERATE WITH ANY OTHER PROGRAMS), EVEN IF SUCH HOLDER OR OTHER PARTY HAS BEEN ADVISED OF THE POSSIBILITY OF SUCH DAMAGES.

   17. Interpretation of Sections 15 and 16.

   If the disclaimer of warranty and limitation of liability provided above cannot be given local legal effect according to their terms, reviewing courts shall apply local law that most closely approximates an absolute waiver of all civil liability in connection with the Program, unless a warranty or assumption of liability accompanies a copy of the Program in return for a fee.

END OF TERMS AND CONDITIONS

How to Apply These Terms to Your New Programs

   If you develop a new program, and you want it to be of the greatest possible use to the public, the best way to achieve this is to make it free software which everyone can redistribute and change under these terms.

To do so, attach the following notices to the program. It is safest
to attach them to the start of each source file to most effectively
state the exclusion of warranty; and each file should have at least
the "copyright" line and a pointer to where the full notice is found.

    <one line to give the program's name and a brief idea of what it does.>
    Copyright (C) <year> <name of author>

    This program is free software: you can redistribute it and/or modify
    it under the terms of the GNU General Public License as published by
    the Free Software Foundation, either version 3 of the License, or
    (at your option) any later version.

    This program is distributed in the hope that it will be useful,
    but WITHOUT ANY WARRANTY; without even the implied warranty of
    MERCHANTABILITY or FITNESS FOR A PARTICULAR PURPOSE. See the
    GNU General Public License for more details.

    You should have received a copy of the GNU General Public License
    along with this program. If not, see <http://www.gnu.org/licenses/>.

Also add information on how to contact you by electronic and paper mail.

    If the program does terminal interaction, make it output a short
notice like this when it starts in an interactive mode:

    <program> Copyright (C) <year> <name of author>
    This program comes with ABSOLUTELY NO WARRANTY; for details type `show
w'.
    This is free software, and you are welcome to redistribute it
    under certain conditions; type `show c' for details.

The hypothetical commands `show w' and `show c' should show the appropriate
parts of the General Public License. Of course, your program's commands
might be different; for a GUI interface, you would use an "about box".

    You should also get your employer (if you work as a programmer) or school,
if any, to sign a "copyright disclaimer" for the program, if necessary.
For more information on this, and how to apply and follow the GNU GPL, see
<http://www.gnu.org/licenses/>.

    The GNU General Public License does not permit incorporating your program
into proprietary programs. If your program is a subroutine library, you
may consider it more useful to permit linking proprietary applications with
the library. If this is what you want to do, use the GNU Lesser General
Public License instead of this License. But first, please read
<http://www.gnu.org/philosophy/why-not-lgpl.html>.

3. Copyright License — Standard Approach

The following summary of copyright license drafting and the annotated sample of a synch license is taken from the Transactional Advisor section of Lexis.com. This group of resources organized by practice area and helpful subsections is a fabulous resource for both a novice and an experienced attorney. Most firms have extensive "form files" from which the attorneys may draw sample agreements similar to the project at hand. Attorneys seldom if ever draft an agreement from scratch.[9] Over time, improved versions are added to the form file and it becomes a valuable commodity. As a general rule, any form agreement you can find on the internet (both free and fee products) are frighteningly bad. This collection on Lexis is surprisingly helpful and is relatively recent; many practicing attorneys are unaware of the resources available here.

Although your time will be subject to enormous demands in practice, it is worth the time to periodically update your training on Lexis and Westlaw research sites. Both companies send reps to offer up-to-date training (and cute logo give-aways) to law firms as well as to law schools where you have doubtlessly already encountered them.

A. Traditional Copyright Licensing Issues

LEXSTAT 2-3 CURRENT LEGAL FORMS FOR INTELLECTUAL PROPERTY § 3.46

Current Legal Forms for Intellectual Property

Copyright 2010, Matthew Bender & Company, Inc., a member of the LexisNexis Group.

Current Legal Forms for Intellectual Property
Chapter 3 PATENTS, COPYRIGHTS AND TRADEMARKS
Part III. Drafting Guidelines

2-3 Current Legal Forms for Intellectual Property § 3.46

AUTHOR: by Frank C. Nicholas and Kevin J. McDevitt

---

[9]   This does of course lead one to wonder when the first versions of the form file agreements were drafted.

§ 3.46 Drafting Guidelines for Copyright License Agreement

[1] Overview

Copyrights are embodied in many different creative mediums, such as literary works; musical works; dramatic works; choreographic works; pictorial, graphic, and sculptural works; motion pictures and other audiovisual works; sound recordings; and architectural works. Additionally, a copyright owner has many exclusive rights in the work, such as the right to reproduce, publicly perform, copy, or record the work. The agreement will set forth with particularity the specific exclusive rights the licensee is afforded, with the remaining rights reserved for the owner.

A copyright license can take many forms, depending on the type of work involved. For example, a mechanical license will be created to allow a licensee to use a song or musical composition in the manufacture and sale of compact discs and phonorecords. Also, a synchronization license will be used to authorize a licensee to include a song in a motion picture in synchronism with the on-screen image.

For public performances, a performance license is created to allow an owner's musical work to be played, whether or not for profit, in a public place. Performance licenses are most commonly used to allow the licensee to play a musical work at a restaurant or club. Because of the difficulty that each copyright owner of each musical work would have to license the thousands of venues that might want to perform or play the work, most owners pay a performance rights society to do so, such as the American Society of Composers, Authors & Publishers ("ASCAP"). ASCAP, in turn, gives each copyright owner a share of the royalties from each license.

Copyright licenses can be created as exclusive or nonexclusive licenses. A nonexclusive license grants the licensee the right to use a copyrighted work in a particular manner. An exclusive license also grants the licensee the right to use the work in a particular manner, but agrees not to allow this right to any other third party. For example, a public performance license will almost always be a nonexclusive license, so that the owner can also allow other venues to perform the musical work.

The fees and royalties associated with a copyright license will vary based on the type of medium, and therefore the type of license. The payment for the license could be in the form of a fixed fee, royalties, or a combination of the two. A fixed fee is a one-time payment for the license usually paid at the time of the agreement. Royalties are based on the number of products sold or a percentage of overall earnings received based on the license.

The provisions of a copyright license will vary directly with the type of medium involved in the license. Drafting the license agreement will be a method of gathering the appropriate provisions based on the medium, as well as the rights licensed to the licensee.

B. *Traditional Approach License — Lexis/Nexis Form*

This form and others like it are available from the Lexis/Nexis Transactional Advisor. The boxed commentary is not part of the actual Form; it is additional, explanatory text. This is a traditional basic form license. Unlike the two examples of Copyleft agreements, this license is crafted to protect and retain an author's rights. There is no concern for the greater good or any higher cause; it is just traditional lawyering with a normal focus on protecting the client. It applies specifically to a **Copyright Synchronization License Agreement** and is therefore more specific in some places than the CC or GNU licenses. Note that while a traditional license would always be tailored this specifically, the CC License is intended to be applicable much more broadly.

[2] FORM: Analysis of a Copyright Synchronization License Agreement

CONTRACT

This agreement is made this _____ day of _____ by and between: LICENSOR, a corporation organized and existing under the laws of the State of _____, with a principal place of business at _____ (hereinafter "Licensor"); and LICENSEE, a corporation organized and existing under the laws of the State of _____, with a principal place of business at _____ (hereinafter "Licensee").

> *COMMENT: The preamble should state the parties with particularity, including the names and addresses as shown. This paragraph should also outline whether the parties are entering into the agreement as entities or individuals.*

WHEREAS the Licensor is the proprietor of the copyright and all rights therein throughout the world in the musical composition entitled "_____," music by _____, lyrics by _____, (hereinafter called the "Composition"); and

> *COMMENT: The recitals should outline the copyright owner's rights in the work, the title of the composition to be licensed, and any limits to those rights. In order to grant the license, the licensor must own the rights in the composition. The licensor must represent and warrant that it is the sole owner of the copyright, and that it has the right to license the work.*

WHEREAS the Licensee is desirous of being authorized by the Licensor to record the Composition in synchronization with one motion picture hereinafter described;

> *COMMENT: This recital has the effect of outlining the specific purpose for the license agreement. The recitals should also state what the purpose of the agreement is, and how the licensee intends on using the transfer of rights.*

NOW, therefore, it is agreed as follows:

1. *Recording Right Grant.* In consideration of, and subject to, the payment by the Licensee to the Licensor of the sum of $_____ within ten days from the date of execution hereof, the Licensor

hereby grants to the Licensee the nonexclusive and limited license, right, and privilege to record the Composition only in synchronization or timed relation with the motion picture here- inafter described, and to make copies of such synchronized recording and to export the same to any country covered by this license, upon and subject to the terms, conditions, limitations, restrictions, and reservations herein contained.

COMMENT: This provision outlines a nonexclusive license grant, but a license grant can be either nonexclusive or exclu- sive. Under a nonexclusive license, the copyright owner licenses the use of the work in a particular manner. An exclusive license allows for the same type of use for a particular manner, but goes further to state that no other licensee will be afforded these rights. An exclusive license gives the licensee of the agreement the sole permission to use the rights granted.

A copyright owner is afforded a bundle of rights, any of which can be assigned or licensed to another party. This license agree- ment grants to the licensee the licensor's right to record the work and the right to copy the work. According to the Copyright Act, a copyright owner has many other exclusive rights in the work, such as the right to reproduce the work, to prepare derivative works, or to perform the work publicly, to name a few.

(a) The motion picture in synchronization with which the Composition my be recorded is "_____," produced by _____ (hereinafter called the "Motion Picture").

COMMENT: This provision should clearly outline the motion picture with which the licensed work will be synchronized.

(b) The type of use to be made of the Composition for such recording is for visual-vocal foreground use. Duration: four minutes, 25 seconds.

COMMENT: The type of use should be very specific so as to limit the grant of license. Some alternatives are a license to use the composition in a movie trailer or for a promotional music video. If the composition is licensed for use in a movie, whether in the body of the movie itself or in a trailer, a separate license is required if the movie is later distributed for private use on videocassette.

> *The type of use might also completely encompass any poten-*
> *tial uses associated with the creation and promotion of the movie,*
> *such as versions translated into foreign languages, television*
> *and radio promotions, and clips or excerpts used in promotional*
> *spots. This provision should also state that the license does not*
> *include any remakes or sequels to the current movie, thereby*
> *limiting the license to the first release.*

(c) The number of such uses is limited to: one.

> *COMMENT: The license agreement used in this example is solely*
> *for the use of a composition once during the movie, either as*
> *background or as a musical number within the movie itself that*
> *adds to the plot or storyline. This provision should be altered as*
> *needed, depending on the use of the composition and the purpose*
> *of the license.*

(d) The territory covered by this recording right license is the United States of America.

> *COMMENT: This license agreement limits the distribution of the*
> *movie containing the composition to the United States. A more*
> *broad territory may list specific countries, or may state that the*
> *territory covered is "the world." It is more common for synchro-*
> *nization licenses to grant a license to the entire world as a terri-*
> *tory, thereby allowing wide distribution of the movie.*

2. *Performing Right Grant.* In consideration of, and subject to, the further payment by the Licensee to the Licensor of the additional sum of $_____ within ten days from the date of execution hereof, the Licensor hereby grants to the Licensee the nonexclusive and limited right to publicly perform, and to authorize others to publicly perform such recordings of the Composition as embodied in the Motion Picture, and in trailers thereof, for the advertising and exploitation thereof, made pursuant to the foregoing recording right grant, only in the territory covered by this performing right grant, and upon the following terms, conditions, limitations, restrictions, and reservations.

> COMMENT: *This provision outlines the grant to the licensee of the right to publicly perform the composition, as limited to the terms of the agreement.*

(a) Such performing right in the Composition shall be limited to the public performance thereof in the exhibition of the Motion Picture to audiences in motion picture theaters and other places of public entertainment where motion pictures are customarily exhibited, including by means of televising motion pictures directly into such theaters or places of public entertainment.

(b) Such performing right in the Composition, in the case of television exhibition of Motion Picture (aside from televising directly to audiences in motion picture theaters or other places of public entertainment, as provided in Subparagraph 2(a) hereof), shall be subject to the express condition that each such television exhibitor shall have obtained, at the time of each such television exhibition, a valid performance license covering each television station over, from, or through which each such television exhibition is to be carried, from the person, firm, or corporation having the right to issue such license, or else directly from the Licensor, separate and apart from this Agreement, and subject to payment of license fees for such separate performance license.

(c) The territory covered by this performing right grant is the United States of America.

3. *Term.* The term of this Agreement shall extend for the remainder of the United States copyright term.

> COMMENT: *An alternative term for this type of license agreement is to allow the license to run in perpetuity. This would be advantageous to the licensor to allow the motion picture to realize its success and profit. This might be important for a synchronization license because some motion pictures don't necessarily become really profitable immediately after release. Additionally, some motion pictures become such long-term classic movies that it would be to a licensor's advantage to allow the term to last in perpetuity.*
>
> *If the medium in which the synchronization license is not a motion picture, but rather with a television program, the term might be limited to several years, depending on the agreement between the parties. A television program would not realize the long-term success that a motion picture might have.*

4. *Cue Sheet.* This Agreement in its entirety (both with respect to recording and performing right grants) shall terminate 30 days after the date of the first public exhibition of the Motion Picture, other than so-called "sneak previews," unless prior to such date the Licensor shall have received from the Licensee a cue sheet of such Motion Picture showing the recorded performance of the Composition licensed hereunder.

COMMENT: When a producer is gathering all compositions for potential use with a motion picture, the synchronization licenses will typically be created before it has ultimately been determined whether the composition will actually be used in the motion picture. The picture will go through many different versions, rewrites and edits, so in the end producers may decide not to use a composition with the picture. The cue sheet provision allows for cancellation of the agreement if the composition is not included in the motion picture. The agreement remains valid if the licensee shows proof to the licensor that the composition, as agreed, was recorded and synchronized with the motion picture. If the composition was not used, the agreement is terminated.

---

5. *Termination.* (a) The Licensor may terminate this Agreement by giving notice thereof to the Licensee if:

COMMENT: The Termination provision will provide for actions that will automatically terminate the agreement, or actions that must be taken to end the agreement before the term end. The termination provision should also include termination resulting from a breach of the agreement. The provision should specifically outline the type of breach required before a party can terminate the agreement based on the breach. Additionally, as shown here, the provision should allow for a period for the party to cure the breach before the agreement is terminated. This option allows for some flexibility for both the licensor and licensee to continue the agreement if the occurrence is unintentional.

(i) The Licensee makes a general assignment of substantially all of its assets for the benefit of creditors; or,

(ii) A petition in bankruptcy or under any insolvency law is filed by or against the Licensee and such petition is not dismissed within sixty (60) days after it has been filed; or,

(iii) The Licensee commits a breach of a material obligation hereunder; provided, however, except for a breach which is a failure to timely make a payment hereunder (in which case the Licensee shall have only 5 days to cure such breach), in the event a breach by the Licensee is capable of being cured, the Licensor may not terminate this Agreement unless and until the Licensee shall have failed to correct such breach within thirty (30) days after it has been served with a notice from the Licensor specifying the breach, requiring its correction, and stating the Licensor's intention to terminate this Agreement if the breach is not corrected within such thirty (30) day period.

(b) In the event this Agreement is terminated by the Licensor pursuant to subsection (a) above, the Licensor and the Licensee shall have the following rights and obligations:

COMMENT: *This section of the Termination provision provides for any further obligations at or after termination for the licensee.*

Some alternative provisions for penalties on the licensee for causing a material breach may be an accelerated payment clause, or a penalty based on fees due, as shown here. This specific provision (b)(i) provides a fee based on the percentage of completion of the motion picture.

(i) The Licensee shall pay to the Licensor a percentage of the prices set forth in Paragraph 1 equal to the percentage of completion, as of the termination date, of the work to be performed hereunder, provided, however, that in no event shall the amount of such payment exceed the total amount remaining unpaid under Paragraph 1 as of the date of the termination hereunder.

(ii) The Licensee shall reimburse the Licensor's actual expenses incurred in terminating any contracts with its subcontractors or suppliers.

(iii) In the event the amounts in Subsections (i) and (ii) above exceed the amounts already paid by the Licensee to the Licensor, the Licensee shall pay the difference to the Licensor within thirty (30) days after receiving from the Licensor an invoice therefore, provided, however, that such invoice must be sent to the Licensee not later than two hundred seventy (270) days after the termination date. If the amounts to be paid to the Licensor are less than the amounts that have already been paid hereunder, the Licensor shall reimburse to the Licensee the difference not later than three hundred (300) days following the date of termination.

6. *Integrity of Composition.* Nothing herein contained shall be deemed to authorize the Licensee or any others to make:

COMMENT: *The terms of this provision are important in limiting the grant of rights in this license agreement. These terms provide that only the music will be utilized in the motion picture, and that the lyrics or storyline will not be copied or adapted in any way for use in the motion picture.*

(a) Any change in the lyrics or in the fundamental character of the music of the Composition;

(b) Any use of the title of the Composition, or any simulation thereof, as the title of the Motion Picture;

COMMENT: *This provision should also state that the licensee has no right to make any translations of the lyrics, unless approved by the licensor. If a translation is allowed, the agreement should provide that any rights in the translated lyrics remain with the licensor.*

(c) Any use of the narrative story of the Composition, or any simulation thereof, as the title of the Motion Picture.

7. *Warranty.* The Licensor makes no warranty or representation, express or implied, except that the Licensor warrants that it has the right to grant the recording and performing license herein granted, subject to the terms, conditions, limitations, restrictions, and reservations herein contained, such licenses being granted and accepted without recourse for any other cause or in any other event whatsoever. If such warranty be breached in whole or in part, the total liability of the Licensor and the sole and exclusive remedy of the Licensee, with respect either to the grant of recording or of performing rights, shall be limited in any event to repaying to the Licensee the consideration theretofore paid hereunder to the extent of such breach.

COMMENT: *It is important for a licensee to secure an agreement that includes the licensor's warranty that it has the right to grant a license in the copyrighted work, and that it is the owner and therefore has this authority. The licensor should also warrant that the license agreement will not infringe any third parties' intellectual property rights. As shown here, the licensor should indemnify the licensee from any damages arising from a breach of warranty by the licensor.*

8. *Reservation of Rights.* The Licensor specifically reserves solely unto itself all rights and uses of every kind and nature whatsoever in and to the Composition, other than the limited rights of recording and performing expressly granted herein, whether now or hereafter known or in existence, including the sole right to exercise and to authorize others to exercise the same at any and all times and places without limitation.

COMMENT: This provision outlines the limitation of the license only to the specific rights outlined in the grant of license. Because a copyright owner is afforded many different exclusive rights, a license agreement should not only specifically outline those rights to be licensed, but also that any other rights not mentioned are reserved for the licensor. This provision is important to make clear the limitation of rights in the license.

9. *Enforcement.* The formation, effect, performance and construction of this Agreement shall be governed by the laws, as though made by two parties residing in the State or Commonwealth of the Licensor so as to be fully performed within the State or Commonwealth of the Licensor.

COMMENT: This is the choice of law provision, stating the jurisdiction under which the agreement will be interpreted. Clearly, this provision favors the licensor, and most agreements will tend to favor the party drafting the agreement, unless the parties negotiate and agree otherwise. Forum selection clauses, if used, are generally enforceable if not unduly burdensome to any party. The forum selection clause states the jurisdiction in which any disputes will be argued.

10. *Entire Agreement.* This Agreement and any attachments hereto constitute the entire agreement and understanding of the parties with respect to the subject matter hereof and supersede all prior agreements and understandings, whether oral or written. No modification or claimed waiver of any of the provisions hereof shall be valid unless in writing and signed by the duly authorized representative against whom such modification or waiver is sought to be enforced.

COMMENT: The Entire Agreement provision prevents any future disputes as to an oral agreement prior to the creation of the written agreement. By including this provision, neither party can dispute a provision included in the agreement based on negotiations or discussions occurring prior to the agreement.

In conjunction with the Entire Agreement provision, the agreement may include procedures for amendment of the agreement, requiring written agreement executed by both parties before any amendments or modifications can be effected.

11. *Other Rights.* Nothing contained in this Agreement shall be construed as conferring by implication, estoppel, or otherwise upon either party any license or other right except the license and rights expressly granted hereunder to that party.

12. *Acceptance.* Each party hereby accepts the licenses and rights granted to it by a party under this Agreement subject to all of the terms and conditions of this Agreement.

In witness whereof the parties hereto have caused this Agreement to be executed the day and year first above written.

[Entity name]

Attest:

_____   by:_____

Secretary   President

[Entity name]

Attest:

_____   by:_____

Secretary   President

C. License Drafting Checklist

This is a very detailed checklist which is available online from the Lexis/Nexis Transactional Advisor. It can be a useful tool to help a novice drafter work through a complex agreement without overlooking any key issues. It also helps explain some of the particular clauses commonly found in a copyright license agreement.

[3] Drafting Checklist — Copyright License Agreement

A. **Parties to the agreement**..................... ❑

    1. Identification of licensor..................... ❑

        a. Give the following information concerning licensor: .... ❑

           (1) Name of licensor..................... ❑

           (2) Entity of Licensor (Individual, Chapter C Corporation, Chapter S Corporation, Partnership, Limited Partnership, Limited Liability Company, Limited Liability Partnership, etc.) .... ❑

           (3) Address or location of licensor .... ❑

           (4) States of incorporation, if a corporation .... ❑

    2. Identification of licensee..................... ❑

        a. Give the following information concerning licensee: .... ❑

           (1) Name of licensee..................... ❑

           (2) Entity of Licensee (Individual, Chapter C Corporation, Chapter S Corporation, Partnership, Limited Partnership, Limited Liability Company, Limited Liability Partnership, etc.)..................... ❑

           (3) Address or location of licensee .... ❑

           (4) States of incorporation, if a corporation .... ❑

B. **Background of the Parties/Agreement** .... ❑

    1. State whether there has been any prior Agreement between the Parties .... ❑

    2. State whether the present Agreement supersedes, novates, incorporates, dominates, etc., any and all prior Agreements between the Parties .... ❑

    3. State whether the present Agreement renders any and all prior Agreements null and void .... ❑

    4. State whether the present Agreement settles any Inferences between the Parties .... ❑

5. State whether the present Agreement settles any pending or future Civil Actions between the Parties .... ❏

C. Preambles or recitals to the agreement .... ❏

1. Subject matter of the license .... ❏

   a. State that the licensor/licensee is the sole owner of the work with respect to which the license is being granted .... ❏

   b. If a statutory copyright has been obtained with respect to the work, specify the registration number and date of registration .... ❏

   c. Recite the nature of the business in which the licensee is engaged................. ❏

   d. Give a brief summary of the purpose for which the agreement is being entered into................. ❏

      (1) The above should be consistent with the matters to be provided in accordance with Section [E] of this checklist .... ❏

D. Definitions. [Practitioner's Note: At this point, any and all Definitions used in the Agreement should be entered and explicitly defined. As an example, this section should include the following *non-exhaustive* list of definitions (or some version thereof more specific to the Agreement).]................. ❏

1. Confidential Information .... ❏

2. Effective Date of the Agreement .... ❏

3. Know-How, especially with regard to software .... ❏

4. Improvements, especially with regard to software .... ❏

5. Territory ....❏

6. Words and phrases used in this Agreement, which are not otherwise defined, shall be interpreted in accordance with the common usage for such words and phrases within the United States of America. Technical terms unless otherwise defined shall be interpreted consistent with their common usage in the Field. Words in the singular include the plural and *vice versa,*unless expressly or implicitly limited ....❏

E. Grant and scope of license....................❏

1. Exclusivity of license....................❏

   a. State whether the license is exclusive or nonexclusive ....❏

   b. If exclusive, specify any limitations thereof, if any [see Section [E].3]............❏

2.   Purpose of license.....................❑

a.   Specify the purpose of the license and the nature of the rights granted, such as:.....................❑

(1) To print, reprint, publish, copy, and sell the work ....❑

(2) To translate the work into other languages or dialects, or make any other version thereof.....................❑

(3) To dramatize any nondramatic work ....❑

(4) To convert any drama into a novel or other nondramatic work ....❑

(5) To perform any drama publicly ....❑

(6) To perform any musical composition publicly, and to make any arrangement or adaptation thereof ....❑

(7) To exercise other rights.....................❑

3.   Restrictions and limitations upon rights ....❑

a.   Specify any and all restrictions, reservations, or limitations upon the exercise of any rights granted under the license, such as whether they are: ....❑

(1) Limited to a specific field or medium ....❑

(2) Limited to a specific geographical territory............ ❑

(3) Subject to specific prior license(s) ....❑

(a) State whether the specific prior license is an exclusive license option .... ❑

(b) State whether the specific prior license is limited to a field of use .... ❑

(c) State whether the specific prior license is limited to a geographic area .... ❑

(d) State whether the specific prior license is limited to the claim(s) of a patent .... ❑

(e) State whether the specific prior license is limited to a time period .... ❑

(4) Subject to the grant of future licenses except to the extent, if any, of the exclusive rights of the licensee ....❑

(5) Subject to any rights which the licensor may retain for his own benefit.....................❑

(6) Permitted to be assigned by licensee, and if so: .... ❑

(a) Whether licensee requires the prior written consent of licensor................. ❏

(b) Whether the Agreement and/or Assignment provides for the license of background inventions ....❏

(c) State the limitations of the Agreement and/or Assignment (i.e., products, units, monetary limitations, percentage limitations, etc. ....❏

(d) State what happens to Assignment upon the termination of the primary license .... ❏

(e) State any other conditions ....❏

(7) Permitted to be sublicensed and, if so, whether ....❏

(a) The prior written consent of licensor is required ....❏

(b) The sublicense terminates automatically upon termination of primary license....................❏

(c) The licensor participates with licensee in any royalties payable under the sublicense .... ❏

(i) Specify the nature and extent of any such participation ....❏

(d) Licensee must give licensor an executed copy of the sublicense ....❏

(e) The sublicense is governed by any limitations (i.e., products, units, monetary limitations, percentage limitations, etc.)....................❏

(f) The sublicense terminates automatically upon the termination of the primary license .... ❏

(g) There are any other conditions .... ❏

(8) Limited to a period of time less than the life of the copyright .... ❏

F. **Consideration or royalty for grant of license** ....❏

    1. Consideration .... ❏

      a. List the monetary amount of consideration due ....❏

      b. List the method of payment, including the currency (Dollars, Pounds, Euros, Pesetas, Yen, Deutsch Marks, etc.).................... ❏

    c.   List the date of payment .... ❏

    d.   List any other factors concerning the payment of consideration .... ❏

2.   Amount of royalty (if any) and method of payment .... ❏

    a.   Specify the royalty to be paid and when the same is payable, which may be expressed in terms of:................❏

       (1) A fixed amount; or....................❏

       (2) A variable amount based upon the number or percentage of units sold, or the monetary value thereof; or....................❏

       (3) A combination of the above....................❏

3.   Fixed royalty....................❏

    a.   Specify the amount which is to be received and when the same is payable.................... ❏

       (1) If the royalty payment is not an installment payment, specify .... ❏

          (a) When the payment is due .... ❏

          (b) The method of payment, including the currency (Dollars, Pounds, Euros, Pesetas, Yen, Deutsch Marks, etc.)..................... ❏

          (c) The date of payment .... ❏

          (d) Any other factors concerning the payment of consideration .... ❏

       (2) If payable in installments, specify: .... ❏

          (a) The number of installments..................... ❏

          (b) The amount of each installment .... ❏

          (c) When each installment is payable; and .... ❏

          (d) Provide for the acceleration of the entire unpaid amount upon: .... ❏

             (i) Failure to pay any installment when due; or .... ❏

             (ii) Breach of any other covenant made by licensee .... ❏

          (e) Adjustments for foreign exchange rate fluctuations .... ❏

          (f) Whether any penalty would apply upon the failure to pay any installment when due. Additionally, state any interest rate application in such cases, and/or the time for the accrual of the interest .... ❏

(g) Whether the royalties will be adjusted for any other factors, such as, for example, inflation, cost of living, etc................... ❑

(3) Specify whether the Agreement provides for prepayment of the royalties. If so, specify details of the pre-payment provisions .... ❑

4. Variable royalty.................... ❑

    a. Specify the amount which is to be received and when the same is payable.................... ❑

       (1) If the royalty payment is not an installment payment, specify .... ❑

          (a) When the payment is due .... ❑

          (b) The method of payment, including the currency (Dollars, Pounds, Euros, Pesetas, Yen, Deutsch Marks, etc.).................... ❑

          (c) The date of payment .... ❑

          (d) Any other factors concerning the payment of consideration............... ❑

       (2) If payable in installments, specify: .... ❑

          (a) The number of installments.................... ❑

          (b) The amount of each installment .... ❑

          (c) When each installment is payable; and .... ❑

          (d) Provide for the acceleration of the entire unpaid amount upon: ❑

             (i) Failure to pay any installment when due; or .... ❑

             (ii) Breach of any other covenant made by licensee .... ❑

          (e) Adjustments for foreign exchange rate fluctuations .... ❑

          (f) Whether any penalty would apply upon the failure to pay any installment when due. Additionally, state any interest rate application in such cases, and/or the time for the accrual of the interest .... ❑

          (g) Whether the royalties will be adjusted for any other factors, such as, for example, inflation, cost of living, etc.................... ❑

(3) Specify whether the Agreement provides for pre-payment of the royalties. If so, specify details of the pre-payment provisions .... ❑

b. Specify the formula which will determine the royalty to be paid, such as:.............. ❑

   (1) A fixed price or rate per unit, multiplied by the total units sold.................. ❑

   (2) A variable price or rate which increases or decreases in accordance with the number of units sold...................... ❑

   (3) A fixed percentage of the net selling price or net sales .... ❑

   (4) A variable percentage of net sales .... ❑

   (5) If royalty is based upon net sales, define "net sales," such as:...................... ❑

      (a) The total amount received on account of invoices billed for the accounting period, less the sum of the following: .... ❑

         (i) Receipts allocable to freight .... ❑

         (ii) Receipts allocable to sales or other taxes or excises .... ❑

         (iii) The amount of all units returned .... ❑

c. State whether the base against which the rate is to be applied: .... ❑

   (1) Is to be recomputed for each specified royalty accounting period, such as:............... ❑

      (a) Monthly...................... ❑

      (b) Quarterly...................... ❑

      (c) Semiannually...................... ❑

      (d) Annually, or...................... ❑

   (2) Is to be cumulative during the term of the license .... ❑

d. State that variable royalties are to be paid within a specified period after the expiration of each royalty accounting period .... ❑

5. Minimum and maximum royalties .... ❑

a. State whether a minimum royalty is payable, and if so, specify the amount thereof and whether:................. ❑

    (1) Such royalties are..................... ❑

        (a) In addition to further royalties payable; or .... ❑

        (b) To be credited on account of further royalties payable .... ❑

            (i) State whether applied to the first royalties payable or in inverse order.................... ❑

    (2) Such royalties are payable:.................... ❑

        (a) In each accounting period for which royalties are to be computed .... ❑

        (b) For any other designated period or periods ...... ❑

        (c) Specify the exact day(s) or date(s) that such royalties become due............... ❑

    (3) The payment of such royalties is .... ❑

        (a) In satisfaction of the licensee's duty to exploit the work; or .... ❑

        (b) An obligation which is imposed in addition to licensee's duty to exploit the work.................... ❑

    (4) Royalty default gives the licensor the option to: .... ❑

        (a) Convert an exclusive license into a nonexclusive license; or .... ❑

        (b) Terminate the license and sue for royalties due .... ❑

  b. State whether and to what extent royalties paid in any period may be credited to royalties payable in the ensuing period(s) .... ❑

  c. State whether the licensee's obligation to pay royalties terminates upon having paid a specified amount .... ❑

    (1) In each accounting period for which royalties are to be computed; or..................... ❑

    (2) In any other designated period(s) .... ❑

  d. Adjustment to minimum and maximum royalties .... ❑

    (1) State whether any minimum or maximum royalty payable is to be adjusted:............... ❑

        (a) By the percentage increase (or decrease) in prices reflected in a specified price index as compiled by the Bureau of Labor Statistics, of the U. S. Department of Labor, or.................... ❑

      (b) In accordance with other specified formula....... ❑

      (c) By any other factors, such as, for example, inflation, cost of living, etc...................... ❑

6.   Accounting for variable royalties .... ❑

    a.   Provide that each variable royalty payment shall be accompanied by a written statement which shall:.......... ❑

      (1) Contain a certification as to the base figure for the royalty accounting period with respect to which payment is made .... ❑

      (2) Be signed by a designated officer of the licensee; and .... ❑

      (3) Bear a notarial acknowledgement as to the signature of such officer...................... ❑

    b.   Specify other information essential to the certification .... ❑

7.   Verification of royalties payable .... ❑

    a.   Licensee shall keep accurate books and records which .... ❑

      (1) Contain all information necessary for an exact determination of all royalties payable for all periods...................... ❑

      (2) Are located at licensee's principal or other designated office; and.............. ❑

      (3) Are available for copying, audit, and examination by any representative or auditor designated by licensor .... ❑

          (a) At any time during normal business hours; or .... ❑

          (b) At other times agreed upon in advance........... ❑

      (4) Are available for the above purposes during a specified period subsequent to the termination or expiration of the agreement .... ❑

      (5) State who bears costs of auditing, including in cases of underpayment..................... ❑

      (6) State whether the licensor receives a written report of the audit............... ❑

8.   Most favored licensee clause..................... ❑

    a.   State whether licensee is entitled to the same benefits of all more favorable provisions contained in each license agreement subsequently entered into by licensor and others covering the same patent or invention .... ❑

        (1) Require that licensor give licensee written notice of each such agreement or modification thereof and a copy of such agreement or modification .... ❏

        (2) Require that licensee give licensor written notice within a specified period in order to obtain such benefits .... ❏

        (3) Provide, where appropriate, that, if licensee desires the benefits of the more favorable provisions, then, at the licensor's option, the licensee must be bound by all provisions which are less favorable .... ❏

        (4) Provide that licensor need not give licensee any such benefits if licensor has previously given licensee written notice of a default which has not been cured........... ❏

  9. Miscellaneous Royalty Provisions. State applicable details of the following items:.................. ❏

    a. Net Amounts of Royalties. That is, specify who pays the tax .... ❏

    b. Type of currency (Dollars, Pounds, Euros, Pesetas, Yen, Deutsch Marks, etc.)...................... ❏

    c. Whether the Agreement provides for automatic and/or electronic payments. If so, specify routing and ABA numbers .... ❏

    d. Whether the Agreement provides for initial/up-front royalty payments .... ❏

    e. Specify what happens to the paid and unpaid royalties if either party terminates the Agreement .... ❏

    f. Specify the effect of the royalty payment upon the expiration of the Copyright .... ❏

    g. Specify when the royalty starts with regard to the reception of the licensed product (i.e., time of sale, F.O.B., etc.)...................... ❏

G. Other rights and duties of the parties .... ❏

  1. Warranties and representations of licensor: .... ❏

    a. Licensor is the sole owner of .... ❏

        (1) The work; and...................... ❏

        (2) Any statutory copyright which has been obtained with respect to the work............... ❏

    b. Licensor has full right, power, and authority to enter into the agreement with licensee............. ❏

    c. The work and any copyright issued with respect thereto does not infringe upon any rights of others................. ❏

2.   Promotion and exploitation of the work .... ❏

    a.   Promotion..................... ❏

       (1) State whether licensee is to use its best efforts to cre-ate a demand for the work............... ❏

       (2) State whether licensee is required to promote or advertise the work in specified media..................... ❏

         (a) Specify whether licensor has the right to approve the format and substance of all promotional material..................... ❏

       (3) State whether licensee is required to expend specified sums for promotional purposes..................... ❏

    b.   Production and sales of the work .... ❏

       (1) Specify whether the licensee is required: .... ❏

         (a) Either to produce or sell a specified number of units during designated periods; or............... ❏

         (b) To satisfy public demand for the work .... ❏

       (2) Specify whether either of the following shall consti-tute sufficient performance in lieu of the above: .... ❏

         (a) Licensee's payment to licensor of a minimum royalty .... ❏

         (b) Licensee's exertion of its best efforts to perform .... ❏

3.   Suspension of obligation to exploit the work .... ❏

    a.   State whether licensee's obligation to exploit the work is suspended, if failure to exploit is caused by any event such as: .... ❏

       (1) Fire, floods, earthquakes..................... ❏

       (2) Explosions, failure, or destruction of plant or equip-ment .... ❏

       (3) Riots, war, strikes, labor disturbances, raw material and equipment shortages............... ❏

       (4) Governmental controls, court order; or .... ❏

       (5) Any other event beyond control of licensee ....❏

    b.   Provide that the period of suspension is coterminous with the event causing inability to perform..................... ❏

    c.   State whether minimum royalties, if any, are payable dur-ing any period of suspension................. ❏

d. Provide that, if the period of suspension exceeds a specified duration, the licensor has the option:.................... ❑

   (1) If an exclusive license, to convert the same into a nonexclusive license; or................. ❑

   (2) To terminate the license.................... ❑

4. Infringement claims and actions .... ❑

  a. Defense of infringement claims and indemnification .... ❑

   (1) State whether licensor is required to indemnify licensee for all damages sustained by it arising out of a claim made or action brought against it for copyright infringement............. ❑

   (2) State whether licensor's obligation to indemnify is: .... ❑

    (a) Limited to the amount of royalties paid by licensee; or.................... ❑

    (b) Limited to another specified amount; or ....❑

    (c) Unlimited in amount.................... ❑

   (3) Provide that licensor's obligation to indemnify is conditioned upon the following:.................... ❑

    (a) Licensee shall give licensor prompt written notice of any claim made or action brought for copyright infringement .... ❑

    (b) Licensee shall not have made any voluntary payment in settlement of the claim or action for which it seeks indemnification .... ❑

    (c) Licensor shall have the right: .... ❑

     (i) To settle or defend the claim or action with counsel of licensor's choice; and............. ❑

     (ii) Require that licensee cooperate with licensor in such settlement or defense........... ❑

     (iii) Require that licensee defend such claim or action: .... ❑

      (a) With counsel of licensor's choice; and................. ❑

      (b) With licensor's cooperation in such defense; and............... ❑

      (c) That licensee make no voluntary payment in settlement of such claim or action.................... ❑

           (d) Licensee shall have paid all costs and fees incidental to the settlement or defense of such claim or action to the extent, if any, required by the license agreement.................... ❏

    b.   Prosecution of infringement claims .... ❏

        (1) Specify whether any action for third-party copyright infringement is to be filed and prosecuted by:..................... ❏

            (a) Licensor, or..................... ❏

            (b) Licensee, or..................... ❏

            (c) Licensor and licensee acting jointly .... ❏

        (2) Specify whether the party required to prosecute any infringement claim shall be given written notice by the other party of information it obtains concerning possible infringement by others .... ❏

        (3) Specify whether any claim or action for copyright infringement may be settled by:..................... ❏

            (a) Licensor, or..................... ❏

            (b) Licensee, or..................... ❏

            (c) Licensor and licensee acting jointly .... ❏

        (4) Specify whether all amounts received in settlement or pursuant to judgment are to be applied............. ❏

            (a) For the benefit of licensor; or .... ❏

            (b) For the benefit of licensee; or .... ❏

            (c) Allocated between licensor and licensee in accordance with specified percentages................. ❏

        (5) Specify whether all costs and fees incidental to the prosecution or settlement of any claim or action are to be paid by: .... ❏

            (a) Licensor, or..................... ❏

            (b) Licensee, or..................... ❏

            (c) Licensor and licensee in accordance with specified percentages .... ❏

  5.   Copyright notice..................... ❏

    a.   Provide, where applicable, that each copy of the work shall bear an appropriate copyright notice............... ❏

    b.   **NOTE:** If a work is published without the requisite copyright notice, it may be considered as having been dedicated to the public .... ❏

    c.   Release from Past Infringement .... ❏

    d.   Taxes .... ❏

Legal Topics:

For related research and practice materials, see the following legal topics:

Copyright Law Conveyances Licenses General Overview

EXERCISE

TOPIC: Licensing

    i.   Licensing Agreements

SKILLS:

    i.   Critical Reasoning

    ii.   Analysis

ESTIMATED TIME FOR COMPLETING THIS EXERCISE:

Approximately two hours.

ESTIMATED LEVEL OF DIFFICULTY (1–5): 3—Critical Reasoning.

1.   Prepare a memo comparing the traditional synch license to the CC license and the GNU GPL. What major differences are apparent? Are there any particular protections beyond copy protection that the traditional license provides that are not present in the CC and GNU licenses? How do the drafting styles compare over all?

2.   Prepare a guidance memo outlining under what circumstances, if any, you would recommend the Creative Commons license to a client. The GNU GPL?

Review the Self-Assessment on the LexisNexis webcourse.

> even though it closely resembles other works so long as
> the similarity is fortuitous, not the result of copying. To
> illustrate, assume that two poets, each ignorant of the
> other, compose identical poems. Neither work is novel, yet
> both are original and, hence, copyrightable.
>
> Originality is a constitutional requirement. The source
> of Congress' power to enact copyright laws is Article I,
> § 8, cl. 8, of the Constitution, which authorizes Congress
> to "secure for limited Times to Authors ... the exclusive
> Right to their respective Writings." In two decisions
> from the late 19th century ... this Court defined the cru-
> cial terms "authors" and "writings." In so doing, the
> Court made it unmistakably clear that these terms
> presuppose a degree of originality.[16]

It need not be unique or non-obvious or even clever or tasteful, but
in order to earn a copyright, a work must fall within one of the eight
statutory categories; it must be an original, creative work of authorship
and it must not fall within the proscribed list of excluded items.[17]

In analyzing the copyrightability of software, then, one first looks to
the threshold requirements. Doing so, one may easily conclude that
some software should fall within the copyright's boundaries. A program
can be viewed accurately as a set of instructions, which can fit within
the first statutory category, Literary Works. The programmer created it,
so it is an original work of authorship, and so long as there is sufficient
detail of expression, one can easily imagine a protectable program. This
is not, however, the same as concluding that all software is presumptively protectable. A program must undergo the same scrutiny that any
literary work does before it may be deemed suitable for copyright. As
has been discussed above, ideas and information are not protectable.
Under patent law, any use of the protected information or process must
be with the patent holder's permission. In copyright, however, the written expression that conveys the information may be copyrighted, but
the underlying information is freely useable by any party. The *Hadley
v. Baxendale* of this idea/expression dichotomy is the 1879 case *Baker
v. Selden*.[18]

In *Baker v. Selden*, which Congress incorporated into Section 102(b)
of the Copyright Act, the Court conclusively outlined the key distinction
between an unprotectable idea and protected expression in copyright
law. In *Baker*, the work at issue was a book detailing a new form
of accounting. It was a fairly revolutionary advance in accounting

---

[16] [n. 18] *See Feist Publ'ns, Inc. v. Rural Tel. Serv. Co.*, 499 U.S. 340, 345–46 (1991) (citations omitted).

[17] [n. 19] The requirement of fixation in a tangible medium, while equally required by the Copyright Act in Section 101 is not discussed here for the sake of brevity. It is well and correctly established that any of the digital media are sufficient to satisfy the fixation requirement. 17 U.S.C. 101 (1994).

[18] [n. 20] 101 U.S. 99 (1879).

procedures and was described in detailed text and tables so that any reader of the book would be able to understand and use the accounting system. The defendant produced a competing book describing the same accounting system. The chapters were not copied verbatim, but some of the tables were exactly reproduced in the second work.[19] There was no question that the author of the second book had copied both the information about the new accounting method and the exact tables from the original work. Nevertheless, the Court found that no infringement had occurred because the copyright of the original work extended only to the author's expression of the new system, not to the system itself and the use thereof.

The actual idea of the system, including the details of its function and how to use the system, were not covered by copyright. Even the exact copying of the tables was permitted, because in order to use the accounting method, one must use tables substantially like those in the original work. The Court reasoned that the tables were necessary to the unprotected method, and to protect the tables would in effect extend protection to the method as well. This is commonly referred to as the merger doctrine. Where there is only one (or limited) ways of expressing an idea, no such expression will be protected. If there is really only one way to describe the process of combining flour, sugar, eggs, chocolate chips, and so forth in a way that will result in a certain savory cookie, then that set of instructions[20] will not be protected. The underlying process is excluded from coverage both by *Baker* and by Section 102(b),[21] and if there is really only one way to describe the process or portion thereof, that expression is deemed to be merged with the idea and is therefore unprotectable.[22]

C. Galloping Into the Future — Applying Copyright to Computers

These fundamental copyright concepts could be applied to software without undue difficulty, and once judges became sufficiently familiar with the basics of computer technology, a line of cases would have developed which would have applied the familiar copyright doctrines to the new technology. Courts could distinguish between idea and expression in software cases as they had in previous cases, although this would likely involve some expert technical advice. This is not a departure from established copyright law, merely a new extension. The

---

[19] [n. 21] *Id.* at 99–101.
[20] [n. 22] This is the case for most recipes.
[21] [n. 23] It is important to note that this does not leave all processes totally without protection. Patent is the correct place for useful processes, machines, etc., but the higher standards and more complicated application process leave copyright a tempting option to many erstwhile applicants.
[22] [n. 24] For a more detailed overview of the idea/expression dichotomy and the merger doctrine, see 4 MELVILLE B. NIMMER & DAVID NIMMER, NIMMER ON COPYRIGHT 13.03[B][3] (2004); MARSHALL A. LEAFFER, UNDERSTANDING COPYRIGHT LAW 2.13 (3d ed. 1999).

Unconscionability issues aside, the enforceability and legality of these agreements allow copyright owners to extend their rights beyond those provided in the Copyright Act. This seems at first as if it should violate the doctrine of federal preemption.[36] Generally, however, although states or other jurisdictional entities are proscribed from varying in any way the federally defined bundle of rights,[37] it has been deemed appropriate to allow private parties to arrive at whatever private deal they choose.[38] The theory held that while it would be improper to allow states to change the scope of the rights provided by the federal government, private deals between individuals are more a matter of freedom of contract than of federal concern.[39] This idea is not a new one, but in the past it was not applied to mass market standard form contracts as it is now. Standardized End User License Agreements (EULAs) are not a matter of private contract. They apply to all users of virtually any computer code; the computer industry very quickly adopted the use of EULAs as standard practice, and as a result, none of us actually owns any of the software we use. Thus, we are all restricted well beyond the bounds of copyright law in how we are allowed to use what we commonly, albeit incorrectly, think of as "our" software.

EULAs are thick with restrictions.[40] Some of the most common terms that have significant copyright implications include the following: that only one copy of the software be installed (if the user has more than one computer, she must purchase more than one copy), that no one else be allowed to use the software, that the software may not be resold, rented, or loaned, and that any failure of the user to abide by any terms of any EULA or other license agreement with the software company renders all such contracts void (in other words, miss a payment on one product and you lose your right to use any of that company's products you may have on your system). Most of these provisions, to which users all blithely agree by ripping open a box or clicking "I Agree," run directly counter to Section 109 of the Copyright Act, the First Sale Doctrine.[41]

---

[36] [n. 38] *See* 17 U.S.C. 301 (1994).

[37] [n. 39] *Id.; see, e.g., Nat'l Basketball Ass'n v. Motorola, Inc.*, 105 F.3d 841 (2d Cir. 1997); *ProCD, Inc.*, 86 F.3d at 1453; *Baltimore Orioles, Inc. v. Major League Baseball Players Ass'n*, 805 F.2d 663 (7th Cir. 1986); *Ehat v. Tanner*, 780 F.2d 876 (10th Cir. 1985). For a general discussion of copyright preemption doctrine, see 1 NIMMER & NIMMER, *supra* note 24, at 1.01[B][1]; MARSHALL A. LEAFFER, UNDERSTANDING COPYRIGHT LAW Ch. 11 (3d ed. 1999).

[38] [n. 40] *See ProCD, Inc.*, 86 F.3d at 1455; *Nat'l Car Rental Sys., Inc. v. Computer Assocs. Int'l, Inc.*, 991 F.2d 426 (8th Cir. 1993); *Taquino v. Teledyne Monarch Rubber*, 893 F.2d 1488 (5th Cir. 1990); *Acorn Structures, Inc. v. Swantz*, 846 F.2d 923, 926 (4th Cir. 1988).

[39] [n. 41] *See ProCD, Inc.*, 86 F.3d at 1454.

[40] [n. 42] *See generally* sample EULA, *supra* note 37.

[41] [n. 43] *See* 17 U.S.C. 109(a) (2000) ("Notwithstanding the provisions of section 106(3) the owner of a particular copy or phonorecord lawfully made under this title, or any person authorized by such owner, is entitled, without the authority of the copyright owner, to sell or otherwise dispose of the possession of that copy or phonorecord.").

The First Sale Doctrine, simply stated, provides that once an individual has purchased a copy of a copyrighted work, that individual may dispose of that copy without the permission of the copyright holder. This includes reselling the copy, loaning it out, burning it, or any of a number of other similar actions. This right is not unlimited and is balanced by the express rights of the copyright holder.[42] For instance, although the owner of a book may sell or give away his copy, he may not make copies of his book, nor may he prepare a new work based on the book, such as a sequel or a screenplay. The balance of rights is carefully drawn and allows the owner of the copy maximum dominion over that physical copy without undermining the copyright protection provided to the underlying intangible work. This long-standing balance between the rights of the copyright holder and a purchaser of a copy of the work take on new aspects with the inclusion of software and EULAs in the copyright equation. The vehicle of a software license neatly sidesteps the limitations of the First Sale Doctrine by avoiding any sale transaction. A license does not trigger the sale, and ownership-based First Sale Doctrine, so the software company is able to take advantage of copyright protection by virtue of the 1980 amendments. It is also able to avoid some of the most significant restrictions on that protection through the fiction of a software "license" rather than sale.

In addition to upholding this result by finding license agreements survive preemption, Judge Easterbrook's widely discussed *ProCD v. Zeidenberg* opinion also opened the door for protection of materials previously unprotectable under the Copyright Act.[43] In *Feist Publications, Inc. v. Rural Telephone Service Company, Inc.*, the Court held that in a dispute between competing producers of white pages phone books, the plaintiff's listings were not protectable under copyright law due to a lack of originality.[44]

Because Rural's white pages lack the requisite originality, Feist's use of the listings cannot constitute infringement. This decision should not be construed as demeaning Rural's efforts in compiling its directory, but rather as making clear that copyright rewards originality, not effort. As this Court noted more than a century ago, "'great praise may be due to the plaintiffs for their industry and enterprise in publishing this paper, yet the law does not contemplate their being rewarded in this way.'"[45]

This expressly overruled the so-called "sweat of the brow" doctrine, under which argument for relief was based on the tremendous effort required to prepare the work.[46] It also made clear that a white pages style directory, no matter how useful or valuable, was exactly the sort of

---

[42] [n. 44] *See id.* 106.
[43] [n. 45] *See ProCD, Inc. v. Zeidenberg*, 86 F.3d 1447 (7th Cir. 1996).
[44] [n. 46] *Feist Publ'ns, Inc. v. Rural Tel. Serv. Co.*, 499 U.S. 340 (1991).
[45] [n. 47] *Id.* at 364 (quoting *Baker v. Selden*, 101 U.S. 99, 105 (1879)).
[46] [n. 48] *Id.*

fact-based work that the Copyright Act expressly left in the public domain. *ProCD*, however, ignores this rule and allows the de facto protection of a digital white pages listing through the vehicle of the license agreement.[47] In *ProCD*, the plaintiffs were the producers of a digital database of names, addresses and phone numbers which is licensed for limited individual use. The defendant obtained a copy of the licensed database and used it for commercial purpose in clear violation of the terms of the license agreement.[48] So by virtue of a shrinkwrap agreement, unprotectable material may be mass marketed with copyright equivalent protection. There is no substantive reason that the same could not apply to the standard white pages supplied to each of us by the phone company each year. In fact, they are generally now delivered in shrinkwrap; the addition of a form agreement inside the wrap would be simple and under the law of *ProCD,* enforceable and legal. The shrink-wrapping of copyright is the next step if the logic of *ProCD* is followed.

Nevertheless, in large part, Judge Easterbrook got it just right.[49] ProCD is one of the companies forging the new rules of digital commerce. The traditional rules really do not provide a good fit. Both copyright law and sales law are awkward around these new forms of works and commerce. The old rules and standards cannot fully envelop the new issues presented by digital works and digital commerce, so Judge Easterbrook made a significant step in setting down a basic rule that does make sense for this type of transaction. This is exactly how the common law is supposed to develop along with the merchants and their new practices. His rule of enforceability of shrinkwrap agreements just formalized what the players already knew; the deal is not on an invoice slip anymore. When you click "I agree," it means you agree. It is a questionable result under both copyright and sales law, but the right one for the new commerce. Circumspect judges and subsequent legislators could ensure that *ProCD*'s progeny do not run wild. *ProCD* should have been just one step in the development of common law in this area. Unfortunately, Congress has already leapt ahead with the 1980 amendments and shortly thereafter, instead of learning from the errors of impatient action in the Copyright Act, the ALI and NCCUSL repeated the mistake with a similarly premature attempt to redraft sales law for computer transactions.

B. *Current Status*

Although copyright protection of software and computer programs is well established and is not likely to be reversed by Congress, there is no real cure for the ill fit inherent from using a law intended to protect

---

[47] [n. 49] *See ProCD, Inc.*, 86 F.3d at 1455.
[48] [n. 50] *Id.* at 1449–50.
[49] [n. 51] I have not discussed his interesting interpretation of the mailbox rule and contract formation in general, but my general conclusion applies to those aspects of his opinion as well.

creative expression and exclude functional aspects of any Work to protect the purely functional list of instructions that is software. Programmers are often frustrated by the scope of protection; unlike under Patent law, there is no way to protect against another programmer taking the idea of a piece of code and merely redrafting the code rather than copying it. Copyright protects the expression, but programmers wish to protect the function and idea.

2. *Patent Protection for Software*

Although early cases seemed to deny patentability for computer programs,[50] it is now settled law that some software can be patentable and that software is not expressly excluded from patentable subject matter under 35 U.S.C. 101. The current trend began in 1981 with *Diamond v. Diehr*[51] in which the Court upheld a patent involving a computer in a process for curing rubber. Multiple variables in the curing process were constantly measured and the measurements were fed into a computer which used these variables to calculate and update the length of time remaining in the curing process. Although this process did include an algorithm and seemed similar to a previously denied patent calculating alarm limits in a catalytic conversion process,[52] in *Diehr,* the Court held that the algorithm at issue was merely a step in a patentable process and was therefore not outside the subject matter of 101.

The Supreme Court did not revisit software patents until its 2010 decision in *Bilski v. Kappos.*[53] In *Bilski,* the Court addressed the "machine or transformation test" which had been developed by the lower courts during the Court's nearly two decades of silence on this topic. Under the machine or transformation test, a program is patentable "only if: '(1) it is tied to a particular machine or apparatus, or (2) it transforms a particular article into a different state or thing.'"[54] The *Bilski* Court upheld the general patentability of software and rejected the lower court approach which applied the machine or transformation test as a required threshold for patentability. "This Court's precedents establish that the machine or transformation test is a useful and important clue, an investigative tool, for determining whether some claimed inventions are processes under §101. The machine-or transformation test is not the sole test for deciding whether an invention is a patent-eligible 'process.'"[55]

---

[50] *Gottshalk v. Benson,* 409 U.S. 63 (1972) (holding unpatentable a binary conversion program as an "algorithm" or a "procedure for solving a given type of mathematical problem" at 65); *Parker v. Flook,* 437 U.S. 584 (1978) (holding unpatentable a program for calculating alarm limits of multiple variables in a catalytic conversion process).

[51] 450 U.S. 175 (1981).

[52] *See Benson,* 409 U.S. at 65; *Flook,* 437 U.S. at 595.

[53] *Bilski v. Kappos,* 561 U.S. _____, 130 S. Ct. 3218, 177 L. Ed. 2d 792 (2010) (affirming *In Re Bilski,* 545 F.3d 943 (Fed. Cir. 2008)).

[54] *Id.,* at Slip Opinion p. 6, *citing In Re Bilski,* at 954.

[55] *Id.,* at Slip Opinion p. 8.

Most programmers object to patent as a protection for their product not because of the standards, rather because of the process. It takes prodigious amounts of time and money to pursue a patent. Even assuming the financial barrier is not prohibitive, the nature of software often makes the patent useless for honest users. Software itself does not have a long shelf life. If a programmer develops a potentially profitable piece of software, whether consumer oriented or technical, by the time the patent would issue, it is obsolete. If you are a patent troll and only interested in obtaining the broad patent protections so you can retroactively prohibit other users from continued use without a high license payment, then the time lag is not a concern. If, on the other hand, you want to release a hot product to the public and make a living off of it, the future litigation based income is not a help. Instead the multiple years of time lag between application and issuance makes the protection mostly worthless.

The ability of unscrupulous trolls to profit so nicely from the fruits of litigation is another reason there is a fair amount of anti-patent bias amongst much of the software community. Protecting one's creation is fine. Ambushing others by gaining rights on a piece of code that has become well known and widely adopted is a perversion of the system, but a very common one today.

This does not mean software companies do not seek patents. Far from it. However, an attorney should recognize the shortcomings of the potential protection and be sure the client understands the process and the ultimate scope of protection. In this way the client will be able to make a reasoned and informed decision, which the attorney will then help to implement.

3. *Trade Secret Protection for Software*

Trade Secret protection was originally a common law doctrine which tended to rely on the Restatement of Torts. Now a majority of jurisdictions have adopted some version of the Uniform Trade Secret Act, but it remains a creature of state law, so variations occur from jurisdiction to jurisdiction. The basic concept is implied by the name. To get the protection of trade secret law, keep the thing you are protecting a secret.

There are not the same complex subject matter requirements for Trade Secrets as in Copyright or Patent.[56] A trade secret can be any

---

[56] The Uniform Trade Secret Act defines Trade Secret as:

"Trade secret" means information, including a formula, pattern, compilation, program, device, method, technique, or process, that:

(i) derives independent economic value, actual or potential, from not being generally known to, and not being readily ascertainable by proper means by, other persons who can obtain economic value from its disclosure or use, and

(ii) is the subject of efforts that are reasonable under the circumstances to maintain its secrecy.

information that has economic value and the economic value derives in part from being confidential. Perhaps the most famous trade secret is the formula for Coca Cola. Other examples can be client lists, proprietary business methods, processes, compilations, software or any other information that gives a business a competitive edge over its competitors. As implied above, the basic requirement for maintaining trade secret status for a company's proprietary materials is to have taken adequate steps to keep the confidential material confidential. Vaults, restricted access computer systems and non-disclosure agreements are among the traditional steps, but it will vary on a case by case basis.

Trade secret protection is fairly straightforward in that there is no application or filing process to undertake. However, the protection is somewhat limited in scope. Trade secret law is in some ways a legal application of the honor system. If you take reasonable steps to protect your information, the law will keep people from taking unreasonable and unfair steps to steal it from you. Copyright's DMCA is similar in philosophy. If a rights-holder embeds reasonable, technical anti-copying technology in a copy of the protected work, legal remedy is provided for the act of circumventing that anti-copying technology that is in addition to the underlying protections of Copyright Law.

Trade secret law does not, however, offer any protection against parties learning your secret without taking any wrongful action, discovering it on their own or reverse engineering to discover it. Companies often need to decide at early stages whether they wish to pursue patent or trade secret protection for proprietary information. There are no requirements of novelty and non-obviousness for trade secret, so often it is the default if the information in question may not clear those substantive Patent hurdles. A Patent application by definition requires a full disclosure of the invention, and should the patent not issue, the disclosure cannot be undone. On the other hand, Patent protection is much more sweeping and comprehensive than the enhanced honor code approach to trade secrets. These decisions are ones where a good attorney can add a great deal of value to a client's decision making process by helping outline the pros and cons of each option with respect to the client's particular proprietary information. Clients tend to understand the value of their IP, but they seldom have a comprehensive understanding of the legal options for protecting it.

4. *Grass Roots Protection Options — Anarchy and Copyleft*

Many programmers subscribe to the philosophy that code, like speech, should be free. They are strong proponents of a system in which programmers develop clever code and share it with others who can improve it or incorporate it into new, but presumptively still clever, pieces of code. It is common for even very talented and highly compensated programmers to routinely use the "shareware" available from free sharing groups such as the Free Software Foundation and their "GNU" project, including a user friendly share-alike or "copyleft" license called the GNU General Public License (GPL). Copyleft is a cute term they coined to describe the pro-sharing license agreements promulgated by the Free Software Foundation and the Creative Commons. Both groups are discussed and a copy of the GNU license is reproduced for your reference in Chapter 9, Copyleft and Licensing. Both licenses are also available in the online materials.

A. The GPL Trap

GPL code is often a valuable source for programmers of all skill levels. The Free Software movement has made it possible for anyone to find existing art solving a particular issue or accomplishing a particular task within a larger program, and it allows them to avoid reinventing the wheel in complex digital formats. Unfortunately, there is an embedded danger using GNU materials. The licenses vary in terms of what use is allowed, but all of them carry to some degree the share and share alike provisions which basically provide as a condition of use that any software containing GNU covered programs will ALSO ITSELF be subject to the GNU provisions. *In other words, if a program contains a small piece of GNU shareware, the ENTIRE program is itself transformed into shareware.* You can imagine the dismay of a corporate client learning that its proprietary software is actually not subject to any basic copyright protection.

5. Ownership of Rights — Employee/Employer Relationships

In both Copyright and Patent, it is common for an employee to create protectable works during his or her employment. A prudent employer has in place clear written agreements with all employees setting forth how ownership and compensation will be apportioned.

A. Patent Law and Employee Issues

"The general rule is that an individual owns the patent rights to the subject matter of which he is an inventor, even though he conceived it or reduced it to practice in the course of his employment. There are two exceptions to this rule: first, an employer owns an employee's invention if the employee is a party to an express contract to that effect; second, where an employee is hired to invent something or solve a particular problem, the property of the invention related to this effort may belong to the employer. Both exceptions are firmly grounded in the principles of contract law that allow parties to freely structure their transactions and obtain the benefit of any bargains reached."[57] The human inventor(s) of a patent must be listed on the patent application, and they are the presumptive owners of the patent. An inventor may, however, be required to assign his or her rights to an employer under the terms of a previous agreement.[58] Thus the terms of any agreement between

---

[57] *Banks v. Unisys Corp.*, 228 F.3d 1357, 1359 (Fed. Cir. 2000).
[58] 1 Donald S. Chisum, Chisum on Patents § 22.01 (Matthew Bender 2010).

employee and employer are crucial and will control whether an employer or employee has the rights to a particular patent invented by the employee.

B. Copyright Law and Employee Issues

The analysis under copyright law is rather more complex. Because any transfer or license of rights under the 1976 Act can be terminated by the author under the Termination of Transfer provisions,[59] it is often important to look not only to a transfer or license of rights, but also to the determination of who is the legal "author" of the work. Under 17 U.S.C. 101, in certain circumstances, an employer will be deemed the author of a work that was in fact created through the efforts of an employee. In these cases, the work is deemed a "Work Made for Hire" and is not subject to any termination of transfers down the road by the employee, because there was no transfer; the employer is considered the actual creator or "author" of the work.

There are two ways to establish a Work Made For Hire. Both are set forth in the definition of Work Made For Hire in Section 101:

A "work made for hire" is

(1) a work prepared by an employee within the scope of his or her employment; or

(2) a work specially ordered or commissioned for use as a contribution to a collective work, as a part of a motion picture or other audiovisual work, as a translation, as a supplementary work, as a compilation, as an instructional text, as a test, as answer material for a test, or as an atlas, if the parties expressly agree in a written instrument signed by them that the work shall be considered a work made for hire. For the purpose of the foregoing sentence, a "supplementary work" is a work prepared for publication as a secondary adjunct to a work by another author for the purpose of introducing, concluding, illustrating, explaining, revising, commenting upon, or assisting in the use of the other work, such as forewords, afterwords, pictorial illustrations, maps, charts, tables, editorial notes, musical arrangements, answer material for tests, bibliographies, appendixes, and indexes, and an "instructional text" is a literary, pictorial, or graphic work prepared for publication and with the purpose of use in systematic instructional activities.

i. Scope of Employment

Under sub-section (1), any work authored by an employee may be a work made for hire if it was created by the employee in the "scope of employment." This is a multistep analysis. The first step is to determine if there is an employment relationship. In the case of a formal, salaried

---

[59] 17 U.S.C. 203, 304(c).

job, the determination may be simple, but there are many less well defined relationships. "Scope of Employment" is a term of art in Agency Law and the Court has held that the principles of agency law will apply to the determination:[60]

> In determining whether a hired party is an employee under the general common law of agency, we consider the hiring party's right to control the manner and means by which the product is accomplished. Among the other factors relevant to this inquiry are the skill required; the source of the instrumentalities and tools; the location of the work; the duration of the relationship between the parties; whether the hiring party has the right to assign additional projects to the hired party; the extent of the hired party's discretion over when and how long to work; the method of payment; the hired party's role in hiring and paying assistants; whether the work is part of the regular business of the hiring party; whether the hiring party is in business; the provision of employee benefits; and the tax treatment of the hired party. See Restatement § 220(2) (setting forth a nonexhaustive list of factors relevant to determining whether a hired party is an employee). No one of these factors is determinative.[61]

Once an employee/employer relationship has been established through the agency law references, the next step is to determine whether the work was created in the scope of that employment. The Restatement 2d of Agency provides a three-part analysis. If all three prongs are satisfied, then the work was created in the scope of the employee's employment: (1) it is of the kind of work he or she is employed to perform; (2) it occurs substantially within authorized time and space limits; and (3) it is actuated, at least in part, by a purpose to serve the employer.[62] Obviously, this is a fact-intensive analysis and the result will vary greatly with the particular circumstances of each case.

ii. *Written Work Made For Hire Agreement*

Subsection (2) provides a different route for the creation of a Work Made For Hire.[63] Under this provision, the work itself must fall into one of the classifications listed in the code *and* there must be a written agreement between the creator and the hiring party clearly indicating an agreement that the work to be created will be a Work Made For Hire. Both prongs must be satisfied. If the work does not fall within one of the statutorily defined categories, no agreement will create a Work Made For Hire, regardless of the intention of the parties.

---

[60] *Community for Creative Non-Violence v. Reid*, 490 U.S. 730, 743 (1989).
[61] *Id*. at 751–752 (citations omitted)
[62] Restatement (Second) of Agency 228.
[63] 17 U.S.C. 101.

Of course, in the absence of a Work Made For Hire, the author of a work may transfer any or all of the Section 107 rights, but any such transfer will be subject to the Termination of Transfers provisions of the Act.[64]

6. *Client-Focused Legal Advice*

This exercise focuses not only on the intellectual property implications of starting a new business, but also on client needs. Law practice is a service industry. It does not exist for its own purposes; it exists only to serve and help the client. Many lawyers lose sight of this fundamental truth as they get absorbed by the intellectual challenges and the stresses that go with the job. Law practice is a demanding world, and it is tragically easy for even the most talented attorney to forget that at the end of the day, no matter how brilliant and attorney is, if the client is not happy and has not been helped by the attorney's efforts, that attorney has failed.

Attorneys who have the luxury of working over time with the same client will inevitably learn the business and will quite naturally align their efforts with the client's needs. If you draft and negotiate enough NASCAR license deals for a merchandiser, you will learn what is and is not possible in the production cycle of die cast cars with driver and sponsor logos. You will even learn which driver matches which number car and who the primary sponsors are. No matter what your ultimate area, if you remember to keep yourself open to the needs of the client rather than the call of law as an entity unto itself, you will have contented clients and a successful practice in any area of the law.

Clients know this too. Following is a blog post by David Berkus, a highly successful venture capitalist, CEO and author.[65]

---

[64] 17 U.S.C. 203, 304(c).

[65] © David Berkus 2010. Reprinted with permission. *See www.berkonomics.com* for a full bio and other articles and blog entries on a variety of business issues.

Berkonomics – Business Insights from Dave Berkus

http://www.berkonomics.com

The value of legal advice isn't measured by a law degree.

Oh boy. This one may get me in trouble with my many attorney friends. But there are considerations an executive must face when relying upon an attorney for either legal or business advice. And the less experience the executive has in an area under discussion, the more likely it is for that person to accept advice from a trusted attorney that may go beyond the attorney's expertise or experience.

That said, attorneys are one of the very best resources for finding all sorts of connections to people, money, potential strategic partners and more. Most all attorneys work diligently to network among their peers, potential clients and within a number of associations. Their position within the community as trusted advisors gives them access to lots of opportunities to connect clients with others as a gesture of goodwill. As always, the problem is at the margins, requiring experience to discern the point where advice offered goes beyond the need or into a dark hole.

Read on for the challenge and click through for a story about one such problem relationship.

All the best,

Dave Berkus

Berkonomics – Business Insights from Dave Berkus

The value of legal advice isn't measured by a law degree.

by Dave Berkus on Aug.09, 2010, under Depending upon others, Surrounding yourself with talent

Over the years in business and as a member of over forty boards, I have received good advice from corporate attorneys and on occasion bad advice as well. There is a line that should be drawn in a relationship between corporate attorney and CEO or board. Attorneys are paid to protect the corporation, not to give business advice. Some are experienced enough to provide great business advice. But the law degree they earned does not assure that, even though most CEO's respect the advice they receive from their attorney highly enough not to doubt the conclusions or the experience behind the conclusions offered.

And since attorneys are paid to protect, often they will give a litany of warnings about what could go wrong when accepting a contract clause they have been trained to challenge. There comes a time when a CEO must decide to reject what may seem like important good advice from the attorney and chance acceptance of terms within a contract that may cause risk, but controllable risk or risk that is so remote as to be worth the acceptance of the business represented by the contract at hand.

I was chairman of a company that had been offered an investment by a Fortune 500 company making a strategic investment in our business, which was capable of driving new demand to the large company though a series of new web services creating a greater need for the large company's products. The business terms had been agreed to between the business development officer of the investing company and our board, as both companies turned the details over to their respective attorneys for documentation.

The attorney for the investor was a member of a large, respected law firm in Silicon Valley, and certainly was full of himself as sole legal protector of the rights of his very significant investor. As drafts of the otherwise standard investment agreements passed from him to our attorney and our management, we immediately spotted a significant number of terms we not only had not agreed to but were contrary to the spirit of the investment. The attorney held fast at every challenge, stating that "these terms are standard for our client and cannot be changed." We appealed to the business development executive, who deferred to the attorney restating that the terms were unchangeable as far as the big company was concerned.

After conferring between our attorney and board, we walked away from what would have been a fine strategic partnership, killed by an attorney who probably understood the client requirements but was unwilling to offer flexible solutions to problem areas. That attorney had made what we considered business decisions on behalf of his client. By the way, we immediately found a willing replacement that had an attorney not quite so full of himself and quickly concluded a similar deal to the acceptance of all. And to this day, I caution my CEO's not to deal with that Fortune 500 firm because of the experience we had with its attorney. You never know how far reaching an action can be, given the speed and extent of communication between CEO's today.

EXERCISE

TOPIC: IP rights in Software (Copyright and Patent)

    i.   Copyright Protection for Software

    ii.   Patent Protection for Software

    iii. Trade Secret

    iv. GNU General Public License

    v.   Employee Creation/Ownership of Rights

SKILLS:

    i.   Critical Reasoning

    ii.   Development of Strategic Plan

    iii. Analysis

    iv. Optional Client Interview

ESTIMATED TIME FOR COMPLETING THIS EXERCISE:

Approximately three hours.

ESTIMATED LEVEL OF DIFFICULTY (1–5): 5—Complex.

CyberAlchemy: Part One

BACKGROUND

You represent CyberAlchemy, LLC., a tech start-up company with limited capitalization and few hard assets. The company's main value is in its founder and President, Andrew Bluemount and the software he has designed. He has written numerous small programs which function invisibly on the back end of many different social networking sites. Most of his early software was designed as a hobby while he was a student and later while he was a frustrated middle manager for several years at a large agro-business conglomerate, AgriGros, Inc. He also did a brief stint as a game developer for about six months after graduation and before joining AgriGros.

So about six months ago, Mr. Bluemount quit his proverbial day job and founded CyberAlchemy. It is currently owned exclusively by him, but he is actively seeking Angel Investors as a first round source of capital, so he will likely have additional shareholders soon. He anticipates wooing venture capitalists for the next stage as well, which will further dilute his ownership and will subject him and CyberAlchemy to detailed scrutiny, so it is important that all of the software is quantifiable and protected. This concern is what has prompted him to come to you.

He has not yet hired any employees, but plans to do so within the next month. He is working on several small but powerful computer programs such as one that will allow companies to cross index their internal databases in a completely new fashion and another that sorts customers automatically based on several indicia of purchasing likelihood which combine basic demographic information with prior purchasing history analysis and a credit record search which utilizes several insidious web crawlers to invisibly obtain a shocking amount of publicly available information about individuals from a panoply of different websites. He plans to package these programs in various compilations of software to license to retail businesses in both the brick and mortar world and online vendors. Some of these compilation products will include earlier pieces of software that he developed prior to founding CyberAlchemy. He mentions that he did not seek a patent for any of the prior programs, but he did post them in a few programmer intensive discussion boards online. He posted all of them under a GNU license because at the time he didn't believe it was moral to own ideas and he wanted to share his brilliant programming with anyone who could use it. Now that he owns a business, however, he has experienced a bit of a viewpoint shift and no longer has any moral conflicts with the concept of exclusivity, provided it works in his favor.

He has engaged experienced securities counsel to advise him on the Angel Investor and Venture Capital process, but he has not had any legal help focused on protecting his and his company's intellectual property.

QUESTIONS

1.   What do you advise him about protecting his software?

2.   What else should you discuss with Andrew? What related steps should he take to protect his company's intellectual property?

Prepare an outline of issues to discuss with Andrew, including how best to address them.

Practice Pointer: This is something of an open-ended question, but it is typical of how clients present their situations. This is where those issue spotting skills from countless law school exams come into play in actual practice. Especially when working with a start up client or other less sophisticated consumer of legal services, you will probably want to address not just the narrow issues the client may have asked about, but also identify and follow up on related concerns that you discover in your review. Here, for example, the client may have just asked about protecting his software, but there are other related issues that he should be contemplating as well. A good lawyer will talk with the client a bit and make sure that the client does indeed need (and want) a comprehensive strategy, then will work towards making sure the client is fully protected on all fronts. If the client does not want to look at any but the immediate issue, it may be a poor decision or it may be a financial one (even unsophisticated clients tend to know that the more things an attorney looks into, the higher the final bill will be).

If the client turns down your advice beyond his specifically framed question, it is always a good idea to record this either in the written memo you prepare for the client or in a file memo of the conversation in which he declined your comprehensive advice. This helps protect you down the road from the indignant cry of "Why didn't you warn me about this?!?" Good practice like file memos of phone conversations and notations in written product allow you to point to it and remind the client that you did indeed warn him of the existence of other issues but he directed you to ignore them. This practice can help divert the downstream wrath of partners as well.

CyberAlchemy: Part Two

CyberAlchemy founder Andrew Bluemount has called you and asked to meet with you to discuss an IP issue that is unrelated to the overall corporate IP protection strategy you are handling for him. He says it involves an old game design idea that he wants to exploit, but he has a few questions that he wants to run by you before he gets too deep into the project because the original idea was created while he was working for another company and teaming up with another employee. You may want to brush up on Work Made For Hire and related issues before your meeting with your client.

Once you have completed your outline, review the Self-Assessment on the LexisNexis webcourse.

Chapter 11
WHERE NO MAN HAS GONE BEFORE — LICENSING

EXERCISE

TOPIC: Trademark Licensing

    i.   Name and Likeness Protection

    ii. Product Endorsement

    iii. Trademark Licensing Agreement

SKILLS:

    i.   Contract Drafting

    ii. Critical Reasoning

    iii. Analysis

ESTIMATED TIME FOR COMPLETING THIS EXERCISE:

Approximately three hours.

ESTIMATED LEVEL OF DIFFICULTY (1–5): 5—Complex.

    You represent a well known and recently retired NASA astronaut, Dave Lightfall. Col. Lightfall successfully completed several space shuttle and international space station missions over the course of his illustrious career.

    Col. Lightfall has been approached by TSS, LLC, a North Carolina company which has manufacturing facilities in many third world countries and a close relationship with QVC (a cable TV based shopping channel). TSS would like to enter into a license deal with Col. Lightfall for the use of his name and likeness on a variety of merchandise which it will sell on QVC and through other retail outlets. Of course, they are counting on the Col.'s participation in the marketing, both with guest appearances at retail outlets or industry conventions and on the "space hour" merchandise show on QVC. The products currently suggested are: freeze dried ice cream, blue flavored Tang, die cast rocket ships of various fanciful and accurate designs, children's costumes, computer games (for Xbox or Nintendo style platform, not internet) and comic books about his adventures. This list is expected to change over time as the parties add and subtract items.

Col. Lightfall is planning on writing his memoirs and hopes to land a gig with The Science Channel narrating a documentary series about space exploration, so he wants to make sure that he does not ruin his reputation by endorsing low quality junk. He also wants to make sure that none of his appearances or products are in poor taste or would undermine his ability to hold himself out as a real scientist. Col. Lightfall also remembers reading about various celebrity products that ended up being a public relations nightmare due to various child labor and sweat shop production facilities. He wants to make sure that nothing like that can be attached to his name.

He has registered his name and domain name as trademarks. He is often referred to in the tabloids and 24-hour television news channels as Star Stud, due in large part to his colorful personal life. He doesn't mind the nickname and, as long as he can control how it's used, he doesn't mind it being part of the deal. It may help sell stuff.

His social life has always been paparazzi-worthy, but he has always stayed in the category of entertaining playboy rather than tasteless scandal. He holds degrees in Aerospace Engineering and Astrophysics, so he does have a respectable science background, but he is not an academic or theoretical scientist. His career has been in practical applications in space flight and media relations. He is pragmatic enough to want to exploit his fifteen minutes of fame, but he does not want to destroy his reputation or in any way reflect poorly on NASA.

The Licensing Agreement that follows is what you have found in your firm's form file. You may assume it is an adequate but not stellar basic form. You noticed that it does not fully address issues such as ownership of any marks or works created in the course of the agreement and that the Licensor is not adequately warranting the products for IP issues or quality. Please edit the agreement as much as necessary to be a good starting point for negations with TSS. You have been told by more experienced attorneys in your firm that the royalty rate for a deal like this would probably be between 8 and 11% of gross sales. The client expressed some hesitation about this deal. The guys from TSS seemed to be promising an awful lot of wildly successful profits, and it seemed a little too good to be true. He wants to make sure that he would not be trapped in this Agreement for a long time if he wants to get out of it, but he understands that they need at least some promise of a reasonable term since there is a lot of start-up cost on their side that they need to be able to recoup. He doesn't want to be unreasonable.

This Licensing Agreement is also available in the Online Materials as a Word document so you can edit it easily.

LICENSING AGREEMENT

This Licensing Agreement (this "**Agreement**") is made this _____ day of _____, 20_____, by and between VRRROOOM, Inc. ("**Licensor**") and Putputput, Inc. ("**Licensee**").

W I T N E S S E T H

WHEREAS, Licensor is engaged in the business of motorsports, including race team ownership and race team marketing and promotion, including Le Mans teams sponsored by William Shatner;

WHEREAS, Licensee is engaged in the business of manufacturing action figures and collectable holographic trading cards;

WHEREAS, Licensor desires to grant to Licensee and Licensee desires to receive from Licensor the non-exclusive rights to produce merchandise bearing the name and likeness of William Shatner.

NOW THEREFORE, in consideration of the covenants contained herein and other good and valuable consideration, the receipt and adequacy of which are hereby acknowledged, the parties hereto hereby agree as follows:

1. Definitions.

    1.1. *Advertising Materials*. All promotional or advertising materials produced by Licensee in connection with this Agreement or the Licensed Products.

    1.2. *Licensed Marks.* The name and likeness of William Shatner, including images related to horseback riding and training, and all marks listed on **Exhibit A** hereto, but excluding all references or images relating to Star Trek, Captain Kirk, ripped shirts, Denny Crane, TJ Hooker, Price Line and any other third party marks with which William Shatner has been associated.

    1.3. *Licensed Products.* Die Cast race cars, t-shirts, caps, sports drinks, clothing, toys, apparel, action figures, holographic trading cards, trading cards, phone apps, pop up ads, ringtones, bumper stickers and home radon test kits.

    1.4. *Related Marks.* All current and future trademarks, tradenames, logos, slogans, artwork, copyrighted materials or other intellectual property of Licensor, its subsidiaries and affiliates, expressly excluding the Licensed Marks.

2. General Grant of License. Subject to the terms and conditions contained in this Agreement, Licensor hereby grants to Licensee the non-exclusive, right, during the Term hereof, to use the Licensed Marks in connection with the production, distribution and sale of the Licensed Products.

3. Territory. The Licensee's use of the Licensed Marks is limited to the following geographic territory: The United States, including

territories thereof, Germany and Guatemala (the "Territory"). No Licensed Products shall be sold or distributed outside the Territory.

4.   Term.

4.1. The initial term of this Agreement shall be ten (10) years from the date hereof. The Agreement shall automatically renew for additional one year terms unless either party hereto gives written notice of its intention to terminate this Agreement at least thirty (30) days prior to the expiration of the then current term. (The initial term together with any renewal terms to be referred to as the "Term" hereof.)

4.2. Licensee shall cease all use of the Licensed Marks and all production of the Licensed Products upon any termination or expiration of this Agreement; provided, however, that Licensee shall be allowed to continue to sell any existing inventories of Licensed Products for a period of six (6) months following the date of the termination or expiration of this Agreement (the "Sell Off Period").

5.   Use of Marks. Licensee shall use the Licensed Marks in connection with the Licensed Products only in such manner as is approved by Licensor pursuant to the terms of this Agreement.

6.   Approvals.

6.1. *Proposed Design Approval*. Prior to any distribution or sale of each Licensed Products, Licensee shall submit to Licensor a detailed plan, schematic, diagram, drawing or other such representation of the form and appearance of each Licensed Product and all related Advertising Materials (a "Proposed Design"). Licensor shall give written notice to Licensee of its approval or rejection of the Proposed Design.

6.2. *Product Approval.* Following Licensor's approval of the Proposed Design, but prior to any full production run or distribution of a particular Licensed Product, Licensee shall submit to Licensor ten (10) samples of such Licensed Product and one (1) sample of all related Advertising Materials for Licensor's approval. Licensor shall give written notice to Licensee of its approval or rejection of the submitted samples.

6.3. *Post Approval Compliance.* Licensee warrants that all Licensed Products and Advertising Materials shall conform in all ways to the samples approved by Licensor. In the event that any non-conforming Licensed Products ("Non-Conforming Goods") are distributed, Licensee agrees to immediately recover such Non-Conforming Goods and notify Licensor. Licensor shall then determine, in its sole judgment whether such Non-Conforming Goods shall be destroyed by Licensee, delivered to Licensor for destruction (at Licensee's sole expense) or distributed as discounted "Seconds" (subject to License Fees).

6.4. *Licensor Termination Rights*. Any failure of Licensee to fully conform to the requirements of this Approvals Section shall give Licensor the right to Terminate this Agreement.

7. License Fee and Report.

7.1. Licensee agrees to pay to Licensor a License Fee equal to fifteen percent (15%) of Licensee's Gross Revenues from sales of the Licensed Products. The License Fee shall be paid on a monthly basis with each Month's License Fee to be due on the fifteenth day of the following month and to be made by check or wire transfer. No deductions, discounts or charge-back of any kind shall be deducted from Gross Revenue prior to the calculation of the License Fee, nor shall any adjustments to Gross Revenues be made for any taxes, tariffs, or other charges related to the production, distribution or sale of the Licensed Products, all of which shall be the sole responsibility of Licensee.

7.2. Each monthly payment of the License Fee shall be accompanied by a report showing all sales of Licensed Products during the previous month, including date of sale, sale price and buyer.

7.3. Licensee agrees to keep, maintain and preserve complete and accurate books, records and accounts of the transactions contemplated by this Agreement and such additional books, records and accounts as are necessary to establish and verify compliance under this Agreement. All such books, records and accounts shall be available for inspection by Licensor and its authorized representatives during reasonable business hours and upon reasonable notice during the term of this Agreement. In the event of Licensor's audit or review resulting in the discovery of an under-reporting or under-payment, in addition to paying any unpaid amounts, Licensee will pay all reasonable costs of Licensor's audit or review, including all costs, auditor's fees and related legal fees.

8. Compliance with Laws.

8.1. Licensee represents warrants and guarantees that all Licensed Products are in compliance with all federal, state and local laws, statutes, ordinances, rules, regulations and orders.

8.2. Licensee intends that the Licensed Products and Advertising Materials will not violate or infringe any Federal or State law or the rights of any third party, including without limitation any copyright, trademark, patent, trade name, trade dress or other intellectual property or proprietary right.

9. Indemnity. Licensee agrees to protect, defend, indemnify and to hold Licensor, and its respective subsidiaries, affiliates, directors, officers and employees ("Indemnitees") harmless from any and all losses, liabilities, damages, costs or expenses (including attorneys'

fees and other expenses of litigation) related to or arising out of (i) any personal/bodily injury, including death at any time resulting therefrom, or damage to property, including loss of use thereof and downtime, caused by any Licensed Product; (ii) any misrepresentation, breach of warranty or covenant or other breach or default by Licensee under this Agreement or (iii) any and all actions, suits, proceedings, claims, demands, assessments, judgments, costs and expenses, including reasonable legal fees and expenses, incident to any of the foregoing or incurred in investigating or attempting to avoid the same or to oppose the imposition thereof, or in enforcing this indemnity; provided, however, that Licensee shall not be obligated under this Agreement to defend, indemnify or hold harmless any Indemnitee from any such loss, liability, damage, cost or expense which results solely from that Indemnitee's willful misconduct or gross negligence. Additionally, without limiting the generality of the foregoing, Licensee shall defend, indemnify and hold harmless Indemnitees from and against any liability, damage, cost or expense arising out of any claim of copyright, patent or other intellectual property infringement relating to any Licensed Product unless such claim relates solely to the Licensed Marks. The indemnifications provided in this Section shall survive any termination or expiration of this Agreement.

10. <u>Insurance.</u> Licensee shall obtain and maintain at its sole expense all times during the Term hereof a product liability policy from a reliable insurance company in an amount not less than $1,000,000.00 per occurrence and shall provide a copy of the current declarations page to Licensor within fifteen (15) days of the execution hereof. Licensee further agrees to give Licensor written notice prior to any modification of the policy.

11. <u>Property Rights.</u> Licensee acknowledges that no right, license or ownership of any kind in or of Licensed Marks is being transferred or granted to Licensee except the limited use license granted by the express terms of this Agreement.

12. <u>Representations and Warranties.</u>

   12.1. Licensor represents and warrants that it has the full right and power to enter into this Agreement and to perform the obligations and grant the rights set forth in this Agreement.

   12.2. Licensee represents and warrants that it has the full right and power to enter into this Agreement and to perform the obligations and grant the rights set forth in this Agreement.

13. <u>Independent Contractor Status.</u> It is understood and agreed by the parties hereto, that the parties shall be and act as independent contractors, and under no circumstances shall this Agreement be construed as one of agency, partnership, joint venture or employment between the parties. Each party acknowledges and agrees

that it neither has nor will give the appearance or impression of having any legal authority to bind or commit the other party in any way.

14. <u>Notices</u>. Any notice, request, demand, waiver or other communication required or permitted to be given under this Agreement will be in writing and will be deemed to have been duly given only if delivered in person, by first class, prepaid, registered or certified mail, sent by courier or by commercial overnight delivery:

If to Licensee:

Legal Department

Putputput, Inc.

9843 Windfall Lane

Winston Salem NC 29872

If to Licensor:

VRRROOOM, Inc.

3245 Sonny Bono Lane

Palm Springs CA 92108

With a copy to:

William Shatner

2 Enterprise Compound

Santa Barbara CA 90210

Or to such other address(es) of which the parties may from time to time give notice. All notices will be deemed to have been received on the actual date of delivery for personal delivery or the receipt date indicated by U.S. Postal Service, courier or overnight delivery company.

15. <u>Right to Specific Performance</u>. Licensee acknowledges that the subject matter of this Agreement is unique, and in the case of any breach of the terms, covenants or conditions to this Agreement by Licensee, Licensor will have, in addition to all other remedies available at law or equity, the right to a decree of specific performance of this Agreement.

16. <u>Waiver</u>. This Agreement or any of its provisions may not be waived except in writing. The failure of any party to enforce any right arising under this Agreement on one or more occasions will not operate as a waiver of that or any other right on that or any other occasion.

17. <u>Headings</u>. The section headings of this Agreement are for convenience only and do not constitute a part of this Agreement.

18. <u>Governing Law</u>. This Agreement shall be governed by and construed in accordance with the substantive laws of the State of North Carolina which apply to a contract executed and to be performed entirely within the State of North Carolina, without regard to principles of conflicts of laws. Licensee irrevocably consents to the exclusive jurisdiction and venue of the Federal Courts in North Carolina or State Courts of North Carolina.

19. <u>Entire Agreement; Amendments</u>. It is understood and agreed that this Agreement constitutes and contains the complete and only agreement between the parties as to the transactions contemplated hereby or the subject matter hereof and that it cancels any and all previous licenses or agreements between the parties as to the transactions contemplated hereby or the subject matter hereof and that it shall not be modified or changed except in writing signed by all parties.

20. <u>Binding Effect; Assignment</u>. This Agreement shall be binding upon and inure to the benefit of the parties hereto and their respective successors and permitted assigns. Licensee may not assign this agreement without the express written consent of Licensor.

21. <u>Relationship of the Parties</u>. Nothing in this Agreement or anything done hereunder shall make or constitute any party hereto the partner, agent, employee or servant of the other, and no party shall be the agent, employee or servant of any other party hereto with respect to the subject of this Agreement. Nothing in this Agreement or anything done hereunder shall create or be deemed to create any relationship of agency, partnership or joint venture between the parties hereto.

22. <u>Severability</u>. In the event that any provision of this Agreement or any word, phrase, clause, sentence or other portion thereof should be held to be unenforceable or invalid for any reason, such provision or portion thereof shall be modified or deleted in such a manner so as to make this Agreement, as modified, legal and enforceable to the fullest extent permitted under applicable laws.

23. <u>Further Assurances</u>. Each party covenants that at any time, and from time to time, it will execute such additional instruments and take such actions as may be reasonably requested by the other parties to confirm or perfect or otherwise to carry out the intent and purposes of this Agreement.

IN WITNESS WHEREOF, the parties hereto have caused this Agreement to be properly executed on the date first written above.

LICENSEE:

PUTPUTPUT, INC.

By:_____

Name:_____

Title:_____

LICENSOR:

VRRROOOM, INC.

By:_____

Name:_____

Title:_____

EXHIBIT A

Licensed Marks

William Shatner

WilliamShatner.com

The Shat

Shatner Automotive

Shatner Racing

Shatner Crew Chiefs

"Shatner: the man, the myth, the legend. AND he can ride horses!"

Chapter 12

LEGACY OF THE CLUEFALL — NEGOTIATING A LICENSING AGREEMENT

OVERVIEW: LICENSING TERMS AND NEGOTIATION TACTICS

Whether you end up in litigation or corporate practice, you will find that negotiation is an important part of your job. This exercise is set up as an opportunity for you to work through a full negotiation involving a commercial deal between an author and a computer game developer.

Just as in practice, everyone involved here has both business and legal concerns. Often, the client is most concerned with the business side of the deal, but one of your responsibilities is to educate the client as to the impact of the various legal terms over which you will be negotiating. If your client does not understand the impact of the legal issues, she will not be able to make an educated decision about whether to go forward if the issues cannot be resolved as you would like. You will not meet with your client in this exercise, but as you negotiate you should keep in mind that your job is to make the deal that your client wants, while, at the same time, making sure there are adequate legal protections in place to minimize your client's risk and exposure. This is not always easy or straight forward, but it is what your client has a right to expect from you.

1. *Negotiation: The Basic Steps*

Negotiating in the legal environment has sometimes been likened to dancing with a partner. While you are learning the steps, it is difficult to keep track of the big picture, much less relax and enjoy yourself. Once you are experienced and confident, you may find it rather jarring if your partner (aka opponent) does not know the steps.

During the learning process, however, it is helpful to have some guidance. Rather than footprint outlines on the floor or a count of "ONE two three four" in your head, following is a basic outline of the stages and steps of a legal negotiation:

A. *Preparation*

Law students and rookie associates often resist this step of negotiations, but they do so at their peril. It is natural to cling to the belief that when the chips are down, you will be struck with a bolt of brilliance and will pull out a stunning legal triumph like Andy Griffith in a Matlock rerun. Unfortunately he had script writers on his side. Failing to fully prepare in advance of a negotiation is like failing to study for an exam. You might manage to scrape by, but you will not excel.

Instead, the first and arguably most important part of your negotiation is the preparation that happens before your first meeting with the other side. You must make yourself completely familiar with (a) your client's situation, (b) her bottom line, absolute requirements for the deal, (c) her aspirations, (d) what your client's back up plan[1] is, *i.e.*, what will she do if you do not reach a deal here and (e) any relevant law, either statutory or case law. Notice that traditional legal research is not the bulk of your preparation. This does not mean it is any less important than in drafting a research memo, rather it means that you have a lot of other things to be thinking about in *addition* to the more familiar legal issues.

After working through the basics of your client's situation, the next task is learning as much as you can about the same issues with respect to the *other* side. You probably will not be able to fully ascertain the other side's needs, alternatives, aspirations and over-all situation, but your client may have some information, and if the deal/other party is significant enough, you may find relevant information on-line, maybe even on the other party's own website.

When you have gathered as much information as you can, it is time to figure out what you do not yet know. You will try to fill in those gaps during the first stage of the actual negotiation. Before you get there, however, you will need to take a little time and work out a strategy of how to approach the negotiation.

Do you have a fairly strong position? Does your opponent seem to have a better situation? Relative power in a negotiation is really all about which party has the better alternatives. If you have another offer waiting in the wings, you do not need this deal as much, and you can afford to hold out for better terms. The same, of course, is true in reverse. If your opponent needs the deal less than you do, you will have a harder time wrestling concessions out of him. If your opponent is rather desperate in comparison to you, you will find you do not need to be as forthcoming with attractive offers.

No strategy survives the first engagement with the enemy.[2] Nevertheless, without preparation and strategy, defeat is virtually assured.

---

[1] In negotiations parlance, this is referred to as your client's BATNA, or Best Alternative To a Negotiated Agreement. By knowing what the client will do if this deal does not come through, you will be better able to know when the deal is not good enough. If your client has a great alternative, then you know going in that if the deal does not look very good, it will not be advantageous to sign. Alternately, if your client is rather desperate and has only fairly unattractive alternatives, then you will need to pursue even a deal that falls far short of ideal.

[2] This axiom has been attributed to nearly every notable military expert from Clausewitz, Napoleon and Moltke to Sun Tsu, MacArthur and Petraeus. It likely originated in the pithy quotable form with Moltke, but certainly all of them said it at some point and knew it to be true.

B. *Introduction and Information Exchange*

This is the first stage of the actual face to face negotiation. Many impatient attorneys dismiss the introductory stages and niceties that waste valuable time; however, it is during the early, more informal stage of the exchanges that often the best opportunities for gathering information will arise. Most lawyers (and law students) are very good at talking; few are equally adept at listening, but it is only by listening that you will be able to start to fill in the blanks in your information about your opponent. You will find that you are much better able to put together a creative, successful deal if you are willing to listen to the other side.[3] Pay attention to what they are willing to tell you without pointed questions. And do not be afraid to provide some information to them as well. This stage of the process is generally referred to as the "information exchange" step; if you do not offer any information, there cannot be an "exchange" at any meaningful level. Do not, of course, reveal sensitive or confidential details, but if you are willing to work *with* the other side on at least some levels, a mutually beneficial deal is much more likely.

Notwithstanding the popularity of military imagery in describing negotiation tactics,[4] diplomacy is arguably more important than aggression. A negotiation, after all, only results in a deal if both sides agree. A congenial approach, especially in a corporate setting where cooperation is virtually required, will be much more likely to lead to success than a take no prisoners approach. Indeed there is a wealth of negotiation experts who hold cooperative or "integrative" techniques to be much more effective even in inherently confrontational situations.[5] Do not mistake this approach for weakness. Only through an understanding of the other side's needs and a willingness to find ways acceptable to both sides to meet them will a negotiated agreement be possible. And that is, after all, why you are both at the table in the first place.

If you waste all your time arguing about why you are right or have the stronger position, at the end of the day, you will have spent a lot of time but made no progress in meeting your client's needs. If, on the other hand, you focus on the issues that each party needs to address and then work with the other side to find a combination of options that will satisfy both, *then* you will be able to bring home the deal for which your client is eagerly hoping.

---

[3] You are not really listening if you are paying attention with half your brain while crafting a retort with the other.

[4] And you need look no further than note 2. *supra*, for an example.

[5] *See, generally,* CARRIE MENKEL MEADOWS, DISPUTE RESOLUTION: BEYOND THE ADVERSARIAL MODEL (2005); ROGER FISHER, WILLIAM URY, & BRUCE PATTON, GETTING TO YES: NEGOTIATING AGREEMENT WITHOUT GIVING IN (2d ed. 1991); RUSSELL KOROBKIN, NEGOTIATION THEORY AND STRATEGY (2d ed. 2009).

C.   Offer and Counter-Offer

This is perhaps where the process begins to look like the horse trading that often comes to mind when picturing a negotiation. Seldom will it be as simple as arguing over a price; generally if there are lawyers involved, there are multiple issues. Here you will find that instead of one series of offer and counter-offer, you will have a complicated series of multi-issue offers. This process is sometimes called Logrolling.[6] Each negotiator keeps several different issues in play, linking concessions on one point to demands on a different, often unrelated one. You may have heard the common advice in car shopping not to negotiate the price of your trade in and the price of the new car at the same time. That advice is only valid if you assume the car salesman has a greater ability to keep track of multiple issues than you do. Contrary to that rather insulting assumption, in a complex legal negotiation, you will need to keep track of many issues at once. A concession on your part with respect to warranties can be matched by a concession from your opponent on indemnities and a moderate concession by both parties on royalty rates and payment schedules.

During this process, you are still gathering information about the other side. As they make offers and counter-offers and justify their positions, you will continue to hone your understanding of the other side's needs. With that information, you can figure out what you can offer them that will meet their needs with the least negative impact on your client. For instance, if you learn that they are absolutely bound to a certain payment schedule, perhaps you will be able to concede that point if your client is not time pressured. Then you tie that concession to a reciprocal request for a favorable definition of the scope of the license. The two issues are not logically related, but each party has a strong need in one of the issues. By identifying each party's needs, a deal satisfying both with minimal concessions can be crafted. Eventually.

This stage of the process is not all cut and dried quid pro quo offers however. Information is still being exchanged. Positions are still being justified. As you discuss the issues with the other side, you will find that although your first instinct may be to argue forcefully for the merits of your position, that approach is more useful in a courtroom than at a negotiation table. Persuasion is an important part of negotiation, but persuading another lawyer and her client is not the same as persuading a judge or jury. Anyone, including opposing counsel, will quite naturally respond more reasonably to requests or demands if you can explain why they are important or fair. Rather than stating loudly that your client could not possible accept anything less than a specific, random-sounding royalty level, you can explain about the opportunity costs inherent in tying up the author's rights to the books for so many years.

---

[6]   ROGER FISHER, WILLIAM URY & BRUCE PATTON, GETTING TO YES: NEGOTIATING AGREEMENT WITHOUT GIVING IN (2d ed. 1991).

If you can show the other side that there are valid reasons for the positions you are taking, you will inevitably get a more positive response from the other side. Persuasion in this form of negotiation is gentle. Panzer Tanks are seldom found in most corporate board rooms.

Note, however, that this stage is called Offer and Counter-Offer. Generally, the parties take turns making concessions and crafting offers. This is where the dance analogy comes back into play. Even if one party seems to be leading, if they are not each taking cues and giving direction, the pair will inevitably get tripped up.

D. Agreement

Once you have come to an agreement on the terms of your deal, you have one crucial step remaining: formalizing the agreement. In the most simple of agreements, there may literally be a handshake and little more, but if lawyers are involved, there should always be some written memorialization of the terms. This can be a simple memo with little more than bullet points and signatures, or it can be a formal legal contract with literally hundreds of pages. Any time, however, that you come to an agreement, it is crucial to write it down in some form and have both parties acknowledge it, albeit informally. Sometimes in the process of reducing the understanding to writing, the parties discover that they have not quite come to a complete meeting of the minds. Misunderstandings or assumptions can be corrected much more easily if they are identified quickly. If both sides have gone back to their clients and reported their understanding of the deal, it is much harder for either to then yield and give up something they thought they had already won. Also, a written memorandum, even a very basic one, is a good insurance policy against either party having imperfect memory of exactly what it was that the parties had in fact agreed.

In more complex corporate deals, it is not uncommon for the negotiation to actually be done in two rounds. First the business oriented folks, often the clients, meet and make agreements on the major economic terms, and then they hand it off to the lawyers to work out the details. Of course those "details" can prove to be more important than the key price terms in the event of a dispute arising in the future, but perhaps that is why it is left to the lawyers.

EXERCISE

TOPIC: Copyright/Trademark Licensing

   i.   Name and Likeness Protection

   ii.   Publishing Rights

   iii.   Licensing

SKILLS:

   i.   Negotiation

   ii.   Contract Drafting (optional)

   iii.   Critical Reasoning

   iv.   Analysis

ESTIMATED TIME FOR COMPLETING THIS EXERCISE:

Approximately three hours.

ESTIMATED LEVEL OF DIFFICULTY (1-5): 5—Complex.

Legacy of the Cluefall Negotiation

Introduction

In this exercise, you will be representing one of the sides in a proposed deal between an author and a video game company. The company wishes to develop a new computer game based on a successful series by the author. Both parties want to make the deal, but each has reasonable concerns about protecting their interests. For instance, on a basic level, the game company needs to make sure they have been granted enough rights, and have received sufficient assurances of help from the author, comfort with respect to the strength of the Author's rights in his own works, and related issues. Similarly, the author wants to make sure that he does not transfer away any more of his valuable book rights than are reasonably necessary to allow the company to make the new games. He will want assurances that the game will not harm either his reputation or the good will associated with the books. Some level of approval and control will need to be distributed between the parties. Finally of course, how much money is going to change hands and on what terms is of key interest to both sides.

Whether you will be formalizing your deal with a short memorandum of understanding or a formal license agreement, the two forms reproduced below will help you identify and understand the issues on a deeper more detailed level than you will see in the confidential information document you receive from your client.

Both draft agreements are drafted as a first "offer" from the game company. The first one is provided as a draft from which the parties can begin their negotiation. It is favorable in many ways to the game company, but that is how the dance goes when formal agreements are involved. One party drafts a first version of the agreement and gives it to the other side, which reviews it and marks it up to reflect more closely what that side would like to see. This, of course, is done in conjunction with sometimes protracted negotiations. The ongoing revision of the agreement is in itself a part of the larger negotiation for the deal.

The second agreement is included to provide you with an example of bad drafting. It is taken (almost) directly from a real negotiation.[7] If you take the time to compare it to the first, more solid, agreement form, you will be able to see more clearly some of the effective and ineffective drafting in each form. The second form is also annotated with some explanatory remarks.

Student Instructions (all students)

You will be assigned to represent either the Author or the Game Developer in this exercise. You will be given information from your client; please keep this information confidential. Do not discuss it with other students in your class, except with a partner if you will be negating in pairs. Treat this information as confidential client information which is protected by attorney-client privilege.

You will be working through a number of complex and realistic licensing issues in this exercise. Please comport yourself at all times during the negotiation process with a professional attitude that would be appropriate for a practicing attorney. (No, you don't have to dress the part — no need to break out the interview suit.)

Remember that your job is to bring home the deal your client wanted if it is possible; you should not let frustration or difficulty with the other side distract you from serving your client's interests at all times.

There are two sets of instructions for the exercise. Your professor will tell you which of them will apply:

I.   Negotiation and Drafting:

    a.   After having sufficient time before hand to prepare, you will either spend a class period or an out-of-class meeting negotiating

---

[7]   Of course, the names have been changed to protect the guilty.

the terms of a license agreement between the author and the game developer. As a starting point for your negotiations, you have a draft license agreement (found in the print materials and on*line) which was prepared by a different lawyer in the game developer's legal department. The author has not agreed to any of the terms in that draft — it is a first draft only and is not binding on either side.

b.   In the time allowed during the negotiation, you should do your best to come to a comprehensive agreement with the other side. Do not try to draft and revise the agreement at this point; focus on working out as detailed an understanding as possible with the other side while you are face to face.

c.   After the negotiation, the game developer's lawyers will incorporate the negotiated terms into the original draft. Your professor will tell you when this revision is due. By the deadline, the game developer's attorney will email the revised draft to the author's attorney, with a copy to the professor. <u>Throughout this exercise, you should copy your professor on all of your email correspondence with the other side.</u>

d.   The Author's attorney will review the revised Agreement and mark the changes he or she thinks are needed to make it acceptable. Your professor will tell you when this mark up is due. By the deadline, the author's attorney will email the marked up draft to the game developer's attorney, with a copy to the professor.

e.   In practice, this process would be repeated several times with a number of phone calls interspersed into the process. For this exercise, the final step will be for the game developer's attorney to accept or reject each of the revisions in the author's mark up. The two parties are allowed to communicate and negotiate a bit with each other to discuss which changes will make it into the final document and in what form, but no further substantial revision or mark ups should be made. Again, your professor will tell you when this process must be completed, and the game developer's attorney will bring a hard copy of the final document to be signed and handed in during class. If the final agreement is not acceptable to the author's attorney, he or she will bring a short summary of why the agreement is not acceptable and will hand that in rather than signing the License Agreement.

f.   PLEASE NOTE: There will be no opportunity for any last minute negotiation or changes in class. All editing and drafting efforts will be cut off as of the time indicated by your professor (i.e., close of business the day before class). The version of the Agreement brought in to be executed in class must be IDENTICAL to the last copy exchanged before the deadline.

Once the exercise in concluded, review the two alternative agreements in the Self-Assessment on the LexisNexis webcourse.

II. Negotiation Only:

a.   After having sufficient time beforehand to prepare, you will either spend a class period or an out-of-class meeting negotiating the terms of a license agreement between the author and the game developer. As a starting point for your negotiations, you have a draft license agreement (found in the print materials and on-line) which was prepared by a different lawyer in the game developer's legal department. The author has not agreed to any of the terms in that draft — it is a first draft only and is not binding on either side.

b.   In the time allowed during the negotiation, you should do your best to come to a comprehensive agreement with the other side. Do not try to draft and revise the agreement; focus on working out as detailed an understanding as possible with the other side while you are face to face.

c.   When you have either reached an agreement or acknowledged that you will not be able to reach an agreement with the other side, you should prepare a short Term Sheet with your opposing counsel, either setting forth the terms of the agreement if one was reached or outlining the terms to which you were able to agree and the terms that were not reconcilable and which led to the impasse. If you were on the path to a resolution but ran out of time, please indicate this and set forth how far you got and which issues were still outstanding. Both parties will sign this short Term Sheet and hand it in to the professor as instructed in class.

Legacy of the Cluefall

Form Licensing Agreements

You will be given a set of Confidential Information from either an author or a game developer whom you will represent. The following Licensing Agreement will be used in the exercise as you negotiate a licensing deal on behalf of your client. A copy of this form is also available in the online materials.

I.　Initial Draft of Licensing Agreement — drafted by Spastic Publishing, Inc. (for use in exercise)

LICENSING AGREEMENT

This Licensing Agreement (this "**Agreement**") is made effective as of the _____ day of _____ 20_____ (the "**Effective Date**") by and between JOHN STARKEY, a resident of Chattanooga, Tennessee ("**Licensor**") and SPASTIC PUBLISHING, INC., a Delaware corporation ("**Licensee**").

W I T N E S S E T H

WHEREAS, Licensor is an author of, among other things, a bestselling series of books known as the *Legacy of the Cluefall*;

WHEREAS, Licensee is engaged in the business of creating and publishing online entertainment communities, core and co-branded gaming content, CD-ROM game titles and other media products, including but not limited to computer, console, online and mobile platform games, card games, board games, books, movies, TV productions, and other products and media;

WHEREAS, Licensor desires to grant to Licensee and Licensee desires to receive from Licensor the exclusive rights to develop certain video and other games based on certain of Licensor's *Legacy of the Cluefall* series;

NOW THEREFORE, in consideration of the covenants contained herein and other good and valuable consideration, the receipt and adequacy of which are hereby acknowledged, the parties hereto hereby agree as follows:

1. Definitions.

    1.1. *Advertising Materials.* The "**Advertising** Materials" shall be all promotional or advertising materials produced by Licensee in connection with this Agreement or the Licensed Products.

    1.2. *Licensed Marks.* The "**Licensed Marks**" shall be any name, likeness, trademark, service mark, logo and other intellectual property rights including copyright, relating to the Legacy of the Cluefall series, consisting of *A Song of Death, Stormy Day, Party in Hell, Archetype, Power Play, Kitty's War, Mozell Clock, Hello Oblivion, How's the Wife and Kids, Diablo, Requiem for Adventure, First Pony Ride* and any future books in the series developed by Licensor during the term of this Agreement (all such titles and the series shall be referred to as the "**Work**").

1.3. *Licensed Products.* The "**Licensed Products**" shall be any computer games, video games, electronic games, card games, online games, coin operated games, board games and other forms of game entertainment based on the Work.

2. General Grant of License. Subject to the terms and conditions contained in this Agreement, Licensor hereby grants to Licensee the exclusive, right, during the Term hereof, to use the Licensed Marks in connection with the production, distribution and sale of the Licensed Products.

3. Territory. The Licensee's use of the Licensed Marks is limited to the following geographic territory: WORLDWIDE (the "Territory").

4. Term. The initial term of this Agreement shall be Five (5) years from the date hereof. Upon the payment of each Initiation Bonus (as such term is described in Section 7) from Licensee to Licensor, the Termination Date shall be extended to the date that is five (5) years after the date of the payment of such Initiation Bonus. Notwithstanding any Termination of this Agreement, Licensor agrees that Licensee may continue to sell a Licensed Product in accordance with the Royalties provision of this Agreement for so long as such License Product continues to sell or for ten (10) years from the product release of such Licensed Product, whichever is longer. (The initial term together with any renewal terms to be referred to as the "Term" hereof.)

5. Use of Marks. Licensee shall use the Licensed Marks in connection with the Licensed Products only in such manner as is approved by Licensor pursuant to the terms of this Agreement.

6. Approvals.

6.1. *Proposed Design Approval.* Prior to any distribution or sale of each Licensed Products, Licensee shall submit to Licensor a detailed plan, schematic, diagram, drawing or other such representation of the form and appearance of each Licensed Product and all related Advertising Materials (a "Proposed Design"). Licensor shall have fifteen (15) business days to approve or reject the Proposed Design. If Licensor fails to reject the Proposed Design within that period, the Proposed Design shall be deemed approved. If Licensor rejects the

Proposed Designs, such rejection will be accompanied with sufficiently detailed explanation of such rejection to allow Licensee to correct the Proposed Design in such as way as to be acceptable to Licensor.

6.2. *Product Approval.* Following Licensor's approval of the Proposed Design, but prior to any full production run or distribution of a particular Licensed Product, Licensee shall submit to Licensor ten (10) samples of such Licensed Product and one (1) sample of all related Advertising Materials for Licensor's approval. Licensor shall have fifteen (15) business days to approve or reject the samples. If Licensor fails to reject the samples within that period, the Proposed Design shall be deemed approved. Licensor may only reject the samples if such samples vary materially from the approved Proposed Design.

6.3. *Post Approval Compliance.* Licensee warrants that all Licensed Products and Advertising Materials shall materially conform to the samples approved by Licensor.

7. License Fee and Report.

7.1. Licensee agrees to pay to Licensor a License Fee equal to Six percent (6%) of Licensee's Net Revenues from sales of the Licensed Products. "**Net Sales**" means the amounts received by Licensee from the sale of the Licensed Products to third parties, less (a) cost of goods, (b) discounts or rebates actually allowed from the billed amount, (c) credits or allowances actually made on claims or returns, (d) taxes or other government charges included in the billed amounts, and (e) freight, postage, insurance charges, packing charges, and any other additional special charges included in the amounts billed. License fees shall be paid on a quarterly basis.

7.2. Each payment of the License Fee shall be accompanied by a report showing all sales of Licensed Products during the previous month, including date of sale, sale price and buyer.

7.3. Licensee agrees to keep, maintain and preserve complete and accurate books, records and accounts of the transactions contemplated by this Agreement.

8. Indemnity. Licensor agrees to protect, defend, indemnify and to hold Licensee, and its respective subsidiaries, affiliates, directors, officers and employees ("Indemnitees") harmless from any and all losses, liabilities, damages, costs or expenses (including attorneys' fees and other expenses of litigation) (i) related to or arising out of any misrepresentation, breach of warranty or covenant or other breach or default by Licensor under this Agreement and (ii) any

and all actions, suits, proceedings, claims, demands, assessments, judgments, costs and expenses, including reasonable legal fees and expenses, incident to any of the foregoing or incurred in investigating or attempting to avoid the same or to oppose the imposition thereof, or in enforcing this indemnity. The indemnifications provided in this Section shall survive any termination or expiration of this Agreement.

9. Property Rights. Licensee acknowledges that no right, license or ownership of any kind in or of Licensed Marks is being transferred or granted to Licensee except the limited use license granted by the express terms of this Agreement.

10. Representations and Warranties.

   10.1. Licensor represents, warrants and covenants as follows: (a) Licensor is the sole author of the Work; (b) Licensor has full power, free of any prior contract, lien or rights of any nature in any person or entity that may interfere with the its ability to i) grant the rights hereby conveyed to Licensee, ii) fulfill its obligations in accordance with the terms of this Agreement or iii) enter into this Agreement; (c) the Work does not contain matter that is libelous or otherwise unlawful or that infringes on the right of privacy, proprietary right or copyright (whether statutory or at common law) of any person or entity.

   10.2. Licensee represents and warrants that it has the full right and power to enter into this Agreement and to perform the obligations and grant the rights set forth in this Agreement.

   10.3. Licensee represents and warrants that the Licensed Products and all versions thereof will be merchantable and of sufficient quality in performance and appearance to pass in commerce.

11. Independent Contractor Status. It is understood and agreed by the parties hereto, that the parties shall be and act as independent contractors, and under no circumstances shall this Agreement be construed as one of agency, partnership, joint venture or employment between the parties. Each party acknowledges and agrees that it neither has nor will give the appearance or impression of having any legal authority to bind or commit the other party in any way.

12. Notices. Any notice, request, demand, waiver or other communication required or permitted to be given under this Agreement will be in writing and will be deemed to have been duly given only if delivered in person, by first class, prepaid, registered or certified mail, sent by courier or by commercial overnight delivery:

If to Licensor: John Starkey
                         2331 Liberty Lane
                         Chattanooga TN 36854

If to Licensee: Spastic Publishing, Inc.
                         206 Cheerwine Drive
                         Cary, North Carolina 27513
                         Attention: John W. Standrop

Or to such other address(es) of which the parties may from time to time give notice. All notices will be deemed to have been received on the actual date of delivery for personal delivery or the receipt date indicated by U.S. Postal Service, courier or overnight delivery company.

13. Right to Specific Performance. Licensee acknowledges that the subject matter of this Agreement is unique, and in the case of any breach of the terms, covenants or conditions to this Agreement by Licensee, Licensor will have, in addition to all other remedies available at law or equity, the right to a decree of specific performance of this Agreement.

14. Waiver. This Agreement or any of its provisions may not be waived except in writing. The failure of any party to enforce any right arising under this Agreement on one or more occasions will not operate as a waiver of that or any other right on that or any other occasion.

15. Headings. The section headings of this Agreement are for convenience only and do not constitute a part of this Agreement.

16. Governing Law. This Agreement shall be governed by and construed in accordance with the substantive laws of the State of North Carolina which apply to a contract executed and to be performed entirely within the State of North Carolina, without regard to principles of conflicts of laws. Licensee irrevocably consents to the exclusive jurisdiction and venue of the Federal courts in North Carolina or State Courts of North Carolina.

17. Entire Agreement; Amendments. It is understood and agreed that this Agreement constitutes and contains the complete and only agreement between the parties as to the transactions contemplated hereby or the subject matter hereof and that it cancels any and all previous licenses or agreements between the parties as to the transactions contemplated hereby or the subject matter hereof and that it shall not be modified or changed except in writing signed by all parties.

18. <u>Binding Effect; Assignment</u>. This Agreement shall be binding upon and inure to the benefit of the parties hereto and their respective successors and permitted assigns. Licensee may not assign this agreement without the express written consent of Licensor.

19. <u>Relationship of the Parties</u>. Nothing in this Agreement or anything done hereunder shall make or constitute any party hereto the partner, agent, employee or servant of the other, and no party shall be the agent, employee or servant of any other party hereto with respect to the subject of this Agreement. Nothing in this Agreement or anything done hereunder shall create or be deemed to create any relationship of agency, partnership or joint venture between the parties hereto.

20. <u>Severability</u>. In the event that any provision of this Agreement or any word, phrase, clause, sentence or other portion thereof should be held to be unenforceable or invalid for any reason, such provision or portion thereof shall be modified or deleted in such a manner so as to make this Agreement, as modified, legal and enforceable to the fullest extent permitted under applicable laws.

21. <u>Further Assurances</u>. Each party covenants that at any time, and from time to time, it will execute such additional instruments and take such actions as may be reasonably requested by the other parties to confirm or perfect or otherwise to carry out the intent and purposes of this Agreement.

IN WITNESS WHEREOF, the parties hereto have caused this Agreement to be properly executed on the date first written above.

LICENSEE:

SPASTIC PUBLISHING, Inc.

By:_____

Name:_____

Title:_____

LICENSOR:

_____

JOHN STARKEY

Legacy of the Cluefall

Form Licensing Agreement

II.   Instuctional Example—Poor Drafting

NOTE: This is an actual contract submitted by a game development company to an author at the beginning of the negotiation process for a deal quite similar to that presented in this Exercise. Specific terms have been adapted and some sections have been deleted for the sake of the exercise, but the errors, inconsistencies and oddly illogical payment provisions are exactly how the Licensee drafted them. Even the formatting is in its original form, complete with inconsistencies. As you read through this Agreement, you should be able to clearly see the pro-publisher bias in the substantive sections. It is provided here to both parties as an example of a fairly one-sided, but not well drafted, Agreement. As you read it, be thinking of not only what provisions are in the agreement, but what important issues are ignored. Some editorial remarks are added in boxes.

This agreement is provided here as a tangible lesson that you can never assume the other side's attorneys are more experienced or have better drafting skills than you. It is not the worst agreement you will see in your practice, but it is an example of fairly poor drafting.

LICENSING AGREEMENT

This Licensing Agreement (this "**Agreement**") is made effective as of the _____ day of September, 2009 (the "**Effective Date**") by and between John Starkey, a resident of Chattanooga, Tennessee ("**Licensor**") and SPASTIC PUBLISHING, INC., a Delaware corporation ("**Licensee**").

WHEREAS, Licensee is a publisher of online entertainment communities, core and co-branded gaming content, CD-ROM game titles and other media products, including but not limited to computer, console, online and mobile platform games, card games, board games, books, movies, TV productions, and other products and media.

WHEREAS, Licensor owns all rights, including, without limitation copyright, to a series of books known as the Legacy of the Cluefall series, consisting of *A Song of Death, Stormy Day, Party in Hell, Archetype, Power Play, Kitty's War, Mozell Clock, Hello Oblivion, How's the Wife and Kids, Diablo, Requim for Adventure, First Pony Ride* and any future books in the series developed by Licensor during the term of this Agreement (collectively, the "**Work**").

WHEREAS, Licensee desires to license the rights to the Work from Licensor and Licensor desires to license such rights to Licensee.

WHEREAS, Licensee desires to create and sell computer games, video games, electronic games, card games, online games, coin operated games, board games and other forms of game entertainment based on the Work (collectively, the "**Licensed Products**").

NOW THEREFORE, in consideration of the mutual promises contained herein, and other good and valuable consideration, the receipt and sufficiency of which are hereby acknowledged, the parties agree as follows:

1. **License**. Licensor hereby grants to Licensee an exclusive, worldwide license to create and sell the Licensed Products, subject to the terms and conditions of this Agreement.

This is a very broad grant of rights. No exclusions are made here, so all rights related to the works and the broad description of the Licensed Products *above* are presumptively transferred.

---

2. **Omission or Modification of Work**. Licensor agrees to assist Licensee to insure the quality of product and storyline of the Licensed Products and Licensee agrees to collaborate with Licensor on any changes desired by the Licensee's development teams. Licensor will use his best efforts to implement any such changes and authorizes Licensee, in its sole discretion, to modify, change or omit all or part of the Work for the development of the Licensed Products as required to make high quality Licensed Products.

Licensor agrees that Licensee has the exclusive and unrestricted right to alter, embellish, add to, delete from, rearrange or combine the content of the Work for the purpose of proper development application of the Licensed Works.

> Best Efforts is a very high standard. Some courts have interpreted best efforts to be equivalent to anythingz possible regardless of the detrimental effect on the actor, up to and including insolvency. This paragraph is rather vague (i.e. *"assist Licensee to insure the quality of product and storyline"*) and does not give the Author any meaningful ability to control or even guide the interpretation of his books.

3. **Use of Name, Titles and Cover Art**. Licensor, to the extent that Licensor may grant such rights, agrees to Licensee's use of his name, image, or both in connection with the marketing of the Licensed Products during the term of this Agreement. Furthermore, Licensor, to the extent that Licensor may grant such rights, agrees to Licensee's use of the book titles and cover art associated with the Work for the packaging and marketing of the Licensed Products during the term of this Agreement. Licensee, at its sole discretion, has the right but not the obligation to use this Licensed Art in the promotion, packaging, or marketing of the Licensed Products.

> This paragraph contains no protection for the Author's interest in protecting his name and the goodwill (i.e., commercial value) associated with it. An author or other public figure can be significantly harmed by low quality advertising or any sort of promotions or products that are either bad or in poor taste. The language "to the extent that Licensor may grant such rights" is here in the original and is presumptively an acknowledgement that other entities may have some control over these rights. Most certainly, the publisher has rights, probably exclusive, over the cover art and maybe title of the books. It would be better lawyering to actually find out what rights the Author has so the parties know what he is in fact conveying here. Uncertainty and vagueness are cardinal sins in contract drafting.

4. **Royalty**. Licensee agrees to pay to Licensor a royalty of Six Percent (6%) on Net Sales of the Licensed Products ("**Royalties**"). "**Net Sales**" means the amounts received by Licensee from the sale of the Licensed Products to third parties, less (a) cost of goods, (b) discounts or rebates actually allowed from the billed amount, (c) credits or allowances actually made on claims or returns, (d) taxes or other government charges included in the billed amounts,

and (e) freight, postage, insurance charges, packing charges, and any other additional special charges included in the amounts billed.

> Royalties are calculated here from net rather than gross sales. The distinction is important, as is the actual definition of net sales. The music industry is especially notorious for deducting ludicrous amounts of "related expenses" from the gross sales figures. It was particularly endemic in the first waves of non-concert footage rap videos. The production values were high, but in many cases the artists were stunned to find out that all the costs, including absurd levels of overhead, were not in fact coming out of the studios' pockets as they had been led to believe. The studios were able to retain virtually all of the profits from record sales by defining net sales expansively, and only a lawyer or accountant would notice the provisions and their ultimate effect. The provision here is actually fairly reasonable.

Payment.

5.1　Royalties are payable within thirty (30) days after the end of the calendar quarter in which they become due. Any Royalties which are unpaid 30 days after the end of the calendar quarter shall bear simple interest accrued at the annual rate of ten percent (10%). Any taxes required to be withheld by Licensee from payments otherwise due under this agreement in order to comply with the tax laws of the United States or any other country shall be promptly paid by Licensee to the appropriate tax authorities.

5.2　Licensee shall pay to Licensor a total of Fifty Thousand Dollars ($50,000) in non-refundable advances towards Royalties in scheduled progress payments for each book in the Work that Licensee uses to develop Licensed Products as set forth in the following table (the "**Advance Payments**"):

Description	Event	Advance Payment
*For the **first book** in the Work that Licensee uses to develop Licensed Products, the following applies:*		
Signing Bonus	Execution and Delivery of this Agreement	Five Thousand Dollars ($5,000.00)
Approval	Licensee's Approval of the Design for the Licensed Products	Ten Thousand Dollars ($10,000.00)
*For any **subsequent book** in the Work that Licensee uses to develop Licensed Products, the following applies:*		

Initiation Bonus	Licensee notifies Licensor of Licensor's intent to create Licensed Work from such subsequent book	Ten Thousand Dollars ($10,000.00)
Approval	Licensee's Approval of the Design for the Licensed Products	Ten Thousand Dollars ($10,000.00)
For _each book_ in the Work that Licensee uses to develop Licensed Products, the following applies:		
Start of Development	Minimum of Three (3) Programmers Begin Working on the Development of the Licensed Products	Five Thousand Dollars ($5,000.00)
Stage 1 Development	Minimum of Three (3) Programmers Working on the Development of the Licensed Products for Three (3) Months After the "Start of Development"	Five Thousand Dollars ($5,000.00)
Stage 2 Development	Minimum of Three (3) Programmers Working on the Development of the Licensed Products for Three (3) Months After the "Stage 1 Development"	Five Thousand Dollars ($5,000.00)
Stage 3 Development	Minimum of Three (3) Programmers Working on the Development of the Licensed Products for Three (3) Months After the "Stage 2 Development"	Five Thousand Dollars ($5,000.00)
Development Completion	Completed Development of the Licensed Products	Ten Thousand Dollars ($10,000.00)

This is a key provision. There is nothing wrong with it, per se, but as an attorney it is important that you realize that these Advance Payments are being deducted from future royalties. They are not in addition to the 6%. Not only should you notice this, you should make sure your client is aware of it as well. It is a significant financial term, and although it may not have any legal issues attached, you cannot assume your client (on either side) is aware of it. Clients are notorious for claiming to have read agreements even when at best they skimmed the first few lines and checked the royalty rate. This is true of even sophisticated clients.

5.3   Licensor and Licensee agree that, for the purpose of calculating Advance Payments, Licensed Products that are developed from a combined content of various books in the Work shall be deemed to have been developed only from one book in the Work. The total of Advance Payments that Licensee shall be obligated to pay to Licensor relating to any one book in the Work shall not exceed Fifty Thousand Dollars ($50,000.00).

5.4 Any Advance Payments toward Royalties from Licensee to Licensor shall be credited towards Royalties due or to become due to Licensor.

> If you had trouble understanding this table, you are not alone. It is unnecessarily complex and rather baffling. The development stages are not referenced anywhere else in this agreement and are questionable at best as benchmarks. They are vaguely defined and are totally in the control of the Publisher. Arguably, by assigning only two programmers to the project, the Publisher would not be obligated to make any payments during the development stages. A simpler calculation and more objective stages would be a big improvement here.

5.5 All payments under this Agreement represent the full and complete compensation for all rights granted to Licensee by Licensor under this Agreement. Licensor acknowledges and agrees that he has no expectancy with respect to any payment other that the Royalties and Advance Payments expressly set forth in this Agreement.

6. **Financial Reports**. With the payment of each quarterly Royalties, Licensee will provide Licensor with a statement setting forth the basis of calculation. Licensor will have the right to audit the royalty records of Licensee no more frequently than once per year, during normal business hours. All information of Licensee will be held strictly confidential by Licensor and he will not disclose any financial information of Licensee to any third party.

> Royalty disputes are not uncommon. If, down the road, the Author thinks he is being underpaid, he will need a meaningful right to review all the relevant financial documents of the Publisher. Note here the right to review is not a full audit right and it attaches only to royalty records. Author would be wise to insist on a more comprehensive set of rights here, including an obligation on the part of the Publisher to keep accurate and comprehensive records relating to the Licensed Products.

7. **Term and Renewal**.

7.1 This Agreement shall terminate five (5) years after the Effective Date (the "**Termination Date**"). Upon the payment of each Initiation Bonus (as such term is described in the payment table of Section 5.2) from Licensee to Licensor, the Termination Date shall be extended to the date that is five (5) years after the date of the payment of such Initiation Bonus. Notwithstanding the Termination of this Agreement, Licensor agrees that Licensee may continue to sell a Licensed Product in accordance with the Royalties provision of this Agreement for so long as such Licensed Product continues to sell or for ten (10) years from the product release of such Licensed Product, whichever is longer.

> Notice that this provision gives the Publisher the ability to extend the term of the agreement unilaterally without actually being required to undertake any new development. The Initiation Notice advanced payment must be made, but no new product really has to be developed.

7.2 Licensee shall have twelve (12) months after the Effective Date in which to conduct a related fund raising campaign for new capital (the "**Campaign**"). **If LICENSEE is unsuccessful in raising at least two million dollars ($2,000,000.00) during THE campaign, THEN EITHER PARTY MAY TERMINATE this Agreement, UPON WRITTEN NOTICE TO THE OTHER PARTY WITHIN 45 DAYS AFTER THE END OF THE CAMPAIGN, without penalty to or further obligation from any party HERETO and LICENSOR shall retain all ROYALTIES AND ADVANCE PAYMENTS PAID TO-DATE AND ownership rights in the Work, notwithstanding any other provisions of this Agreement.**

> In the world of start up companies and the scramble for funding, this is not an unreasonable provision; the main thing is to be sure that both sides are aware of this term, since it can in effect cancel the entire agreement. The startlingly random capitalization, however, is appalling. It really came from the Publisher's counsel exactly like this. Upon seeing it, you should immediately suspect that the rest of the agreement was drafted with a similar lack of care. Word processing programs are notorious for adding errors like this, especially when terms are subjected to a few levels of cutting and pasting. ALWAYS ALWAYS ALWAYS print out a version of your document and actually LOOK at it and read through it — you do NOT want to be this lawyer!

8.   **<u>Termination</u>**. Notwithstanding any contrary provisions contained in this Agreement, this Agreement may be terminated as follows:

8.1 Licensor may terminate this Agreement immediately upon a material breach of any term or condition of this Agreement by Licensee.

Since this is a fairly broad termination right (usually you would at least expect a notice and cure period) and is in the Publisher's original draft, I have often wondered if the same careful drafter responsible for the previous section didn't inadvertently switch "Licensee" and "Licensor" in this section.

8.2 This Agreement shall terminate automatically and immediately on the occurrence of any of the following events: bankruptcy or insolvency of Licensee or any assignment of Licensee's assets for the benefit of creditors.

8.3 Upon expiration or termination of this Agreement, Licensee shall cease all use of the Work and the Licensed Products, Licensor shall retain all Royalties and Advance Payments paid to-date, and all rights granted to Licensee under this Agreement shall immediately revert back to Licensor, except that Licensee may sell any Licensed Products already distributed to retail sellers or customers.

This provision is a bit vague and doesn't really address all the reasonable needs of either party. A defined sell-off period is standard in agreements of this sort so that the Author does not have to worry about more of the goods entering the market after the agreement is over, especially if he terminated it for cause and so that the Licensee will not end up with a warehouse of unsold products that it has to take a loss on because the agreement expired.

9. **Representations, Warranties and Covenants**. Licensor represents, warrants and covenants as follows: (a) Licensor is the sole author of the Work; (b) Licensor has full power, free of any prior contract, lien or rights of any nature in any person or entity that may interfere with the its ability to i) grant the rights hereby conveyed to Licensee, ii) fulfill its obligations in accordance with the terms of this Agreement or iii) enter into this Agreement; (c) the Work does not contain matter that is libelous or otherwise unlawful or that infringes on the right of privacy, proprietary right or copyright (whether statutory or at common law) of any person or entity.

> It is unlikely an Author could make these warranties; almost certainly some of the rights referenced will implicate previous agreements with the book publisher. It is standard for there to be at least some mutuality of reps and warranties; a one sided provision like this is not generally acceptable.

10. **Indemnification; Limitation of Liability**.

    10.1   Licensor shall indemnify and hold Licensee, its distributors, employees, licensees, partners, agents, advertisers, and any retailers harmless against any suit, claim, demand, proceeding, prosecution, recovery or penalty and any expense, including, without limitation, reasonable attorneys' fees arising out of Licensor's breach of this Agreement.

> As with the previous section, mutuality is standard practice, although it is not at all uncommon for a first draft to be one sided like this. Sometimes the other side might be careless and not ask for mutuality of indemnification, so it is worth a shot starting like this.

    10.2   IN NO EVENT SHALL LICENSEE BE LIABLE TO LICENSOR FOR ANY INDIRECT, INCIDENTAL, SPECIAL, OR CONSEQUENTIAL DAMAGES, INCLUDING LOSS OF PROFITS, REVENUE OR USE INCURRED BY LICENSOR OR ANY THIRD PARTY, WHETHER IN AN ACTION IN CONTRACT OR TORT, OR BASED ON A WARRANTY, EVEN IF THE OTHER PARTY HAS BEEN ADVISED OF THE POSSIBILITY OF SUCH DAMAGES.

11. **Ownership of Intellectual Property**. The trademark rights, copyright(s) and any and all other rights, titles or interests in and to the Work, and any and all derivative works thereof, shall be and remain and constitute the sole and exclusive property of Licensor or Licensor's designee or assignee and Licensee shall acquire no rights thereto other than the license rights granted herein.

> The reservation of rights here is important for the Author, but this is rather awkwardly phrased. The Author will want a more expressly detailed section here.

12. **Miscellaneous**.

    12.1   <u>Force Majeure</u>. No party shall be responsible for any failures or delays that are due to causes beyond its control, including, without limitation, acts of God, acts of government, war, fires, floods, strikes or failure by third parties to comply with their obligations.

12.2 <u>Governing Law</u>. This Agreement shall be construed and interpreted in accordance with the laws of the state of North Carolina.

12.3 <u>Integrated Agreement: Modification</u>. This Agreement contains all agreements of the parties relating to the subject matter hereof, and each party's respective rights and obligations thereto, and cannot be amended or modified except by a writing signed by the party to be bound. No prior agreement, statement, representation, or understanding pertaining to any such matter shall be effective.

12.4 <u>Severability</u>. The unenforceability, invalidity, or illegality of any term or provision of this Agreement shall not render the other terms and provisions unenforceable, invalid, or illegal.

12.5 <u>Counterparts: Copy</u>. This Agreement may be executed in one or more counterparts but all such separate counterparts shall constitute but one and the same instrument. This Agreement is made in duplicate and each such duplicate shall be deemed to be an original Agreement.

12.6 <u>Notices</u>. Any and all notices or other communications required or permitted to be given under any of the provisions of this Agreement shall be in writing and shall be deemed to have been duly given when personally delivered or mailed (postage prepaid) by first-class registered mail, return receipt requested, or sent by a generally recognized guaranteed overnight courier (with all applicable delivery fees prepaid or billing therefor arranged to the sender) addressed to the parties as follows:

If to Licensor

If to Licensee:

Any party may change the person or address to which any notices hereunder are to be sent by notifying the other party of such change in accordance with this Section.

IN WITNESS WHEREOF, the parties have executed this Agreement as of the date first written above.

LICENSOR:

_____

LICENSEE:

a Delaware corporation

By: _____

Name:

Title:

As you read an agreement like this, it is important to step back and think in terms of larger issues that you might lose sight of while working on a detailed job of drafting or revising. For instance, this agreement does not define the development process in any meaningful way; the Licensor does not know what to expect nor at what point his input will be relevant. The Licensor will also likely want some assurance that the final products will not be low quality. Not only would such a bad product not sell and therefore not make the Licensor much money on this deal, having his name associated with such a low quality product may harm his reputation and his ability to sell books and make other deals in the future. Licensing agreements should spell out what will happen and when, to the extent possible and relevant. Licensor will almost certainly insist on some meaningful assurances from the Licensee as well. At the very least the Licensee should warrant that the Products won't violate any laws or safety standards; indemnity along the same lines is important as well.

The agreement should always include any specific concerns the individual Licensor may have. There may not be anything particularly unusual, but some Licensors have particular concerns stemming from personal preferences or previous bad experiences with other Licensees. At the very least, a wise Licensor will want to have the ability to approve or reject anything that will have his Marks on it.

On a more superficial level, not only does the random formatting of the numbers and indentations make the agreement look sloppy, it makes it somewhat hard to follow if you are working with it closely. Even the font in the original (Arial) was unprofessional looking for a legal document. It is certainly not required that all legal documents be written in Times New Roman, but it has been the gold standard of legal drafting for quite some time. Many partners expect to see it, and it generally looks more professional. This can, of course, be a matter of personal taste, but for a legal document, trendy fonts do not improve the overall impact.

PART IV

PATENT

Chapter 13

FLINGWING — PATENT APPLICATION

OVERVIEW: FILING A PATENT

Applying for a patent is a very detailed process which typically consumes a great deal of both time and money. Non-attorneys typically have no problem filing copyright applications. Trademark applications with the USPTO are a bit more complicated, but non-specialist attorneys as well as non-attorneys are perfectly capable of completing the basic process. If they have questions, the help lines at the USPTO are really quite helpful and are usually sufficient to clear up any confusion during a filing. An experienced trademark attorney will be able to draft a more complete and finessed application, but the process is possible without counsel. Patents are a completely different matter. Drafting a patent application is much more complex process and is well beyond a layman's ability.

1. *Patent Standards*

A. *Patentable Subject Matter*

Patent claims[1] fall into two basic categories: Process and Product.[2] "Process" is one of the three express categories of patentable subject matter and encompasses a "process, art or method, and includes a new use of a known process, machine, manufacture, composition of matter, or material."[3] The term "Product" is used to cover the other three categories listed in section 101 as patentable subject matter: machines, articles of manufacture and compositions of matter.[4]

i. *Process claims*

Process claims are somewhat more amorphous than the tangible product claims. Two fairly recent evolutions, software and business method patents, are both process claims and have both generated a great deal of disagreement over the scope of patentable subject matter. Generally an abstract idea is not patentable, so a process should be tied to a physical product in some way. For instance, a newly developed chemical component for strengthening long fingernails could be patentable, as would a method for creating it. An abstract mathematical algorithm by itself, however, would not be patentable.[5] The extent to which a tangible element must be related to an intangible process is not exactly clear. The statute expressly excludes abstract ideas, but in *Bilski*

---

[1]   This section addresses only Utility Patents and does not discuss Design or Plant Patents.
[2]   STEPHEN M. MCJOHN, INTELLECTUAL PROPERTY (3d. ed. 2009).
[3]   35 U.S.C. 100(b).
[4]   35 U.S.C. 100.
[5]   *See Diamond v. Diehr*, 450 U.S. 175 (1981); *State Street Bank & Trust Co. v. Signature Financial Group, Inc.,* 149 F.3d 1368 (Fed. Cir. 1998); *In re Alappat*, 33 F.3d 1526 (Fed. Cir. 1994).

v. Kappos,[6] the Supreme Court rejected the "machine or transformation" test as a necessary requirement for certain processes. Prior to *Bilski,* many lower courts as well as the USPTO had required that these processes be tied to a particular machine or accomplish a specific transformation of matter in order to pass statutory muster. The opinion does not, of course, change the statutory standard, and the machine-or-transformation test remains a "a useful and important clue"[7] to be used by the lower courts. The Court held, however, that it is not the exclusive test, which necessitated an updated USPTO order "Interim Guidance for Determining Subject Matter Eligibility in light of *Bilksi v. Kappos*"[8] because the USPTO's internal procedures had just been held invalid. Obviously, the correct way to draw the boundaries for an acceptable process claim is difficult to discern in some cases.

The newly issued USPTO guidelines on this provide, in part:

101 Method Eligibility Quick Reference Sheet

The factors below should be considered when analyzing the claim **as a whole** to evaluate whether a method claim is directed to an abstract idea. However, not every factor will be relevant to every claim and, as such, need not be considered in every analysis. When it is determined that the claim is patent-eligible, the analysis may be concluded. In those instances where patent-eligibility cannot easily be identified, every relevant factor should be carefully weighed before making a conclusion. Additionally, no factor is conclusive by itself, and the weight accorded each factor will vary based upon the facts of the application. These factors are not intended to be exclusive or exhaustive as there may be more pertinent factors depending on the particular technology of the claim. For assistance in applying these factors, please consult the accompanying "Interim Guidance" memo and TC management.

Factors Weighing Toward Eligibility:

- Recitation of a machine or transformation (either express or inherent).
  - Machine or transformation is particular.
  - Machine or transformation meaning fully limits the execution of the steps.
  - Machine implements the claimed steps.
  - The article being transformed is particular.

---

[6] *Bilski v. Kappos*, 561 U. S. _____, 130 S. Ct. 3218, 177 L. Ed. 2d 792 (2010).
[7] 130 S. Ct. at 3227, 177 L. Ed. 2d at 803.
[8] USPTO Memorandum, "Interim Guidance for Determining Subject Matter Eligibility in light of Bilksi v. Kappos" 27 July 2010.

- ◦ The article undergoes a change in state or thing (e.g., objectively different function or use).
- ◦ The article being transformed is an object or substance.
- The claim is directed toward applying a law of nature.
  - ◦ Law of nature is practically applied.
  - ◦ The application of the law of nature meaningfully limits the execution of the steps.
- The claim is more than a mere statement of a concept.
  - ◦ The claim describes a particular solution to a problem to be solved.
  - ◦ The claim implements a concept in some tangible way.
  - ◦ The performance of the steps is observable and verifiable.

Factors Weighing Against Eligibility:

- No recitation of a machine or transformation (either express or inherent).
- Insufficient recitation of a machine or transformation.
  - ◦ Involvement of machine, or transformation, with the steps is merely nominally, insignificantly, or tangentially related to the performance of the steps, e.g., data gathering, or merely recites a field in which the method is intended to be applied.
  - ◦ Machine is generically recited such that it covers any machine capable of performing the claimed step(s).
  - ◦ Machine is merely an object on which the method operates.
  - ◦ Transformation involves only a change in position or location of article.
  - ◦ "Article" is merely a general concept (see notes below).
- The claim is not directed to an application of a law of nature.
  - ◦ The claim would monopolize a natural force or patent a scientific fact; e.g., by claiming every mode of producing an effect of that law of nature.
  - ◦ Law of nature is applied in a merely subjective determination.
  - ◦ Law of nature is merely nominally, insignificantly, or tangentially related to the performance of the steps.
- The claim is a mere statement of a general concept (see notes below for examples).
  - ◦ Use of the concept, as expressed in the method, would effectively grant a monopoly over the concept.
  - ◦ Both known and unknown uses of the concept are covered, and can be performed through any existing or future-devised machinery, or even without any apparatus.

- ° The claim only states a problem to be solved.
- ° The general concept is disembodied.
- ° The mechanism(s) by which the steps are implemented is subjective or imperceptible.

NOTES

1) Examples of general concepts include, <u>but are not limited,</u> to:

- ☐ Basic economic practices or theories (e.g., hedging, insurance, financial transactions, marketing);
- ☐ Basic legal theories (e.g., contracts, dispute resolution, rules of law);
- ☐ Mathematical concepts (e.g., algorithms, spatial relationships, geometry);
- ☐ Mental activity (e.g., forming a judgment, observation, evaluation, or opinion);
- ☐ Interpersonal interactions or relationships (e.g., conversing, dating);
- ☐ Teaching concepts (e.g., memorization, repetition);
- ☐ Human behavior (e.g., exercising, wearing clothing, following rules or instructions);
- ☐ Instructing "how business should be conducted."[9]

It is too early to fully appreciate the changes, if any, this will have on the patents issued by the USPTO, but the *Bilski* opinion dashed the hopes of many who hoped the Court would forbid the issuance of business method patents altogether.[10]

ii. *Product claims*

Product claims are easier on a basic level. Prof Mc John summarizes the three statutory categories of Product claim well:

> *Machine* A "machine" does something. "The term machine includes every mechanical device or combination of mechanical powers and devices to perform some function and produce a certain effect or result." *Corning v. Burden*, 56 U.S. 252, 267 (1853). Machines would include a piano, a hammer, a compact disc player, and a merry go round.
>
> . . . .

---

[9] *Id.* at 3–4.
[10] Free Software activists were also harboring hope that software patents would be overruled in *Bilski* but few outside their circles thought that was likely. Indeed, the Court did not even address the idea of such a reversal.

(Article of) Manufacture The Supreme Court has read "manufacture" as "the production of articles for use from raw or prepared materials by giving to these materials new forms, qualities, properties, or combinations, whether by hand-labor or by machinery." *Chakrabarty,* 447 U.S. at 306. This is a very broad category. Clothing, furniture, toys, food, and anything else made by man could potentially fall within the category of "article of manufacture."

. . . .

Composition of Matter A "composition of matter" includes "all compositions of two or more substances and . . . all composite articles, whether they be the results of chemical union, or of mechanical mixture, or whether they be gases, fluids, powders or solids." *Chakrabarty,* 447 U.S. at 308. Like the other categories, "composition of matter" is very broad. It reaches from human genes to toothpaste.[11]

B. Originality

In copyright, the subject matter standard is much more likely to be an issue than the level of creativity required. Unlike the copyright standard of a small modicum of original creation, the standard for patents is significant. To be patentable, the process or product must be New, Useful and Non Obvious.

i. Novelty

An invention is *new* or "*novel*" if it is not (a) already known or or used publically in the United States,[12] (b) already patented or described in print anywhere in the world[13] (that earlier patent would be said to have "priority"), (c) already invented by someone else in the United States who did not abandon, suppress or conceal the earlier invention[14] or (d) derived from some other source.[15] It is important to note that patent applications, which are published 18 months after their filing, are considered prior art as of their *filing* date, not their publication date.[16] These standards are set forth in the code[17] and are the subject of voluminous case law. The analysis of anticipation, priority and derivation can be quite detailed, and a failure of one or several of these requirements has disappointed and surprised many a hapless inventor. An invention can also fail the Novelty inquiry if the claim is filed more than one year after the invention had first been described in print or

---

[11] MCJOHN, *supra* note 2, at 203–205.
[12] 35 U.S.C. 102(a).
[13] *Id.*
[14] 35 U.S.C. 102(g).
[15] 35 U.S.C. 102(f).
[16] 35 U.S.C. 102(e).
[17] 35 U.S.C 102.

publically used. This one year window in which to file is often called the statutory bar and is enforced to encourage prompt application.

ii. Utility

Usefulness, or utility, originally was treated as little more than a truism. Why would an inventor go through the hassle and expense to create, much less patent an invention that had no purpose? It was deemed pretty much a self-enforcing standard. At one point, Justice Story took the doctrine a step further by imposing a level of morality.[18] He wrote that "All the law requires is, that the invention should not be frivolous or injurious to the well-being, good policy or sound morals of society.... . For instance, a new invention to poison people or to pro-mote debauchery, or to facilitate private assassination, is not a patent-able invention."[19] Little more attention was paid to this element until the advent of biotech research with scientists racing to patent chemical innovations although even the scientists themselves did not yet know what, if any, real purpose the discovery would serve. This led to sudden relevance for the utility requirement. Although the modern expression is not as poetic as Justice Storey's, now in order to be patentable an invention must provide "a significant and presently available benefit to the public."[20]

iii. Non-obviousness

This standard is another substantial hurdle for an invention. It must not be something that, although new, would have been obvious to some-one working in the relevant field if that person took into account all the relevant prior art.[21] Prior art is therefore relevant to both a determina-tion of novelty as well as to the non-obviousness analysis. Although logical arguments can be made to the contrary, courts have held that all prior art under the Section 102 definition (Novelty) will also apply to the Section 103 (Non-obviousness) determination.[22] Section 103 does not offer its own definition of prior art, so the same body of materials is applied to both determinations. The artificial construct of the "person having ordinary skill in the art" sets the standard at which the analysis of obviousness is to occur. Something may be obvious to an expert in the field and simultaneously completely non-obvious to a layman. This person of ordinary skill seems often to get a job as a patent examiner, but the patent examiner's judgment of obviousness is supposed to be made in light of a skilled practitioner in the relevant field. Although patent examiners are entitled to take Official Notice of "common knowl-edge,"[23] more often the examiners will identify each and every claim

---

[18] *Lowell v. Lewis*, 15 F. Cas. 1018, 1019 (No 8568) (C.C.D. Mass 1917).
[19] *Id.*
[20] *In re Fisher*, 421 F.3d 1365 (Fed. Cir. 2005).
[21] 35 U.S.C. 103; McJohn, *supra* note 2, at 253.
[22] *Id.*
[23] Manual of Patent Examining Procedure § 2144.03.

limitation as being described in a piece of prior art as Applicants are entitled to request supporting evidence of any fact of which the Examiner takes such notice. Furthermore, Examiners must be able to cite specific reasons why multiple prior art references would be combined to render the claimed invention obvious;[24] typically such references should be drawn to solving the same problem as the claimed invention. In addition to challenging the Examiner's interpretation of the prior art references, applicants and courts may rely on marketplace related factors in challenging or validating the Examiner's assertions. Courts tend to rely on marketplace related factors in making this determination. An invention is likely to be non-obvious if it (a) satisfies a long felt commercial need, (b) enjoys commercial success, (c) is the subject of expressions of surprise or admiration from professionals in the relevant field, (d) is widely licensed, (e) is something that other inventors tried without success to create and (f) was unexpected or counterintuitive.[25]

2. *Role of the Patent Attorney*

Unlike other specialties, where expertise is gained purely through experience and practice, a patent attorney is required to have a hard science education background and must pass the specialized Patent Bar. The goal is for these highly specialized attorneys to have technical understanding of the subject matter involved in their clients' patents. Obviously no one attorney can be sufficiently experienced in the full spectrum of the sciences, but the intention is for members of the Patent Bar to have scientific and technical expertise superior to that of their liberal arts educated colleagues. This understanding, together with the same sort of practical experience gained in other areas of practice, allow patent attorneys to draft artful claims which provide their clients' inventions with the broadest protection possible while still limiting the claims enough to qualify for patent protetion.

---

[24] Manual of Patent Examining Procedure § 2141.01.
[25] *See Greenwood v. Hattori Seiko Co.*, 900 F.2d 238, 241; ROGER E. SCHECTER, INTELLECTUAL PROPERTY 285–86 (2006).

EXERCISE

TOPIC: Patent

    i.   Patent Standards

    ii. Patent Claim Review

SKILLS:

    i.   Document Review

    ii. Critical Reasoning

    iii. Analysis

ESTIMATED TIME FOR COMPLETING THIS EXERCISE:

Approximately three hours.

ESTIMATED LEVEL OF DIFFICULTY (1–5): 3—Moderate
(heavier than average reading).

FLINGWING — PATENT APPLICATION

You represent Jodi Sarnow, a world famous dog trainer and celebrity personality. Jodi's many pooches are Hollywood regulars whenever a script or ad copy calls for a family pet to walk through the scene. Her dogs don't do tricks *per se*, but they are all great at walking by or standing around on camera. This is a surprisingly lucrative niche. Jodi has also written a book, *Stop Blaming the Dog: You're the One With the Issues,* which emphasizes that the number one most effective way to have well-behaved, happy dogs is to give them plenty of fun exercise. The book also implies that the same is true for people, but it stops intentionally shy of becoming a candidate for any Dr. Phil reading lists.

While recovering from surgery six months ago for a severely strained shoulder caused by throwing tennis balls, Jodi improvised a handheld catapult-like ball flinger that rockets balls *way* further than she ever could with even an uninjured shoulder. It is basically a handheld stick with a cup on the end of it and has the bonus characteristic of being able to pick the ball up off the ground after the dog drops it at her feet. This saved her from a lot of bending over which was annoying with the huge sling on her injured shoulder. A passerby with a Newfoundland dog (huge, mellow dogs with a talent for prodigious drool) commented on the odd ball flinging contraption and was in raptures over the idea that the flinger would keep the user from having to pick up soggy, spit-covered balls. Privately, Jodi thought the guy was a bit fussy (dog trainers aren't generally put off by doggie drool), but she acknowledged that she was indeed now insulated from direct contact with the slobbery spheroids that were such an integral part of her day.

After getting TONS of comments from various dog owners whenever she used her invention in public, Jodi realized that there was a definite market for the product. Never one to turn up her nose at profit, Jodi has engaged a marketing and production team for her new dog exercise product and is ready to go to market. A friend suggested that she get the item patented, so she has called you for help.

The device is fairly simple in design. It is roughly 24 inches long, made of durable plastic with enough give in it that when she throws the ball there is a slight whipping action that helps fling the ball farther than the more rigid versions she had first tried. The cup at the end is sized so that it can hold any standard tennis ball, although Jodi plans to market it with a cute, special production ball in bright colors with little doggie paw prints on it. These will also be sold separately for the people that her marketing consultant assures her are willing to pay $7 for a cuter dog ball. Because of its slightly curved shape, the ball flinger sort of vaguely resembles a bird wing, so Jodi has named her invention the FlingWing. Attached is a line drawing of the device she commissioned from a commercial artist that she thought might be helpful to you.

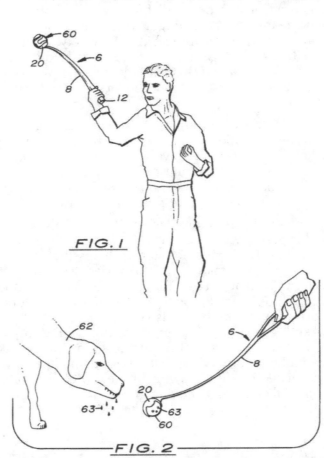

The FLING WING! Top drawing shows basic position for superhuman ball chucking action. Lower drawing illustrates how FLING WING protects the user from the dreaded Doggie Drool effect.

Jodi has asked your opinion on whether her invention is patentable or not. She understands that the patent process can be long, expensive and painful, but she thinks that the pay-off in sales of her ball flinger will be worth it if she can keep others from making knock-off products and selling them cheaper than hers.

1. Is the invention patentable subject matter?

2. Does the invention meet the patent standards of novelty, utility and non-obviousness? You may assume there are no hidden problems or facts not revealed in the text which would bar a patent from being issued. The relevant Prior Art is provided below.

3. Do you think the invention is patentable?

4. Prepare a memo identifying any characteristics or elements of the invention that should be included in the patent claim. Would you make a process claim, a product claim or both? What claims would you make?

Relevant Patented Prior Art:

The following are actual patents from the USPTO files.[26] You may assume they are the totality of the relevant prior art for this application. There is no need to do any original research for this exercize.

---

[26] They have been edited for length; if you would like to view the entire patent including additional drawings you can go to: www.uspto.gov, clicking on "2 search" under the **Patents** text box on the left of your screen. On the right panel on your screen scroll down slightly to "USPTO Patent Full-Text and Image Database (PatFT)" and click on "Patent Number Search." Alternately you can go directly to the search engine at: http://patft.uspto.gov/netahtml/PTO/srchnum.htm

United States Patent	5,390,652
Minneman, et al.	February 21, 1995

Dual thrower

Abstract

A disk thrower is disclosed for simultaneously launching two clay targets. The thrower includes two target holders attached to an adjuster which is mounted to a handle for swinging the thrower. The target holders are adjustable along supports formed on the adjuster. A first one of the target holders is arcuately movable along an arc wherein the first target holder is movable relative to a second target holder while lying in a single pane. The second target holder is movable to different positions on the adjuster whereby the second target holder is adapted to lie in different predetermined planes relative to the adjuster and first target holder such that a target held by the second target holder will follow a predetermined convergent, divergent or parallel trajectory relative to a target held by the first target holder.

Inventors:	**Minneman; Steven W.** (Clayton, OH), **Minneman; Michael C.** (Englewood, OH)
Assignee:	**MTM Molded Products Company** (Dayton, OH)
Appl. No.:	**07/971,073**
Filed:	**November 3, 1992**

Current U.S. Class:	**124/5** ; 12/43
Current International Class:	F41J 9/28 (20060101); F41J (20060101); F41J 009/28 (); F41B 003/04 ()
Field of Search:	124/4,5,42,43

References Cited [Referenced By]

U.S. Patent Documents

831365	September 1906	Masel
1306393	June 1919	Sibley
1445371	February 1923	Vickery
1607874	November 1926	Darton
3095867	July 1963	Kiyuna

3537438	November 1970	Reed
4076004	February 1978	Huelskamp
4233952	November 1980	Perkins
4347828	September 1982	Bridgeman
4730595	March 1988	Glass et al.
4974574	December 1990	Cutlip

Foreign Patent Documents

| 2321107 | March 1977 | FR |

Other References

One page Sales Brochure of the MTM Molded Products Company.

Primary Examiner: Reese; Randolph A.

Assistant Examiner: Ricci; John

Attorney, Agent or Firm: Biebel & French

Claims

What is claimed is:

1. A holder for throwing a first target and a second target, comprising:

   a handle; and

   a plurality of adjustable target holders for receiving said first and second targets;

   said plurality of adjustable target holders being adjustable such that said first target is thrown in a predetermined relationship with respect to said second target;

   said holder further comprising:

   an adjuster for adjustably securing said plurality of adjustable target holders to said handle;

   said plurality of target holders comprising first holder which lies in a first plane and a second holder which lies in a second plane, respectively, said adjuster comprising at least one support for adjustably supporting said first holder in a predetermined angular position relative to said second holder;

   said at least one support comprising an angular support for supporting said first holder in a predetermined angular relationship with respect to said second holder, thereby permitting said first and second targets to be launched at different trajectories.

2. The holder as recited in claim 1 wherein said at least one support further comprises an arcuate support associated with said angular support for supporting said second holder in a predetermined arc-uate relationship with respect to said first holder, thereby permitting said first and second targets to be released at different times from said first and second holders.

3. A holder for throwing a first target and a second target, comprising:

a handle; and

a plurality of adjustable target holders for receiving said first and second targets;

said plurality of adjustable target holders being adjustable such that said first target is thrown in a predetermined relationship with respect to said second target;

said holder further comprising:

an adjuster for adjustably securing said plurality of adjustable tar-get holders to said handle;

said plurality of target holders comprising a first holder which lies in a first plane and a second holder which lies in a second plane, respectively, said adjuster comprising at least one support for adjustably supporting said first holder in a predetermined angular position relative to said second holder, said at least one support further comprising an arcuate support for supporting said second holder in a predetermined arcuate relationship with respect to said first holder.

4. An adjustable dual holder for throwing a first target and a second target comprising:

a handle;

a first holder;

a second holder; and

adjusting means for adjustably coupling said first holder and said second holder to said handle such that said first and second targets may be thrown in a predetermined trajectory;

each of said first and second holders comprising an elongated shaft member having a first end and a second end, said first ends having a target holder thereon; said adjusting means adjustably securing said second ends to said handle,

said adjusting means comprising a support associated with an end of said handle for supporting said first and second holders in a predetermined angular and spaced relationship such that said targets may be thrown in said predetermined trajectory;

said support comprising an angular support for supporting said first holder in a predetermined relationship relative to said second holder.

5.   The adjustable dual holder as recited in claim 4 wherein said support further comprises an arcuate support for supporting said second holder in a predetermined arcuate relationship with respect to said second holder.

6.   The adjustable dual holder as recited in claim 4 wherein said adjustable dual holder further comprises:

fastening means for adjustably fastening said first and second holders to said support.

7.   A method for adjustably coupling a first target holder and a second target holder together such that a first target and a second target may be thrown on a first predetermined trajectory and a second predetermined trajectory, respectively, said method comprising the steps of:

(a)   positioning a first target holder in operative relationship with a second target holder;

(b)   adjusting the relative angle of said first and second target holders; and

(c)   adjustably securing said first target holder to a second target holder with an adjuster.

8.   A method for adjustably coupling a first target holder and a second target holder together such that a first target and a second target may be thrown on a first predetermined trajectory and a second predetermined trajectory, respectively, said method comprising the steps of:

(a)   positioning a first target holder in operative relationship with a second target holder; and

(b)   adjustably securing said first target holder to a second target holder with an adjuster, said adjuster comprising a first angular support, said positioning step comprising the step of:

(a)(1)   adjustably positioning the first target holder on said first angular support such that said first target holder is in a predetermined angular relationship with respect to said second target holder.

9.   The method as recited in claim 8 wherein said adjuster comprises a second arcuate support, said positioning step comprises the step:

(a)(2) adjustably positioning the second target holder on the second arcuate support such that said second target holder is in a predetermined arcuate relationship with said first target holder.

10. An adjustable connector for coupling a first target holder to a second target holder, said adjustable connector comprising:

a handle;

an arcuate support located on the end of said handle;

an angular support associated with said arcuate support; and

a fastener for adjustably fastening said first target holder to said arcuate support and said second target holder to said angular support.

11. The adjustable connector as recited in claim 10 wherein said arcuate support comprises a plurality of arcuate support positions for supporting said first target holder in a predetermined arcuate relationship with respect to said second target holder.

12. The adjustable connector as recited in claim 11 wherein said angular support comprises a plurality of angular support positions for supporting said second target holder in a predetermined angular relationship with respect to said first target holder.

13. The adjustable connector as recited in claim 10 wherein said angular support comprises a plurality of angular support positions for supporting said second target holder in a predetermined angular relationship with respect to said first target holder.

Description

BACKGROUND OF THE INVENTION

The present invention relates to disk holders, and more particularly, relates to a disk holder for throwing multiple disks wherein the trajectory of the disks relative to each other may be adjusted.

The use of hand held disk holders for launching disk-shaped clay pigeon targets for trap shooting is well known, and such holders typically include a target holder attached to a handle by means of a thin flexible neck. The handle may be swung to impart a propelling force to the target held within the target holder and at the end of the swinging motion, the neck and target holder are snapped to cause the target to fly out of the holder. In addition, as the target leaves the holder, the holder frictionally engages a side of the target to impart a spinning motion whereby the target is caused to fly along a trajectory from the holder.

Several trap games employ multiple disks discharged simultaneously such that it is desirable to provide a holder which is capable of holding

3698720	November 1972	Gudmundsen
3771794	November 1973	Crockett
3854727	December 1974	Alexander
4787632	November 1988	Nigrelli et al.
4799684	January 1989	Rango
4892314	January 1990	Rango
4925190	May 1990	Learned
4955609	September 1990	Kassen
5116046	May 1992	Pace

Primary Examiner: Marlo; George J.

Attorney, Agent or Firm: Seth; Sandeep

Claims

I claim:

1. A combination ball lift and ball mark repair apparatus for a golf club having an elongated hollow shaft, a ball striking clubhead extending from a clubhead end of the shaft, and an elongated handgrip disposed about an opposite handgrip end of the shaft, the handgrip having an outer surface and a top edge, said apparatus comprising:

   ball mark repair means extending from the top edge of the handgrip for lifting and turning dirt and turf to repair a ball mark when a user operates said apparatus by holding the golf club substantially at its clubhead end;

   internal mounting means for rigidly mounting said ball mark repair means within the hollow shaft to the handgrip end of the golf club to allow the shaft to act as a handle extension which is resistant to torque and translational force produced by repairing a ball mark with said apparatus and which is sufficiently long to allow a user to operate said apparatus while the user is standing substantially upright; and

   ball lift means, removably mountable upon said ball mark repair means, for lifting a golf ball from a surface upon which the golf ball rests when a user operates said apparatus while holding the golf club substantially at its clubhead end;

   wherein, said ball lift means also acts as a protective cover for said ball mark repair means when mounted thereon.

2. An apparatus, as claimed in claim 1, wherein:

   said ball mark repair means and ball lift means are entirely contained within an imaginary cylindrical boundary extending from the outer surface of the handgrip at its top edge parallel to a longitudinal axis of the golf club.

3. An apparatus, as claimed in claim 2, wherein: said passageways adjoin the outer surface of the insert; and

each of said first portions is sized to partially laterally extend beyond the outer surface of said insert and frictionally engage the inner wall of hollow club shaft to further secure the rigid engagement of said mounting means to the inner wall of the shaft.

4. An apparatus, as claimed in claim 2, wherein:

each of said prong members is cylindrical;

each of said prong member's first portions is straight along its length;

each of said prong member's second portions is arcuate along its length; and

each of said prong receiving bores is arcuate along its length.

5. An apparatus, as claimed in claim 1, wherein:

said internal mounting means comprises

an elongated insert having an outer surface and sized for being frictionally received within the hollow shaft, and

a first and a second passageway longitudinally disposed along said insert;

said ball mark repair means comprises

a pair of elongated prong members, each said prong member having a first portion frictionally disposed within one said longitudinal passageway and a second portion extending from said first portion a selectable length beyond the handgrip of the golf club to provide poking surfaces for lifting and turning dirt and turf; and

said ball lift means comprises

a prong member receiving base portion having a pair of bores therein, said bores located and configured to frictionally receive one said second portion of a respective prong member and having a bore length corresponding to the selected length of said second portion such that said base portion is mountable upon said prong second portions generally flush with the edge of the handgrip, and

an arcuate ball lifting surface integral with said base portion to lift a golf ball thereon.

6. An apparatus, as claimed in claim 5, wherein:

each of said second portions extend away from the longitudinal axis of the shaft in a direction opposite to the direction in which the clubhead extends from the longitudinal axis of the shaft;

each of said bores extend in the same direction as said second portions; and said arcuate lifting surface faces the same direction in which the clubhead extends;

wherein the user thus repairs ball marks while holding the golf club at the clubhead end with the clubhead pointing towards the user and lifts a ball from a ball cup while holding the club at the clubhead end with the clubhead pointing away from the user.

7. An apparatus, as claimed in claim 1, wherein:

the inner wall of the hollow shaft narrows at a point along the longitudinal dimension to define a positive stop within the hollow shaft; and

said internal mounting means is sized longitudinally such that a first end of said mounting means abuts the positive stop with an opposite second end of said mounting means disposed generally at the handgrip end of the golf club.

8. A golf club assembly comprising:

an elongated hollow shaft having an inner wall and a clubhead end and a handgrip end;

a ball striking clubhead extending from the clubhead end;

an elongated handgrip disposed about said handgrip end and having an edge and a first outer surface;

an elongated insert rigidly disposed within said hollow shaft at said handgrip end and having a second outer surface, first and second opposed ends, and a pair of longitudinal channels longitudinally disposed along said insert, said longitudinal channels originating at said first opposed end and terminating at a selectable terminal end point between said first and second opposed ends;

a pair of elongated prong members, each prong member having

a first portion, having a third outer surface, rigidly disposed within one said longitudinal channel and abutting said terminal point of said channel, and

a second portion extending from said first portion beyond the edge of said handgrip to provide a poking surface for lifting and turning dirt; and

ball lift and prong cover means, slidably engaged over said second portions of said prong members, for lifting a golf ball from a golf ball cup and holding the golf ball thereon and for covering said second portions of said prong members to prevent injury and damage.

9. A golf club assembly, as claimed in claim 8, wherein each of said second portions extend in a direction opposite to the direction in which the clubhead extends from the shaft and wherein:

said ball lift and prong cover means comprises

a base portion including a pair of bores therein, each bore located sized and configured to frictionally receive one said second portion and extending within said base portion in the same direction as its said received second portion such that said base portion is mountable upon said second portions generally flush with the edge of the handgrip; and

an arcuate ball lifting surface integral with said base portion to cup and lift a golf ball thereon, said arcuate surface facing the same direction in which the clubhead extends;

wherein the user thus repairs ball marks while holding said golf club at the clubhead end with said clubhead pointing towards the user and lifts a ball from a ball cup while holding said club at the clubhead end with said clubhead pointing away from the user.

10. A golf club assembly, as claimed in claim 8, wherein:

said ball mark repair means and said ball lift and prong cover means are sized and cooperate to be entirely contained within an imaginary cylindrical boundary extending from the outer surface of said handgrip parallel to a longitudinal axis of said golf club.

11. A golf club assembly, as claimed in claim 10, wherein:

said first portion of each said prong members is generally straight;

said second portion of each said prong members is generally arcuate; and

said prong receiving bores are generally arcuate.

12. A golf club assembly, as claimed in claim 8, wherein:

the inner wall of said hollow shaft narrows to define a positive stop;

said longitudinal channels are in communication with said outer surface of said insert;

said first end of said insert abuts said positive stop with said second end of said insert disposed at said handgrip end of said shaft; and

a part of said outer surface of said first prong member portion laterally extending beyond its respective channel into frictional contact with the interior of said hollow shaft.

13. A golf club assembly, as claimed in claim 8, wherein:

said internal mounting means is comprised of a wood material;

said ball lift and cover means is comprised of a hardened plastic material; and

said ball mark repair means is comprised of a metal or metal alloy material.

14. A method of manufacturing a golf club assembly comprising the steps of:

providing a golf club having an elongated hollow shaft having an inner wall, a clubhead end and an opposed handgrip end, a clubhead extending from the clubhead end and a handgrip disposed about the handgrip end and having a top edge;

providing an elongated insert having an outer surface, first and second opposed ends, and a pair of channels longitudinally disposed along the insert;

providing a pair of elongated prong members, each prong member having a first portion extendable into one of the passageways and a second portion extending from the first portion to provide a poking surface for lifting and turning dirt and turf;

inserting the insert by its first end, into the handgrip end of the hollow shaft so that the insert is rigidly positioned in the hollow shaft with its first end within the shaft and its second end generally adjacent to the handgrip end of the shaft;

inserting the first portion of each of the prong members into one of the passageways so that the first portion is rigidly positioned in the passageway with the second portion extendable beyond the handgrip end of the golf club;

providing ball lift and prong cover means for lifting a golf ball and for covering said second portions of said prong members to prevent injury and damage when mounted onto the prong members; and

mounting the ball lift and prong cover means over the prong members.

15. A method, as claimed in claim 14, wherein:

the second portion is bent relative to the first portion;

the step of inserting the first portions includes orienting each of the prong members such that when its first portion is inserted, the second portion extends in the direction opposite to the direction which the clubhead extends;

the ball lift and prong cover means comprises a base portion including a pair of bores therein, each bore being located sized and configured to frictionally receive one respective second portion and extending within the base portion in the same direction the second portion it is to receive; and

the step of mounting includes sliding the bores over the prongs such that the base portion is mounted upon the second portions generally flush with the handgrip end of the golf club.

16. A method, as claimed in claim 14, wherein:

the ball lift and cover means includes an arcuate ball lifting surface integral with the base portion for lifting the golf ball thereon, the arcuate surface facing the direction opposite to the direction in which the prong members extend; and

the step of mounting results in the arcuate surface facing in the opposite direction to the direction in which the clubhead extends.

17. A method, as claimed in claim 14, wherein:

said ball mark repair means and said ball lift and prong cover means are laterally sized less than or equal diameter of the outer surface of the handgrip at the handgrip's top edge; and

the steps of inserting the first portion and mounting result in the ball mark repair means and the ball lift means being entirely contained within an imaginary cylindrical boundary extending from the outer surface of said handgrip at the handgrip's top edge generally parallel to a longitudinal axis of the handgrip.

18. A method, as claimed in claim 14, wherein:

the inner wall of the hollow shaft narrows to define a positive stop; and

the step of inserting the insert includes abutting the first end of the insert against the positive stop with the second end of the insert at the handgrip end of said shaft.

19. A method, as claimed in claim 14, wherein:

the longitudinal passageways are in communication with the outer surface of the insert;

the prong members are cylindrical and have a radius substantially equal to the radius of the passageways; and

the step of inserting the first portions and inserting the insert results in each of the first portions frictionally contacting the inner wall of the hollow shaft.

Description

TECHNICAL FIELD

The invention generally relates to golfing apparatus. The invention relates, more particularly, to golf clubs having apparatus for lifting golf balls and repairing ball marks.

BACKGROUND ART

The prior art is replete with golf club mounted apparatus. Examples of such apparatus in a search of prior art for such apparatus are disclosed in U.S. Pat. Nos. 3,239,264; 3,273,927; 3,562, 184; 3,698,720; 4,925,190; 4,787,632; 4,892,314; 4,799,684; 4,955,609 and 5,116,046.

A review of the above patents reveals that none of the apparatus disclosed therein is capable of providing for golfer a safe, durable and convenient golf club mounted device which allows the golfer to lift golf balls and to repair ball marks on a putting surface without needing to bend over. More particularly, no apparatus is disclosed in which a safely shaped ball lifting means is mounted over a ball mark repair means to allow a golfer to lift a ball without bending over and which also acts as a cover to the ball mark repair means. All of the devices disclosed, while suitable for their intended purpose, fall short of the above-stated goal. For example, U.S. Pat. No. 3,293,351 to Dupont discloses a golf club end mounted ball scoop which allows the golfer to pick up a golf ball from a ball cup without bending over. However, this device provides no means for repairing ball marks on the putting green.

U.S. Pat. No. 4,892,314 to Rango discloses a means for repairing divots, or ball marks, which is positioned within a hollow end of a golf shaft. However, the divot repair means is only kept in the shaft for storage and so the device does not alleviate the need for the golfer to bend over to repair a divot. U.S. Pat. No. 4,925,190 Learned overcomes the limitation of Rango by disclosing a combination golf club and turf repair tool in which the turf repair means is mounted on the end of a golf club such that the golf club acts as a handle extension and the golfer can repair the divot without bending over. The turf repair tool further uses a portion of the handgrip as a cover for the repair tool. The tool, however, provides no means to lift a ball from the cup. Furthermore, the mounting configuration for mounting the repair tool to the golf club is subject to failure from repeated use. Specifically, the base is subject to be pushed into the shaft from translational forces produced while repairing a ball mark (e.g., when digging into the turf). Furthermore, the base is subject to rotating or tilting in the shaft from torque forces produced while repairing a ball mark (e.g. while turning the turf), necessitating tool repair costs.

U.S. Pat. No. 4,787,632 to Nigrelli discloses a device which allows the golfer to both lift the ball from the ball cup and to repair ball marks. However, as is easily apparent, the device is cumbersome on the golf club and exposes many dangerous and potentially damaging surfaces. Furthermore, the golf club cannot be readily put into or taken from a golf bag, because of the bulkiness of the device. Finally, the device's mounting is not torque or translation force resistant.

It would be desirable if the device provided the golfer the ability, without having to bend over, to repair a ball mark and to lift a ball out of a ball cup with little or no damage to the cup. It would further be desirable if the ball lifting means could also act as a removable cover for the ball mark repair means to protect against harm and damage from the repair means. It would be a significant advantage if such a device could provide a configuration which took up no more lateral room than the golf club itself, so that a golf club outfitted with the device structure could conveniently fit in the golf bag or in any other place which the unmodified golf club could fit into. It would also be beneficial if the ball mark repair means could be mounted to the golf club with significant resistance to the torsional and translational forces generated by repairing ball marks.

Additional objects, advantages and novel features of the invention shall be set forth in part in the description that follows, and in part will become apparent to those skilled in the art upon examination of the following or may be learned by the practice of the invention. The object and the advantages of the invention may be realized and attained by means of the instrumentalities and in combinations particularly pointed out in the appended claims.

To achieve the foregoing and other objects and in accordance with the purpose of the present invention, as embodied and broadly described herein, the combination ball lift and ball mark repair device of this invention may comprise the following.

DISCLOSURE OF INVENTION

According to the invention, a combination ball lift and ball mark repair apparatus is provided for a golf club having an elongated hollow shaft, a ball striking clubhead extending from a clubhead end of the shaft, and an elongated handgrip disposed about an opposite handgrip end of the shaft. The handgrip has an outer surface and a top edge. In its broadest sense, the apparatus includes ball mark repair means and ball lift means releasably mounted on the ball mark repair means. The ball mark repair means extends from the top edge of the handgrip for lifting and turning dirt and turf to repair a ball mark when a user operates the apparatus by holding the golf club substantially at its clubhead end. The ball lift means is provided for lifting a golf ball from a surface when a user operates the apparatus while holding the golf club substantially at its clubhead end. According to an important aspect of the invention, the ball lift means also acts as a protective cover for the ball mark repair means when mounted thereon.

The apparatus further includes internal mounting means for rigidly mounting the ball mark repair means within the hollow shaft to the handgrip end of the golf club to allow the shaft to act as a handle extension which is resistant to torque and translational force produced by repairing a ball mark with the apparatus and which is sufficiently long to allow a user to operate the apparatus while the user is standing substantially upright. Preferably, the ball mark repair means and ball lift means are entirely contained within an imaginary cylindrical boundary extending from the outer surface of the handgrip at its top edge parallel to a longitudinal axis of the golf club.

In a preferred embodiment of the present invention, the internal mounting means includes an elongated insert having an outer surface and sized for being frictionally received within the hollow shaft, and a first and a second passageway longitudinally disposed along the insert. The ball mark repair means includes a pair of elongated prong members which each have a first portion frictionally disposed within one of the longitudinal passageways and a second portion which extends from said first portion a selectable length beyond the handgrip. The second portions provide poking surfaces for lifting and turning dirt and turf. The ball lift means includes a base portion having a pair of bores therein. The bores are located and configured to frictionally receive one of the second portions such that said base portion is mountable upon the second portions generally flush with the edge of the handgrip. The ball lift means is provided with an arcuate ball lifting surface integral with the base portion to lift a golf ball thereon.

Preferably, each of the second portions extends away from the longitudinal axis of the shaft in a direction opposite to the direction in which the clubhead extends from the longitudinal axis of the shaft, and each of the bores extends in the same direction as the second portions. The arcuate lifting surface faces the same direction in which the clubhead extends. In this preferred but non-exclusive configuration, the user thus repairs the ball marks while holding the golf club at the clubhead end with the clubhead pointing towards the user and lifts a ball from a ball cup while holding the club at the clubhead end with the clubhead pointing away from him.

In accordance with an important aspect of the present invention, the internal mounting means cooperates with the ball mark repair means to provide torsional and translation durablity of the apparatus against forces it experiences while a ball mark is being repaired. Translational durability is provided by using a positive stop defined within the hollow shaft where the inner wall of the hollow shaft narrows to provide the positive stop. Positive stop is defined herein as a point or surface of rigid translational resistance. The internal mounting means, in the form of an insert, is sized longitudinally such that its first end abuts the positive stop to prevent it from being unwantedly pushed into the hollow shaft. To provide the torsional resistance the passageways adjoin the outer surface of the insert and each of the prong first portions is sized to partially laterally extend beyond the outer surface of the insert and frictionally engage the inner wall of hollow shaft.

The foregoing, in combination with a conventional golf club, provides a novel golf club assembly of the present invention which provides the golfer the ability to pick up golf balls and repair ball marks while being convenient and safe because the ball lifting means also acts as a safe cover for the ball mark repair means. Furthermore, the apparatus is not cumbersome, and does not affect the ability of the golfer to store his golf club in a golf bag or golf club tube.

The present invention also provides a method of manufacturing a golf club assembly which includes the step of providing a conventional golf club having an elongated hollow shaft having an inner wall, a clubhead end and an opposed handgrip end, a clubhead extending from the clubhead end and a handgrip disposed about the handgrip end. The method further includes providing an elongated insert having an outer surface, first and second opposed ends, and a pair of channels longitudinally disposed along the insert in communication with the insert outer surface. The method further includes providing a pair of elongated prong members, each prong member having a first portion extendable into one of the passageways and a second portion extending from the first portion to provide a poking surface for lifting and turning dirt and turf. The insert is inserted by its first end, into the handgrip end of the hollow shaft so that the insert is rigidly positioned in the hollow shaft with its first end within the shaft and its second end generally adjacent to the handgrip end of the shaft.

The first portion of each of the prong members is inserted into one of the passageways so that the first portion is rigidly positioned in the passageway with the second portion extending beyond the handgrip end of the golf club. The method further includes providing ball lift and prong cover means for lifting a golf ball and for covering the second portions of said prong members to prevent injury and damage when mounted onto the prong members. The method further includes mounting the ball lift and prong cover means over the prong members.

Preferably, the steps of inserting the first portion and mounting result in the ball mark repair means and the ball lift means being entirely contained within an imaginary cylindrical boundary extending from the outer surface of said handgrip at the handgrip's top edge generally parallel to a longitudinal axis of the handgrip. Preferably, the step of inserting the insert includes abutting the first end of the insert against a positive stop defined within the hollow shaft. The accompanying drawings, which are incorporated in and form a part of the specification illustrate preferred embodiments of the present invention, and together with the description, serve to explain the principles of the invention. In the drawings:

BRIEF DESCRIPTION OF THE DRAWINGS

FIG. 1   is a perspective view illustrating a golf club assembly of the present invention having a combination ball lift and ball mark repair apparatus. [omitted]

FIG. 2   is a partial vertical section, taken along the line 2–2 in FIG. 1, illustrating the insert means and other parts of the combination apparatus. [omitted]

FIG. 3   is a partial exploded perspective view, illustrating the primary elements of the present invention. [omitted]

FIG. 4   is horizontal section, taken along the line 4–4 in FIG. 10, illustrating the cooperation of the prong member and the insert inside of the hollow shaft. [omitted]

FIG. 5   is a partial perspective view illustrating a golfer repairing a ball mark with the clubhead pointing towards the golfer

FIG. 6   is an enlarged partial vertical section, taken along the line 6–6 in FIG. 5, illustrating ball repair motions resulting in torque and translational forces.

FIG. 7   is a partial perspective view illustrating a golfer lifting a ball from a ball cup with the clubhead pointing away from the user.

FIG. 8   is a partial vertical section, taken along the line 8–8 of FIG. 7, illustrating the ball lifting means lifting a ball.

FIG. 9   is a side elevation view illustrating a ball lift and cover means having an ornamental hand shape. [omitted]

FIG. 10   is a partial vertical section, taken along line 10–10 of FIG. 2, showing the cooperation of the insert against the positive stop. [omitted]

BEST MODE FOR CARRYING OUT THE INVENTION

FIGS. 1-10 illustrate a combination ball lift and ball mark repair apparatus 10 of the present invention used as part of a golf club assembly 11 having a hollow shaft 12 to which a conventional clubhead 14 is attached at a clubhead end 14a thereof. The clubhead 14 is a conventional putter type typically used in the final part of play in a round of golf to sink a golf ball 30 into a golf ball cup 31 located in the ground on a putting green.

. . . .

The foregoing is considered as illustrative only of the principles of the invention. Further, since numerous modifications and changes will readily occur to those skilled in the art, it is not desired to limit the invention to the exact construction and operation shown and described, and accordingly all suitable modifications and equivalents may be regarded as falling within the scope of the invention as defined by the claims that follow.

U.S. Patent   June 13, 1995   Sheet 2 of 3   5,423,543

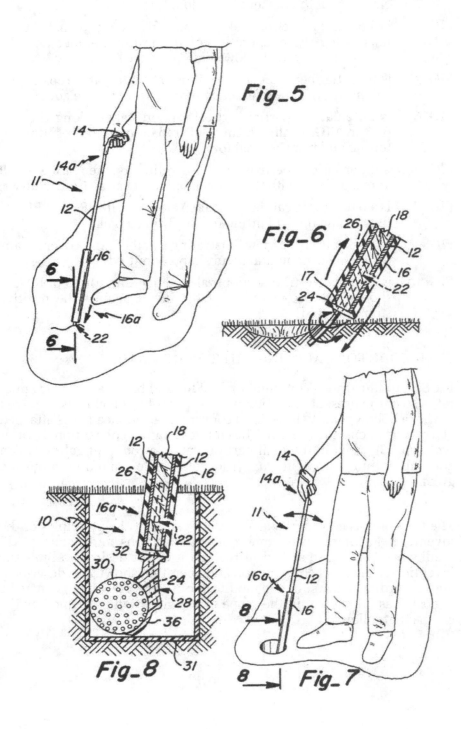

Fig_5

Fig_6

Fig_8

Fig_7

United States Patent	**5,129,650**
Hayman	**July 14, 1992**

Apparatus and method for playing golf

Abstract

A set of flexible throwing rods each have a handle on one end for grasping and a gradual narrowing taper toward the other end. Each throwing rod has a varying length ranging from approximately 15 inches to approximately four feet. One such rod is selected, depending upon the distance to a target, onto which a ball with a diametrical hole therethrough is slid. A whip-like action of the rod forces the ball off of the end, the speed of which is dependent upon the length of the rod.

Inventors: **Hayman; Jesse M.** (Laguna Niguel, CA)

Appl. No: **07/716,994**

Filed: **June 18, 1991**

Current U.S. Class:	**473/289**; 124/5; 273/317; 473/282; 473/409
Current International Class:	A63B 59/02 (20060101); A63B 59/00 (20060101); A63B 067/02 (); A63B 065/00 ()
Field of Search:	273/77R,77A,77B,317,318,327,412 124/5

References Cited [Referenced By]

U.S. Patent Documents

2705148	March 1955	Waller
2902023	September 1955	Waller

Foreign Patent Documents

470791	June 1914	FR

Primary Examiner: Grieb; William H.

Claims

What is claimed is:

1. Apparatus for playing golf on a golf course, comprising:

    a set of flexible throwing rods, each rod of the set having a different flexibility resulting in a different throwing power, each of the rods having a first, and a second ends, a round cross-section, and a taper, the first end having a larger diameter than the second end;

    a round ball having a diameter of a standard golf ball, and a diametrical hole therethrough such that with the second end of the rod inserted into the hole, the second end of the rod protrudes minimally beyond the ball when the ball is wedged thereon;

    whereby an appropriate rod from the set of rods is selected in accordance with the throwing power derivable therefrom, the ball is wedged onto the second end of the rod, the rod is swung in an arc to dislodge the ball from the rod to project the ball into space in a selected direction, the process being repeated in sequence as frequently as required to move the ball incrementally from the tee to the green.

2. The apparatus of claim 1 wherein the overall length of the rods of the set of rods lies between approximately 26 and 64 inches.

3. The apparatus of claim 1 wherein the rods are made of graphite.

4. The apparatus of claim 1 wherein the rods are made of fiberglass.

5. The apparatus of claim 1 wherein the flexibility of the rods lies between 0.1 and 0.25 inches per inch of rod length per pound of side deflection force.

6. The apparatus of claim 1 wherein the rod is graduated to indicate the position of the ball on the rod.

7. A method of playing golf on a golf course using a set of flexible throwing rods, each rod of the set having a different flexibility resulting in a different throwing power, each of the rods having a first, and a second ends, a round cross-section, a taper and graduations on the rod near the second end, the first end having a larger diameter than the second end; and a round ball having a diameter equal to the diameter of a standard golf ball, and a diametrical hole therethrough such that the ball may be mounted upon any one of the rods by inserting the rod into the hole, the second end of the rod protruding minimally beyond the ball when the ball is wedged thereon, comprising the steps:

    a) selecting an appropriate rod from the set of rods, the rod being selected in accordance with the throwing power derivable therefrom;

    b) wedging the ball onto the second end of the rod;

c)   swinging the rod in an arc to dislodge the ball from the rod to project the ball into space in a selected direction;

d)   repeating steps (a), (b) and (c) in sequence as frequently as required to move the ball incrementally from the tee to the green.

8.   The method of claim 7 wherein step (b) further includes the selection of one of the graduations as a positioning point for the ball on the rod thereby controlling the wedge force of the ball on the rod.

Description

FIELD OF THE INVENTION

This invention relates to games and corresponding amusement devices. More particularly, this invention relates to a golf-like game involving the projection of a ball from a flexible throwing rod.

BACKGROUND OF THE INVENTION

Apparati for projecting a ball from a throwing rod are well known. Devices of this type generally employ a ball with a diametrical hole therethrough for slidably engaging a thin, flexible throwing rod. The throwing rod is usually characterized by a handle on one end for grasping and a gradual taper on the other end. In operation, a person slides a ball down the shaft of the throwing rod toward the handle. The ball is thrown by swinging the stick in a whip-like motion toward a target. Centrifugal force causes the ball to slide along the rod and off the end thereof. The speed at which the ball is projected is dependent upon the strength of the throw, the length and flexibility of the throwing rod, and the friction created by the ball sliding along the throwing rod.

Most of the known devices, such as that described in U.S. Pat. No. 2,902,023 issued to Waller on Mar. 29, 1955, utilize a hollow ball, as a solid ball has so much momentum after being projected that it causes great discomfort to a person attempting to catch it. While this may be a concern for some games, clearly not all games require a person on the receiving end of a throw. For example, it has been found that devices of this type are particularly well suited for use on a golf course, following generally the same rules as the game of golf. Because the speeds and distances that can be achieved from such devices are similar to those that can be achieve by striking a golf ball with a golf club, a golf ball with a diametrical hole therethrough can be used with such devices in an extremely entertaining fashion and with a high degree of accuracy.

Using such a device in this manner it was noticed that, as in the game of golf, at each successive throw the target is at a different distance from the ball. No provision is made in the devices of the currently known art for throwing rods with distinct distance ranges, as found in a set golf clubs with varying lengths. Clearly, such a game would be more enjoyable if specific distances could be achieved with consistency. The present invention fulfills these needs and provides further related advantages.

SUMMARY OF THE INVENTION

The present invention is a set of flexible throwing rods, each throwing rod having a handle on one end for grasping, and a gradual narrowing taper toward the other end to allow easy sliding of a golf ball, or the like, with a diametrical hole therethrough. Each throwing rod has a varying length ranging from approximately 15 inches for a rod with relatively small distance ranges, to a rod of approximately four feet for greater distance ranges. The longer throwing rods correspond to longer and more massive golf clubs, referred to as "woods." The shorter throwing rods correspond to shorter golf clubs with ball-striking faces relatively inclined, referred to as "irons" and "wedges."

In operation, the distance to a target, such as to a golf putting green, is estimated by the player. Based on this estimation, an appropriate throwing rod is selected. A ball is slid down the throwing rod until it reaches a point on the rod where the rod is approximately the same diameter as the hole in the ball. The ball is then slightly held in place on the rod by friction, thereby preventing the ball from inadvertently sliding off of the throwing rod during a practice swing, for example. The player, aiming at the target, swings the throwing rod in a whip-like manner with a generally overhead swing. Centrifugal force overcomes the friction holding the ball to the rod, thereby releasing the ball off of the end of the rod toward the target. This process is repeated until the ball has landed in close proximity to the target, for example, on the putting green. A conventional golf putter may then be used to hit the target directly.

One important feature of the present invention is that projecting a ball in this manner is easier to learn and generally easier to perform than hitting a golf ball with a conventional golf club. Lateral spinning of the ball upon release is almost non-existent with the present invention, thereby minimizing the lateral curving actions, known as "hook" or "slice," in conventional golf. As such, the present invention allows more people to enjoy a golf course and the entertainment and psychical challenge that such a course provides.

Use of the present invention does not, however, eliminate the challenge of trying to reach a target with a golf ball or the like. Consistently selecting the amount of pressure that holds the ball in place on the rod is a skill that must be learned. Moreover, the proper selection of the throwing rods and the force used when projecting a ball all require physical consistency to produce consistent results. As such, the present invention provides a similar, if slightly easier, challenge than does the standard game of golf. Other features and advantages of the present invention will become apparent from the following more detailed description, taken in conjunction with the accompanying drawings, which illustrate, by way of example, the principles of the invention.

BRIEF DESCRIPTION OF THE DRAWINGS

The accompanying drawings illustrate the invention. In such drawings:

FIG. 1   is a perspective illustration of one of a set of flexible throwing rods of the invention; [omitted]

FIG. 2   is a top plan view of a set of flexible throwing rods of the invention, illustrating some of the possible relative lengths between each throwing rod; [omitted]

FIG. 3   is a perspective illustration of a ball of the invention, illustrating a diametrical hole therethrough; and [omitted]

FIG. 4   is a perspective illustration of a person throwing the ball of the invention with one of the set of flexible throwing rods, illustrating a backswing position and a releasing position.

DETAILED DESCRIPTION OF THE PREFERRED EMBODIMENT

FIGS. 1 and 2 show a set 10 of flexible throwing rods 20, 30, 40, and 50. For simplicity of explanation in the following description, each rod 20, 30, 40, or 50 may be referred to as rod 5. Each rod 5 of the set 10 has a different flexibility, preferably between 0.1 and 0.25 inches per inch of rod length per pound of side deflection force, resulting in a different throwing power.

. . . .

While the invention has been described with reference to a preferred embodiment, it is to be clearly understood by those skilled in the art that the invention is not limited thereto. For example, any number of rods 5 may comprise a set 10 of such rods 5. Thus, the scope of the invention is to be interpreted only in conjunction with the appended claims.

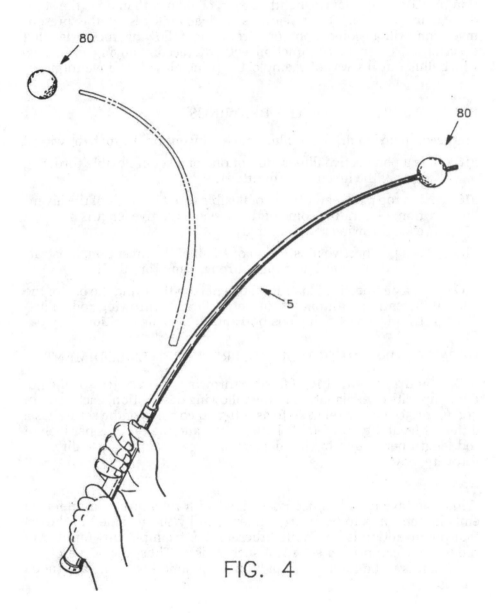

FIG. 4

United States Patent	**4,974,574**
Cutlip	**December 4, 1990**

Multiple disc launcher

Abstract

A multiple disc launcher arrangement includes a single handle and a plurality of spines directed longitudinally of said handle wherein a first spine is of a linear configuration, wherein a second spine is of an arcuate configuration, wherein each spine orthogonally mounts at forward terminal ends thereof respective "C" shaped heads. Each "C" shaped head defines a straight leg and an arcuate leg with a circular pocket defined therewithin. An elongate, continuous "U" shaped groove receives a disc therewithin. A modification of the instant invention includes a sleeve selectively joining a plurality of separate handles, wherein each separate handle is joined to a respective straight and arcuate spine. The sleeve includes a ribbed upper surface to enhance grasping thereof. A further modification includes a resilient leg sleeve selectively positionable about a forward terminal end of each arcuate leg of each head to alter resistance of the head to release a disc when hurled by an individual.

Inventors: **Cutlip; Jeffrey A.** (Goshen, OH)

Appl. No.: **07/439,141**

Filed: **November 20, 1989**

Current U.S. Class:	**124/5**; 124/43
Current International Class:	F41B 3/00 (20060101);
	F41J 9/00 (20060101);
	F41J 9/28 (20060101);
	F41B 003/04 ()
Field of Search:	124/5,4,42,43,81,79

References Cited [Referenced By]

U.S. Patent Documents

831365	September 1906	Masel
1306393	June 1919	Sibley
1445371	February 1923	Vickery
1607874	November 1926	Darton

| 4076004 | February 1978 | Huelskamp |
| 4730595 | March 1988 | Glass et al. |

Primary Examiner: Cuomo; Peter M.

Attorney, Agent or Firm: Gilden; Leon

Claims

What is claimed as being new and desired to be protected by Letters Patent of the United States is as follows:

1. A target disc launcher apparatus for simultaneously and manually projecting a plurality of target discs, wherein said apparatus comprises,

    a unitary handle means for securing a first and second spine member longitudinally thereof, the first spine member defined by a straight linear configuration and the second spine member defined by an arcuate configuration, and

    the first and second spine members each integrally mounting a respective first and second head member thereon at a forward terminal end of each first and second spine members, and

    wherein the first and second head members each include upper and lower surfaces, the upper and lower surfaces of each head member in an aligned parallel relationship relative to one another, and each head member defining a straight leg and an arcuate leg defining a "C" shaped configuration, wherein the "C" shaped configuration includes a circular pocket at a rearwardmost end of the "C" shaped configuration and further defines a continuous "U" shaped groove within a continuous interior surface of the first and second leg members, and

    wherein the unitary handle means is defined as a sheath portion, the sheath portion including a side portion of a ribbed configuration for enhanced manual grasping thereof, and further including an elongate cavity of a generally parallelepiped configuration therewithin, and

    wherein the first and second spine members each terminals at their rearward ends in a first and second handle, the first and second handles are slidably received within the cavity of the sheath member, and wherein the first and second handles define an external configuration complementary to that defined by the cavity, and

    wherein each arcuate leg includes a leg aperture directed orthogonally therethrough spaced from the "U" shaped channel, and further including a resilient sleeve slidably mounted on the arcuate leg and extending forwardly of the arcuate leg, and wherein the sleeve includes a plurality of sleeve apertures directed there-through, and further including a lock pin directed selectively through one of the sleeve apertures and through the arcuate leg aperture to selectively secure the sleeve relative to the arcuate leg.

Description

BACKGROUND OF THE INVENTION

1.   Field of the Invention

The field of invention relates to disc throwers, and more particularly pertains to a new and improved multiple disc launcher wherein the same receives a plurality of discs associated with the games of skeet and trap to direct the discs in a parallel trajectory relative to one another.

2.   Description of the Prior Art

Disc throwers for utilization in shooting sports, particularly the sports of skeet and trap, have been well utilized and known in the prior art. Several skeet and trap games employ multiple discs discharged simultaneously, but heretofore have necessitated the use of elaborate and complex mechanical throwers to effect such discharge. The instant invention attempts to overcome disadvantages of the prior art by presenting an economical and readily transportable multiple manually secured disc thrower to project a plurality of discs simultaneously. Examples of the prior art include U.S. Pat. No. 4,076,004 to Huelskamp illustrating the use of a unitary launcher for disc type targets referred to as "clay pigeons" of conventional configuration.

U.S. Pat. No. 4,233,952 to Perkins sets forth a catapult device for use with target discs utilizing a pivoting head to enhance circulatory motion upon the projection of a target disc by an individual.

U.S. Pat. No. 3,901,208 to Laporte, et al., sets forth a disc type throwing device utilizing a planar plate member with a secondary leg member positioned at an acute angle relative to the plate member relative to a forward terminal end of the plate member, with a notched recess positioned to receive a target disc between the leg and the plate member.

U.S. Pat. No. 2,586,547 to Marley sets forth a hand trap for throwing a disc target defined as an elongate linear plate with a groove formed within each side of the plate to receive a disc between the grooves.

U.S. Pat. No. 4,730,595 to Glass, et al., sets forth a disc launcher of a molded construction with a symmetrical head member with a flexible arm extending from one side of the head member to receive a disc therebetween the arm and the head member.

As such, it may be appreciated that there is a continuing need for a new and improved multiple disc launcher as set forth by the instant invention which addresses both the problems of ease of use and the securement of multiple discs to accommodate specialized shooting game events, as well as effectiveness in construction, and in this respect, the present invention substantially fulfills this need.

SUMMARY OF THE INVENTION

In view of the foregoing disadvantages inherent in the known types of disc launchers now present in the prior art. The present invention provides a multiple disc launcher wherein the same securedly receives a plurality of discs for subsequent launch thereof in spaced trajectories. As such. The general purpose of the present invention, which will be described subsequently in greater detail, is to provide a new and improved multiple disc launcher which has all the advantages of the prior art disc launchers and none of the disadvantages.

To attain this, the present invention includes a single handle and a plurality of spines directed longitudinally of said handle wherein a first spine is of a linear configuration, wherein a second spine is of an arcuate configuration, wherein each spine orthogonally mounts at forward terminal ends thereof respective "C" shaped heads. Each "C" shaped head defines a straight leg and an arcuate leg with a circular pocket defined therewithin. A modification of the instant invention includes a sleeve selectively joining a plurality of separate handles, wherein each separate handle is joined to a respective straight and arcuate spine. The sleeve includes a ribbed upper surface to enhance grasping thereof. A further modification includes a resilient leg sleeve selectively positionable about a forward terminal end of each arcuate leg of each head to alter resistance of the head to release a disc when hurled by an individual.

My invention resides not in any one of these features per se, but rather in the particular combination of all of them herein disclosed and claimed and it is distinguished from the prior art in this particular combination of all of its structures for the functions specified.

There has thus been outlined, rather broadly, the more important features of the invention in order that the detailed description thereof that follows may be better understood, and in order that the present contribution to the art may be better appreciated. There are, of course, additional features of the invention that will be described hereinafter and which will form the subject matter of the claims appended hereto. Those skilled in the art will appreciate that the conception, upon which this disclosure is based, may readily be utilized as a basis for the designing of other structures, methods and systems for carrying out the several purposes of the present invention. It is important, therefore, that the claims be regarded as including such equivalent constructions insofar as they do not depart from the spirit and scope of the present invention.

Further, the purpose of the foregoing abstract is to enable the U.S. Patent and Trademark Office and the public generally, and especially the scientists, engineers and practitioners in the art who are not familiar with patent or legal terms or phraseology, to determine quickly from a cursory inspection the nature and essence of the technical disclosure of the application. The abstract is neither intended to define the invention of the application, which is measured by the claims, nor is it intended to be limiting as to the scope of the invention in any way.

It is therefore an object of the present invention to provide a new and improved multiple disc launcher which has all the advantages of the prior art disc launchers and none of the disadvantages.

It is another object of the present invention to provide a new and improved multiple disc launcher which may be easily and efficiently manufactured and marketed.

It is a further object of the present invention to provide a new and improved multiple disc launcher which is of a durable and reliable construction.

An even further object of the present invention is to provide a new and improved multiple disc launcher which is susceptible of a low cost of manufacture with regard to both materials and labor, and which accordingly is then susceptible of low prices of sale to the consuming public, thereby making such multiple disc launchers economically available to the buying public.

Still yet another object of the present invention is to provide a new and improved multiple disc launcher which provides in the apparatuses and methods of the prior art some of the advantages thereof, while simultaneously overcoming some of the disadvantages normally associated therewith.

Still another object of the present invention is to provide a new and improved multiple disc launcher wherein the same receives a plurality of discs within a single launch thrower to direct a plurality of discs in spaced trajectories.

These together with other objects of the invention, along with the various features of novelty which characterize the invention, are pointed out with particularity in the claims annexed to and forming a part of this disclosure. For a better understanding of the invention, its operating advantages and the specific objects attained by its uses, reference should be had to the accompanying drawings and descriptive matter in which there is illustrated preferred embodiments of the invention.

BRIEF DESCRIPTION OF THE DRAWINGS

The invention will be better understood and objects other than those set forth above will become apparent when consideration is given to the following detailed description thereof. Such description makes reference to the annexed drawings wherein: [Fig. 3 only included here]

FIG. 1   is an isometric illustration of a prior art disc launcher.

FIG. 2   is a top orthographic view of a multiple disc launcher of the instant invention.

FIG. 3   is a top orthographic view of a multiple disc launcher of the instant invention in a loading configuration receiving target discs therewithin.

FIG. 4   is a top orthographic view of the instant invention during a multiple disc launch event.

FIG. 5   is a modified disc launcher assembly utilizing a plurality of individual disc launchers and a securement sheath.

FIG. 6   is an orthographic view taken along the lines 6–6 of FIG. 5 in the direction indicated by the arrows.

FIG. 7   is a top orthographic view of a modified disc launcher utilized in the assembly, as illustrated in FIG. 5.

FIG. 8   is an enlarged top orthographic view of the head assembly of the disc launcher, as illustrated in FIG. 7.

DESCRIPTION OF THE PREFERRED EMBODIMENT

With reference now to the drawings, and in particular to FIGS. 1 to 8 thereof, a new and improved multiple disc launcher embodying the principles and concepts of the present invention and generally designated by the reference numerals 10 and 10a will be described.

....

Therefore, the foregoing is considered as illustrative only of the principles of the invention. Further, since numerous modifications and changes will readily occur to those skilled in the art, it is not desired to limit the invention to the exact construction and operation shown and described, and accordingly, all suitable modifications and equivalents may be resorted to, falling within the scope of the invention.

U.S. Patent   Dec. 4, 1990   Sheet 2 of 4   4,974,574

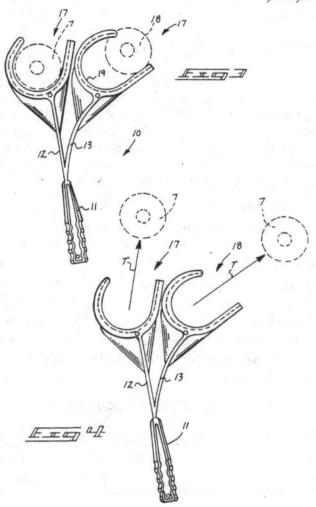

United States Patent   **3,841,292**

Hoffman   **October 15, 1974**

HAND OPERATED CATAPULT TOY

Abstract

A catapult toy, embodying a flexible resilient wand, with a finger grip handle, a tapered whippable shank, and a shaped front end, to receive a mass to be loosely but frictionally fitted on said front end, to be catapulted from said wand by a whipping action by the operator.

Inventors: **Hoffman; John C.** (Delhi, NY)

Appl. No.: **05/222,138**

Filed: **January 31, 1972**

Current U.S. Class:	**124/5**; 124/41.1
Current International Class:	F41B 3/00 (20060101); F41b 003/02 ()
Field of Search:	124/5,4,41 273/95,102

References Cited [Referenced By]

U.S. Patent Documents

1168808	January 1916	Von Hoffmann
2820321	January 1958	Kuhn

Primary Examiner: Oechsle; Anton O.

Assistant Examiner: Browne; William R.

Claims

What is claimed is:

1. A toy comprising

    a flexible wand having a handle grip on one end, and the other or front end having surface irregularities to constitute a frictional surface;

    and a ball-shaped rubber-like mass having an axial opening sized to permit the mass to be co-axially selectively frictionally disposed on said frictional surface, so said wand may be whipped to displace and project the mass in selected direction and with selective force to attempt to place said mass in a preselected area.

2. A toy, as in claim 1, in which the axial opening through said ball mass is of appropriate size to engage the frictional surface with a slight degree of holding pressure to avoid slipping off until whipped off by an operator.

3. A catapult toy, as in claim 1, wherein said wand is resilient and has a tapered whippable shank.

Description

This invention relates to a catapult toy, comprising a flexible wand having a front or free end shaped to frictionally receive a mass, preferably in the shape of a round ball, so the wand can be whipped to project the ball through a selected trajectory and to a preselected distance, to strike a pre-set target area, thereby to test and measure the skill of the operator in controlling the whipping action of the toy.

The wand is provided with a handle at one end which is held by the operator, and the free outer end of the wand may be shaped in any suitable way, such as, by the formation of fluted regions along the front end, to frictionally hold the ball when fitted onto the wand. The ball is provided with a central axis hole diametrically disposed to enable the ball to be fitted onto the front end of the flexible wand, with the ball material having sufficient resilience, and the diametral hole being of such dimensions, that the ball will be frictionally held on the front end of the wand until a whipping operation of the wand will forcibly catapult the ball from the wand.

The construction of the toy and some of the features of its operation are shown in the accompanying drawings, in which

FIG. 1   shows a front elevational view of the wand and the ball in position on the wand; and

FIGS. 1A,

1B and 1C   show sectional dimensional views taken along the shaft of the wand;

FIG. 2   shows the ball positioned on the wand ready to be catapulted from the wand; and

FIG. 3   shows schematically several trajectories through which the ball may be projected from the wand, to illustrate how the skill and dexterity of the operator may be tested and demonstrated by being able to catapult the ball to preselected areas as targets.

As shown in FIG. 1, the toy 10 comprises a wand 12 of resilient flexible material, and a mass in the shape of a ball 14, preferably consisting of a resilient rubber-like material.

The wand 12 embodies a shaped handle 22, with suitable flutes 24, to provide good non-slipping hand grip, and further embodies an elongated shank 26 that extends to a shaped front end 28 whose surface is shaped to embody irregularities 30, to provide frictional characteristics to the surface of front end 28. The wand may be tapered as indicated in the necked region 32 to provide greater flexibility to the wand, for whipping action, when it is operated as a whip to snap the wand for the purpose of operation of the toy, to catapult the ball through a selected trajectory to hit a selected target.

The ball mass 14 may be of any shape, but for the sake of symmetry, is more easily formed as a sphere or ball, and is provided with a hole 40, diametrically and axially through the ball, in order to permit the ball to be applied and pressed onto the irregularly shaped front end surface 28 of the wand 12.

As shown in FIG. 2, when the ball 14 is on the wand 12, the wand may then be whipped as implied by the curved condition of the wand in FIG. 2, and the ball then catapulted and projected off the wand to move in a preselected path of projection, such as one of the many possible paths, of which three are illustrated in FIG. 3, and identified by the numerals 45, 50 and 55.

The toy may be used in the manner illustrated in FIGS. 2 and 3, to test the skill of the operator in being able to catapult the ball through any selected trajectory to reach a predetermined area as the target, as indicated by the regions 60-1, 60-2 and 60-3, under the arrows of the trajectories shown in FIG. 3.

The structural design and formation of the surface irregularities at the front end of the wand may take any desired shape, since their function primarily is to provide sufficient friction to hold the ball against casual displacement, and to require a fair amount of energy in the whipping action to dispel the ball and cause it to travel through a preselected distance, corresponding to some such trajectory as shown in FIG. 3, to reach a selected target area.

The design and construction may be variously modified, without departing from the spirit and scope of the invention, as defined in the claims. For example, the wand may be made of wood or metal, and the mass need not be round and need not be made of resilient rubber-like material, but may be made of non-resilient material and may also be made in other forms and shapes such as longer cylinders or flat shallow cylinders in the shape of a disc.

PATENTED OCT 1 5 1974

3,841,292

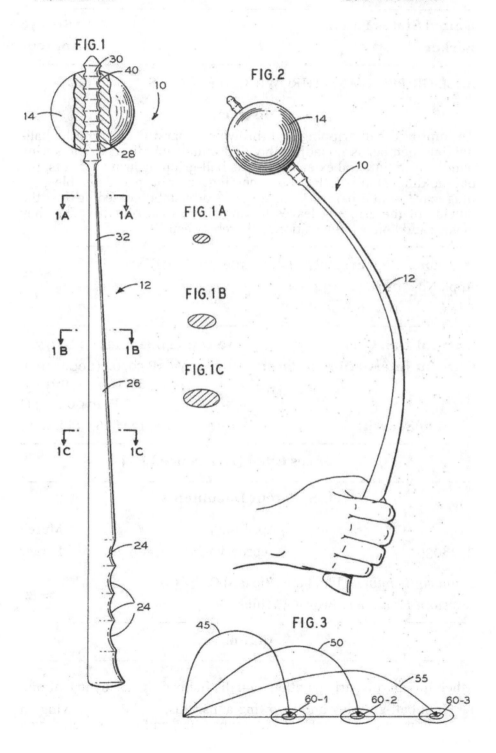

FIG.1

FIG.2

FIG.1A

FIG.1B

FIG.1C

FIG.3

United States Patent	3,589,349
Parker	June 29, 1971

BALL-GRIPPING AND THROWING APPARATUS

Abstract

An improved ball-gripping and throwing apparatus wherein the ball-holding member is nonadjustably and immovably fixed to the spring handle by an integral extension of the ball-gripping arm elements, the ball-holding member otherwise including a pair of spaced flexible gripping leaves and a pair of pressure arms adjustably forced against the outside of the gripping leaves to vary the pressure with which they engage and hold a ball positioned therebetween.

Inventors: **Parker; Robert J.** (Battle Creek, MI)

Appl. No.: **04/840,434**

Filed: **July 9, 1969**

Current U.S. Class:	**124/5**; 124/41.1; 124/7; D21/723
Current International Class:	A63B 59/02 (20060101);
	A63B 59/00 (20060101);
	F41b 003/04 ()
Field of Search:	124/5,6,7,8,9,41,30

References Cited [Referenced By]

U.S. Patent Documents

1535029	April 1925	Murch
3428036	February 1969	Parker

Primary Examiner: Pinkham; Richard C.

Assistant Examiner: Browne; William R.

Claims

I therefore particularly point out and distinctly claim as my invention:

1.   In a ball-gripping and throwing apparatus, of the type having an operating handle, a ball-holding member, and means including a

spring resiliently connecting said handle and said member, and wherein said ball-holding member includes a pair of spaced ball-gripping elements and means mounting said elements for resiliently biased movement toward or away from each other, means for adjustably varying the resilient bias on said ball-gripping elements to change the trajectory characteristics of a thrown ball; said means consisting essentially of an integral bracket having a base and two spaced arms, each extending toward and contacting one of said gripping elements, and threaded shaft means engaging said base for providing reciprocational movement of said arms with respect to said ball-gripping elements, thereby causing said elements to move toward each other for gripping engagement and permit said elements to move away from each other when the bracket moves away from the elements.

2. The improved apparatus defined in claim 1, wherein said spaced ball-gripping elements comprise resiliently flexible finger portions.

3. The improved apparatus defined in claim 2, wherein said finger portions are structurally interconnected.

4. The improved apparatus defined in claim 3, wherein said finger portions comprise an integral arcuate member.

5. The improved apparatus defined in claim 1, and wherein said spaced ball-gripping elements comprise interconnected resiliently flexible finger portions.

6. The improved apparatus defined in claim 1, wherein there is a means for fixedly and rigidly connecting said spring between the handle and the ball-holding member and prohibiting relative movement therebetween.

7. The improved apparatus defined in claim 6, wherein said finger elements include an upper finger extending over the top portion of a ball held in said ball-holding member, and wherein said connecting means includes a generally rigid structure between said spring and such finger.

Description

BACKGROUND OF THE INVENTION

This invention relates broadly to ball-throwing equipment, and more particularly to a device of this nature which is eminently useful in baseball or softball practice sessions. More specifically, in my previous U.S. Pat. No. 3,428,036, I disclosed a ball-gripping and throwing apparatus which is quite successful in throwing a ball with a minimum amount of exertion and a maximum amount of accuracy, and by which various types of throws can be accomplished. However, that apparatus is relatively

complicated from a structural point of view, and thus involves a relatively high cost of manufacture. In particular, both of the embodiments
disclosed in the aforementioned patent, include a means for vertical
adjustment of either the entire ball-holding member or the guide arm
portion thereof, so that in either case the guide arm can be raised and
lowered from the horizontal to vary the grip on the ball and thus vary
the flight of the ball when thrown.

SUMMARY OF THE INVENTION

I have discovered that the ball-gripping and throwing apparatus disclosed in the aforesaid patent can be considerably simplified and still
achieve the basic purpose of accurately and repeatably throwing a ball
to simulate a fly ball, popup, line drive, or a ground ball. Accordingly,
I have provided an improvement for a ball-gripping and throwing
apparatus of the type comprising an operating handle connected to
a ball-holding member by a spring fixed therebetween, wherein such a
ball-holding member comprises gripping leaves, a guide arm, and a
support arm all fixed to each other. Briefly stated, the improvement
comprises a rigid or fixed interconnection between the guide and support arms of the ball-holding member and the spring between the latter
component and the handle, by which relative movement therebetween
is prohibited, and a novel structure for varying the gripping pressure of
the aforesaid gripping leaves, which are preferably integral parts of a
unitary spring element.

Therefore, it is an object of the invention to provide an improved ball-
throwing apparatus wherein various different types of throws can be
accurately obtained by an adjustment mechanism which is structurally
uncomplicated and which does not require extensive or tedious
manipulation.

It is a further object of the invention to provide an improved ball-
gripping and throwing apparatus of the above character which is economical to manufacture.

Other objects and advantages will become apparent upon reference to
the following drawings and detailed discussion.

BRIEF DESCRIPTION OF THE DRAWINGS

FIG. 1   is a fragmentary side elevational view of the apparatus con-
          structed in accordance with the invention.

FIG. 2   is a fragmentary front elevational view of the apparatus.

FIG. 3   is a sectional plan view taken through the plane III-III of FIG. 1.

DESCRIPTION OF THE PREFERRED EMBODIMENT

As in my earlier U.S. Pat. No. 3,428,036, referred to above, this invention concerns a throwing apparatus for projecting a ball 10 in any one

of a number of possible trajectories, usually to simulate a ball hit by a bat, for purposes of training, practicing and the like. The invention specifically provides an improvement in such a ball-gripping and throwing apparatus, which basically comprises a handle 12 having a grip portion 14 at one end and a leaf spring 18 secured to the other end, which may be crimped or sweged to form a spring retainer portion 16. A generally flat, sleevelike coupling 20 is secured to the other end of the spring 18, and serves to attach the latter to a ball-holding member 22.

As in my earlier invention, the ball-holding member 22 comprises generally a pair of spaced lateral gripping leaves 24 and 26, an upper guide arm 28, and a lower support arm 30, all of which are interconnected at a common point 32, in a manner set forth hereinafter. The gripping leaves 24 and 26 are preferably formed from an integral C-shaped member made of relatively thin spring steel or the like, and the guide arm 28 and the support arm 30 are preferably integral extensions of a common element, emanating from a common generally C-shaped rib 34, to the midpoint 32 of which the gripping leaves 24 and 26 are attached.

In accordance with the invention, I have modified and simplified my earlier ball-gripping and throwing apparatus as follows. Firstly, the ball-holding member 22 is fixed to the spring 18 in a rigid manner precluding relative motion therebetween, by means of an integral part of the bracket or rib 34, i.e., an offset end extension 40 of the lower support arm 30, which extends into and is fixed within the sleevelike connector 20. I have found that such a construction provides very good throwing performance with excellent repeatability, and that it is not strictly necessary to be able to vertically adjust the angle of the guide arm 28 or the ball-holding member 22. It is because of the omission of such vertical adjusting structure, and the inclusion of the rigid attachment of the ball-holding member to the spring, that the cost of the apparatus has been substantially reduced.

Also of great importance to the concept of the invention is the presence of a rigid pressure bracket 35 having offset end extremities 36 and 38 which form a pair of spaced pressure arms. Pressure bracket 35 is attached to the ball-holding member 22 by a flatheaded screw 50 countersunk into the rear of the spring member forming the gripping leaves 24 and 26 and passing through both the latter and the upright rib 34, as well as through the pressure bracket. To tighten the pressure arms 36 and 38 down onto the gripping leaves 24 and 26, a wingnut 60 is threaded onto the protruding end of screw 50 and bears against the central portion of bracket 35, thus allowing the pressure of the leaves 24 and 26 on the ball 10 to be varied. In this connection, it is to be noted that the arcuate band forming the gripping leaves 24 and 26 has a curved circumference greater than that of half the ball 10, such that the ball can be gripped by the outermost tips of the leaves while a space is created at the base of the latter, behind the ball, by increased pressure applied to the leaves by tightening the wingnut 60 against the pressure bracket 35. Such adjustment will change the trajectory of a ball thrown with a uniform motion, and it is the only such adjustment which need be done to the device to accomplish this end. Thus, a very considerable simplification in structure is attained by the invention, without sacrificing versatility and variable performance.

It is entirely conceivable that those skilled in the art may well devise certain variations and modifications of the preferred embodiments disclosed and described hereinabove. Consequently, the specific structures which are illustrated and described should be regarded as being for purposes of illustration, and not as determinative of the only practical or desirable way of implementing the concept on which the invention is based.

PATENTED JUN 29 1971   3,589,349

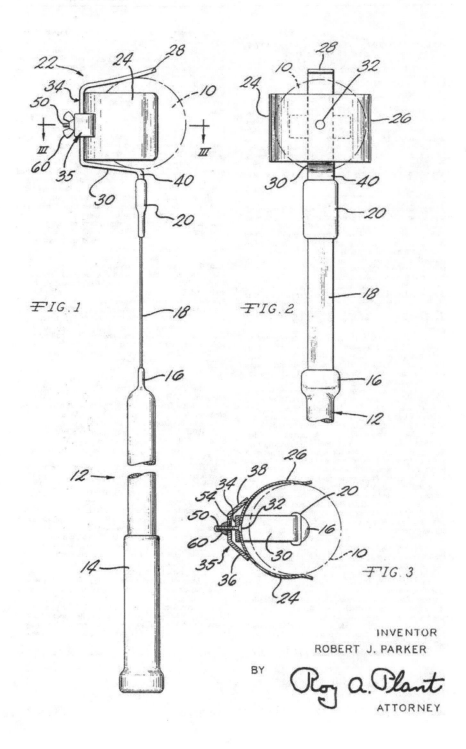

FIG.1

FIG.2

FIG.3

INVENTOR
ROBERT J. PARKER

BY

Roy a. Plant

ATTORNEY

United States Patent Office

3,428,036
Patented Feb. 18, 1969

1

3,428,036

BALL GRIPPING AND THROWING APPARATUS
Robert J. Parker, 58 Mosher Ave.,
Battle Creek, Mich. 49017
Filed Sept. 1, 1965, Ser. No. 484,210
U.S. Cl. 124—5   1 Claim
Int. Cl. F41b 3/04; F41f 7/00; G01n 3/08

ABSTRACT OF THE DISCLOSURE

This adjustable apparatus resiliently but releasably holds a ball or the like in a side opening flange assembly mounted on the end of a resilient member mounted on the end of an operating handle. The resilient member facilitates the ball throwing by flexing backward at the start of the throwing motion and then flexing forward as the end of the throwing motion is approached to provide an improved throwing action.

This invention relates broadly to athletic equipment, and more specifically to a piece of athletic equipment to be used in assisting an individual in throwing a ball.

There is more baseball, soft ball, slow pitch ball, and other types of ball throwing actively being conducted at the present time and at all age levels. This increase of participation is on the increase for many basic reasons. One basic reason for the increase is that we have a continual growth of population. Another reason is that we have a continual expansion in the recreational time available by individuals as a whole. Still another reason is that more of our citizens are living in urban or suburban areas and this type of activity permits a pleasurable means of meeting various exercising desires by the participants.

Because of this increase in ball throwing type activities, there is also a greater opportunity that many more individuals will be participating in this activity on a very limited or sporadic basis. These individuals after being dormant in the field of vigorous physical activities for considerable and varied lengths of time can cause permanent or temporary injuries or inconvenience to develop in their arms and back upon hard throwing of balls, swinging of bats, et cetera. Many times ball throwing activities are conducted when a limited amount of time is available both for practice and participation. This is true both for persons holding down a full-time job and participating, and for individuals attending school full-time and participating. It is difficult even for some good athletes to hit various types of balls such as pop-ups, grounders, fly balls, et cetera, a consistent or controlled distance, speed, direction, et cetera. Professional athletes have been able to acquire fairly expensive equipment which can simulate consistently and under controlled conditions line drives, fly balls, bouncers, et cetera. This equipment is not available to the vast majority of ball playing participants even in organized activities such as high school, college and community recreational programs. It is in recognition of these and other problems and the fact that no wholly satisfactory system has been commercially available that the present invention was conceived.

Accordingly, among the objects of the present invention is to provide a ball throwing assisting device which will permit even unskilled ball players to throw a ball in a controlled manner.

Another object is to provide a ball throwing assisting apparatus having the ability to permit the user to be very consistent in the distance he throws the ball.

A further object is to provide a ball throwing assisting apparatus which can accurately control the direction in which the ball will be thrown.

A still further object is to provide a ball throwing as-

2

sisting apparatus permitting the user to throw various styles of balls and have a controlled direction of curve.

A still further object is to provide a ball throwing assisting apparatus permitting the user to throw various types of balls as he may desire, such as flies, line drives, grounders, or infield pop-ups.

A still further object of the present invention is to provide a ball throwing assisting apparatus for use in throwing pop-ups which a catcher may be faced with in a normal ball game situation.

A still further object of the present invention is to provide a ball throwing assisting apparatus which permits the user to throw a ball continually without having an adverse effect on his arm or back.

Still another object is to provide a ball throwing assisting apparatus which has adjusting means to help accomplish the direction and type of throwing being made and the pressure of grip the apparatus applies to the ball.

Also, an object of the present invention includes the provision of a ball throwing assisting apparatus capable of accomplishing the above objectives with a minimum of material cost and fabricating expense and at the same time being composed of a simple and ruggedly formed structure which is very reliable in application.

Still further objects and advantages of the invention will appear as the description proceeds.

To the accomplishment of the foregoing and related ends, the invention, then, consists of a ball throwing assisting apparatus as hereinafter fully described and particularly pointed out in the claim, the annexed drawings, and the following description setting forth in detail certain means for carrying out the invention, such disclosed means illustrating, however, but one of various ways in which the principles of the invention may be used.

In the annexed drawings:

FIGURE 1 is a side elevational view of a ball throwing assisting apparatus embodying the present invention.

FIGURE 2 is a partial front view of the present invention as disclosed in FIGURE 1.

FIGURE 3 is a partial side elevational view of the present invention illustrating the ball throwing assisting apparatus showing the opposite side of the apparatus as shown in FIGURE 1.

FIGURE 4 is a partial sectional view showing the ball control assembly taken along line IV—IV of FIGURE 3 looking in the direction of arrows IV.

FIGURE 5 is a partial sectional side elevational view of the ball throwing assisting apparatus taken along line V—V of FIGURE 2 viewed in the direction of the arrows V.

FIGURE 6 is an elevational back view of an alternate embodiment of a ball throwing assisting apparatus illustrating the present invention.

FIGURE 7 is a side elevational view of the ball throwing assisting apparatus disclosed in FIGURE 6.

Referring to FIGURE 1 there is disclosed a ball gripping and throwing apparatus generally referred to as 10 which has benefit as a ball throwing assisting device. The ball gripping and throwing apparatus 10 is made up of a shaft assembly 11 which is made up generally of a handle member 12 and a shaft member 14. The handle member 12 has two general portions. The lower portion is a hand grip 15 and the upper portion is a rigid shaft member 16. The hand 15 can be made of various materials such as metal, wood, et cetera, or some type of material such as rubber or leather which would give the user a firm gripping surface in a preferred embodiment. The rigid shaft member 16 has a support ring 17 positioned near its upper end. The support ring 17 could be a separate piece or part of rigid shaft member 16; in the present illustration it is shown as a separate piece and brazed to the rigid shaft member 16. The support ring 17 supports a locking member 18. The

3,428,036

3

locking member 18 has a locking arm 19 which includes a securing finger 21 and an actuating member 22. The locking arm 19 is pivotally supported by flange members 24 or support ring 17. A pivot pin 25 passes through and supports locking arm 19 to flange members 24. A spring member 26 acts on locking arm 19, as viewed in FIGURE 5, holding the securing finger 21 in contact with rigid shaft member 16 in its free condition, the purpose of which will be explained below in detail.

A clamping member 27 connects flange members 24, holding them in a proper spaced position so that locking arm 19 is free to move about pivot pin 25 when actuating member 22 is depressed and released. Rigid shaft member 16 has a receiving hole 28 which receives securing finger 21 of locking arm 19. Shaft member 14 can slide up and down along an inside surface 29 of rigid shaft member 16. Adjusting holes 31 are provided on shaft member 14 to receive securing finger 21. When the securing finger 21 is in position, as illustrated in FIGURE 5, the shaft member 14 is locked in its adjusted position with respect to rigid shaft member 16. The shaft member 14 depending upon its length, the intended use of the equipment, et cetera, may have as many adjusting holes 31 as may be needed to give the necessary length adjustment. A positioning slot 32 runs the length of shaft member 14 and acts with a positioning pin 33 which is embedded in rigid shaft member 16, as viewed in FIGURES 2 and 5, to hold the proper alignment of adjusting holes 31 with the securing finger 21. At the upper end of shaft member 14 is secured a cylindrical helical spring 37. The cylindrical helical spring 37 can be secured to the shaft member 14 in various manners. For the present illustration, a securing wire 38 is provided which extends across the shaft member 14, gripping a turn of the cylindrical helical spring 37. A ball control assembly 40 is mounted to the upper end of cylindrical helical spring 37. The ball control assembly 40 has a head support member 41 which is mounted to the cylindrical helical spring 37 by a securing wire 42 in a similar manner as the securing wire 38 mounts the shaft assembly 11 to the cylindrical helical spring 37. The ball control assembly 40 has a flange assembly 44 which can be mounted to the head support member 41 in various manners well known in the art. For the present illustration, rivet members 43 are shown. Flange assembly 44 has a flange hinge 45 at its upper end which connects flange assembly 44 to flange member 46. Flange member 46 is made up of rib member 47, guide arm 48, and gripping arm 49. A holding member 51 is connected to flange member 46. This can be accomplished in various ways. However, for the present illustration, rivet members 50 are used. Holding member 51 has gripping leaves 52 and 53. The gripping leaves 52 and 53 have back-up support means in the form of pressure arms 54 and 55, respectively. Pressure arms 54 and 55 are secured to rib member 47 by hinge members 56 and 57, respectively. The pressure arms 54 and 55 have end assemblies 58 and 59, respectively. End assemblies 58 and 59 are connected together by an adjusting bolt 61. The adjusting bolt 61 is freely connected to end assembly 58 and threadably connected to end assembly 59. The adjusting bolt 61 is provided with a turning tip 62. When turning tip 62 is turned in one direction it will move end assemblies 58 and 59 towards each other which causes pressure arms 54 and 55 to move away from each other. When turning tip 62 is turned in the opposite direction end assemblies 58 and 59 will move away from each other which causes pressure arms 54 and 55 to move towards each other. When the pressure arms 54 and 55 move towards each other, they apply pressure on the gripping leaves 52 and 53 and as they move away from each other they reduce the pressure which they apply on the gripping leaves 52 and 53, the purpose of which will be explained below.

Gripping leaf 53 is provided with a pressure gauge assembly 65. Pressure arm 55 acts on the gripping leaf 53 through pressure gauge assembly 65. The pressure gauge

4

assembly 65 has a gauge fluid housing 66 which is acted upon and is in actual physical contact with pressure arm 55. The gauge fluid housing 66 holds the main portion of the gauge fluid used in the pressure gauge assembly 65. A gauge tube 67 is provided below the gauge fluid housing 66 and is marked off with graduation marks. The gauge tube 67 is provided with a confined gas at its lower tip. As the pressure arm 55 is moved towards gripping leaf 53 it will apply additional pressure on the gauge fluid housing 66 forcing more fluid into the gauge tube 67 compressing the confined gas at the tip of gauge tube 67 and giving a relative reading along its graduated side. This will provide a reading which will be beneficial to the user as will be explained below in more detail.

Rib member 47 is provided with a contacting means 71. Contacting means 71 receives an adjusting bolt 72. The adjusting bolt 72 is pivotally connected to flange assembly 44 by pivot nut assembly 73. The adjusting bolt 72 is in threaded contact with pivot nut assembly 73 and has turning knob 74 connected at its opposite end from contacting means 71. When the turning knob 74 is turned in one direction, it will move flange member 46 in a counterclockwise direction about flange hinge 45 as viewed in FIGURE 1. When the turning knob 74 is turned in the opposite direction it will move flange member 46 in a clockwise direction about flange hinge 45 as viewed in FIGURE 1. A gauge flange 77 is mounted to flange assembly 44 and has a graduated scale 78 secured to it toward gripping arm 49. Gripping arm 49 has an indicator member 79 secured to its bottom side which extends adjacent to graduated scale 78 giving an indicated relative reading when turning knob 74 is turned, moving flange member 46 about flange hinge 45. The purpose of this adjustment will be explained below in more detail.

Gripping leaves 52 and 53 are used to grip a projectile, in the present illustration a ball is shown in phantom and indicated as 80. The gripping arm 49 also acts on the ball 80 gripping it between itself and guide arm 48. To utilize the present invention, a ball 80 is positioned within gripping leaves 52 and 53 and gripping arm 49 and guide arm 48 and the user will grasp the hand grip 15 and swing the ball gripping and throwing apparatus 10 in a movement pattern similar in manner to that used in the normal throwing of a ball. Depending upon the user and the adjustments, the ball 80 will take various paths in its flight; examples would be fly balls, line drives, grounders, pop-ups, et cetera. Each user will have to accustom himself to the adjustments to get the results they may desire.

As the ball 80 is being released from the ball control assembly 40, it will get part of its direction of flight from the guide arm 48. The gripping arm 49 merely assists in holding the ball 80 in position within the ball control assembly 40 before it is released. Depending upon the snap the user puts in the ball gripping and throwing apparatus 10, the guide arm 48 will control the type of projectory. As the turning knob 74 is turned to move the flange member 46 in more of a counterclockwise direction along flange hinge 45, the projectory of the ball will become higher because the guide arm 48 will be raised. If the turning tip 62 is turned in one direction adjusting bolt 61 will cause the end assemblies 58 and 59 to move towards each other and increase the pressure to be applied against the ball 80 by the gripping leaves 52 and 53, thus requiring more force to be exerted to get the ball 80 out of holding member 51. If the turning tip 62 is turned in the opposite direction the pressure on ball 80 will be reduced allowing it to come out of the holding member 51 with less force.

To throw the ball in a straight direction, the follow-through of the user should be such that the arm will have the holding member 51 extending forward in a direction indicated by arrow 82 of FIGURE 4. The ball 80 will then be released with substantially no spinning motion about its up and down axis. If the thrower wishes to have

3,428,036

5

the ball **80** curve to the right, the up direction as viewed in FIGURE 4, he should have holding member **51** cocked and the follow-through be in the direction of arrow **83**, as shown in FIGURE 4. This will cause the ball **80** to be released by rolling off gripping leaf **53** giving the ball a clockwise spinning motion, as viewed in FIGURE 4. If he wishes the ball to curve to the left, the down direction as viewed in FIGURE 4, he should have holding member **51** cocked and the follow-through be in the direction of arrow **84**, as shown in FIGURE 4. This will cause the ball **80** to be released by rolling off gripping leaf **52** giving the ball a counterclockwise spinning motion, as viewed in FIGURE 4.

Users, because of their various heights and swinging motions, may want to change the length of the shaft assembly **11**. This, of course, will be accomplished by pushing actuating member **22** toward rigid shaft member **16** which removes securing finger **21** from contact with adjusting holes **31**. Then the shaft member **14** can be moved either in or out along inside surface **29** of the rigid shaft member **16** until the desired length is found. Then actuating member **22** can be released so that securing finger **21** may again contact adjusting holes **31**, securing the ball gripping and throwing apparatus **10** at this desired length. The cylindrical helical spring **37** permits the ball control assembly **40** to have a certain amount of resilient freedom in any direction. It also adds a good deal of the snap necessary to provide the type of throw a user may desire and permitting him to throw for considerable lengths of time without tiring or injuring his arm or back.

The shaft assembly **11** also provides for completely releasing the shaft member **14** from the rigid shaft member **16** so that an alternate shaft member could be placed in the rigid shaft member **16**, giving great flexibility as to the size ball any one ball gripping and throwing apparatus **10** could be used to throw.

Referring generally to FIGURES 6 and 7, an alternate ball gripping and thowing apparatus **110** is illustrated. The ball gripping and throwing apparatus **110** has a unitary shaft assembly **111**, at the upper end of which is secured a leaf spring **137**. This can be done in various manners well known in the art. For the presenf illustration rivet members **138** are shown. A gripping portion **115** is provided at the bottom end of the shaft assembly **111**. A ball control assembly **140** is secured to the upper end of leaf spring **137**. This can be done in various manners well known in the art. For the present illustration rivet members **142** are shown. Ball control assembly **140** has a flange assembly **144** which is in actual secured contact with leaf spring **137**. A holding member **151** with gripping leaves **152** and **153** is secured to the flange assembly **144**. This can be done in various manners well known in the art. For the present illustration rivet members **150** are used, only one is viewable in FIGURES 6 and 7. A pair of pressure arms **154** and **155** are in contact with gripping leaves **152** and **153**, respectively. Hinge members **156** and **157** connect pressure arms **154** and **155**, respectively, to flange assembly **144**. Pressure arms **154** and **155** are provided with end assemblies **158** and **159**, respectively. End assemblies **158** and **159** are provided with pressure control rods **161** and **162**, respectively. The ends of pressure control rods **161** and **162** extend away from their end assemblies **158** and **159**, respectively, and are connected together by tension spring **163**. Tension spring **163** tends to move the ends of pressure control rods **161** and **162** towards each other which causes a predetermined pressure to be applied on the projectile held by the holding member **151**. Thus, pressure arms **154** and **155** are continually urged into contact with gripping leaves **152** and **153**, respectively. A flange member **146** is connected to flange assembly **144** by flange hinge **145**. A contacting means **171** is mounted on flange assembly **144** and receives one end of an adjusting bolt **172**

6

which has a turning knob **174**. The adjusting bolt **172** passes through and is in threadable engagement with pivot nut assembly **173**. The flange member **146** has a rib member **147** and a guide arm **148**. If the turning knob **174** is turned in one direction, it will move flange member **146** in a clockwise direction about flange hinge **145**; and if it is turned in the opposite direction, it will move flange member **146** in a counterclockwise direction about flange hinge **145**. This adjustment by positioning guide arm **148** helps control the course a ball or projectile will take as it leaves holding member **151** in the same manner that guide arm **48** helps to determine the path that ball **80** will take as it leaves holding member **51**.

While but two forms of the invention have been shown and described, other forms within the spirit and scope of the invention will be apparent to those skilled in the art. Therefore, the embodiments shown in the drawings are to be considered as merely being set forth for illustrative purposes and are not intended to limit the scope of the invention described and shown.

Other modes of applying the principle of my invention may be employed, instead of those explained, change being made as regards the apparatuses herein disclosed, provided the means stated by the following claim or the equivalents of such stated means be employed.

I therefore particularly point out and distinctly claim as my invention:

1. A ball gripping and throwing apparatus comprising, in combination:

(a) a unitary shaft assembly having a gripping handle at its lower end,

(b) a leaf spring secured to said unitary shaft assembly's upper end,

(c) a flange assembly secured to one end of said leaf spring,

(d) a flange hinge connecting a flange member to said flange assembly,

(e) a connecting means secured on said flange assembly above said flange hinge,

(f) said flange member having a rib member connected to said flange hinge at one end,

(g) said flange member having a guide arm connected to the end of said rib member away from said flange hinge,

(h) a pivot nut assembly connected to said flange member between its ends,

(i) an adjusting bolt threadably connected with said pivot nut assembly and rotatably connected with said contacting means,

(j) a ball holding member secured to said flange assembly,

(k) said ball holding member having ball gripping leaves, and

(l) pressure arm connected to said flange assembly applying pressure on said gripping leaves.

References Cited

UNITED STATES PATENTS

663,090	12/1900	Pike et al.	124—5
1,253,700	1/1918	McLaughlin	273—81.2
1,535,029	4/1925	Murch	124—5
3,058,341	10/1962	Heintzmann	73—141

FOREIGN PATENTS

307,797	2/1920	Germany.

RICHARD C. PINKHAM, *Primary Examiner.*

W. R. BROWNE, *Assistant Examiner.*

U.S. Cl. X.R.

73—94, 141; 124—41

Feb. 18, 1969   R. J. PARKER   **3,428,036**

BALL GRIPPING AND THROWING APPARATUS

Filed Sept. 1, 1965   Sheet ___/___ of 2

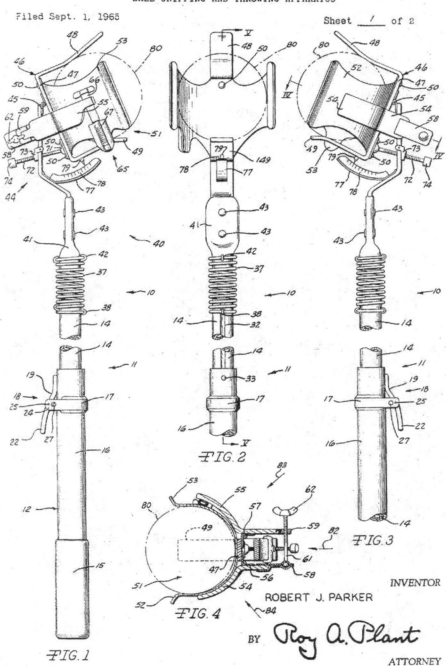

FIG. 1

FIG. 2

FIG. 3

FIG. 4

INVENTOR

ROBERT J. PARKER

BY *Roy A. Plant*

ATTORNEY

Patented Apr. 21, 1925.   **1,535,029**

UNITED STATES PATENT OFFICE.

WILLIAM W. MURCH, OF BROOKLYN, NEW YORK.

TOY.

Application filed May 9, 1924. Serial No. 712,074.

To all whom it may concern:

Be it known that I, WILLIAM W. MURCH, a citizen of the United States, and a resident of the city of New York, borough of 5 Brooklyn, in the county of Kings and State of New York, have invented new and Improved Toys, of which the following is a full, clear, and exact description.

This invention relates to toys and more 10 particularly to an improved device for picking up, holding and throwing a ball.

An object of the invention is to provide a toy of this kind which is adapted to grip the ball with sufficient resiliency to hold it 15 under normal conditions but which will release the ball when a throwing action is imparted thereto so that the ball can be projected with great force and accuracy.

A further object is to provide a toy con- 20 sisting of a handle of any suitable length having a ball receiving socket at one end and at an angle thereto, the socket being so constructed as to resiliently engage and hold a ball but which will permit the re- 25 lease of the ball when a throwing action is imparted to the handle to allow the ball to be projected as may be desired.

With these and other objects in view, the invention consists in certain novel features 30 of construction and combinations and arrangements of parts which will be more fully hereinafter described and pointed out in the claims.

In the accompanying drawings—

35 Figure 1 is a view in side elevation illustrating my improved toy;

Figure 2 is a view in longitudinal section through the socketed end of the toy showing a ball in position therein;

40 Figure 3 is a view in transverse section on the line 3—3 of Figure 2;

Figure 4 is a plan view of one of the ball-gripping jaws before the latter is bent.

1 represents a handle which may be of any 45 suitable length and to which at one end a ferrule 2 is secured and provided with a pair of spring tongues 3, 3 projecting therefrom. A pair of holding wings 4, 4 is secured to the free ends of the spring tongues 3 and a 50 pair of tension springs 5 bears against the leaves 4 giving them sufficient inward pressure to hold the ball 6. A casing 7 is located around the leaves and springs above described and encloses them with the ex- 55 ception of the forward ends of the leaves which are in the form of a plurality of tongues 8. The tongues project slightly beyond the forward end of the casing so as to provide an entrance grip to receive the ball when the latter is forced into the casing be- 60 tween the leaves.

It will be noted that the casing 7 with the parts enclosed therein is located at an angle of approximately 135° to the handle 1, and this is important in that it properly posi- 65 tions the ball so as to guide its discharge in flight.

The parts above described are assembled as follows: The ferrule 2 is inserted on the end of the handle 1, the spring tongues 3 70 which constitute strips of metal are located at opposite sides of the ferrule 2, a bolt 9 is projected through the registering openings in the tongues 3 and ferrule 2, and this bolt 9 is screw-threaded at both ends and 75 receives nuts 10 and 11 which are tightly clamped against the strips or tongues 3.

The outer extremities of the respective ends of the bolts 9 receive nuts 12 which project through relatively large openings 80 13 in the casing 7 and at their inner ends are concaved or cupped so as to conform to the curvature of the springs 5 and bear against said springs and held by said connection against accidental removal. Fur- 85 thermore, the free ends of the ferrule 2, strips 3, and springs 5 are secured by a rivet 14 which projects through the handle 1. The casing 7 is secured to the handle by means of a pair of screws 15 or other secur- 90 ing devices projected therethrough and into the handle.

Figure 4 illustrates on a reduced scale one of the leaves 4 in plan before it is bent into shape. These leaves are bent upon any 95 number of longitudinal lines or given any desired transverse shape so that they will receive the ball 6 and hold the same with sufficient resilient or frictional resistance to prevent the accidental dropping of the ball. 100

When the handle 1 is swung in the arc of a circle to give a throwing motion to the ball great leverage and accuracy can be had, and as the forward motion or swing of the handle is stopped the ball 6 will fly out of 105 its position between the leaves 4 and be directed with great accuracy and can be thrown at a great distance.

Furthermore, it will be noted that the device can also be used for picking up the 110 ball as it is simply necessary to position the leaves 4 over the ball and then the handle

2   1,535,029

downward when the ball will find its position between the leaves ready for another operation of throwing the same.

It is of course to be understood that the invention is not limited to the precise construction set forth but I believe that I have illustrated a preferred embodiment which will most efficiently perform the functions intended and hence various slight changes might be made in the general form of the parts described without departing from my invention, and hence I do not limit myself to the precise details set forth but consider myself at liberty to make such slight changes and alterations as fairly fall within the spirit and scope of the appended claims.

I claim:

1. A toy of the character described, comprising a handle, a pair of springs fixed to the handle, a pair of ball-holding leaves connected to the springs, and other springs secured to the handle and exerting inward pressure against the leaves.

2. A toy of the character described, comprising a handle, a pair of springs fixed to the handle, a pair of ball-holding leaves connected to the springs, other springs secured to the handle and exerting inward pressure against the leaves, a casing surrounding the leaves and springs, a bolt projected through the handle and through the leaves and springs, nuts on the bolts pressing the first-mentioned springs toward the handle, and cap nuts on the outer ends of the bolts projected through the casing and engaging the last-mentioned springs.

3. A toy of the character described, comprising a handle, a pair of inwardly spring-pressed leaves secured to the handle and located at an angle to the handle, said leaves having a plurality of tongues at their outer ends flared outwardly constituting an entrance for a ball.

4. A toy of the character described, comprising a handle, a socket member on the handle, spring tongues against the socket member, ball engaging leaves connected to the tongues, springs secured to the socket member and exerting inward pressure against the leaves, a casing located around said springs and leaves and secured to the handle, a bolt projected through said handle, socket, spring tongues, springs and casing, and a plurality of nuts on both ends of said bolt securing the parts in their proper relative positions.

WILLIAM W. MURCH.

April 21, 1925.   1,535,029

W. W. MURCH

TOY

Filed May 9, 1924

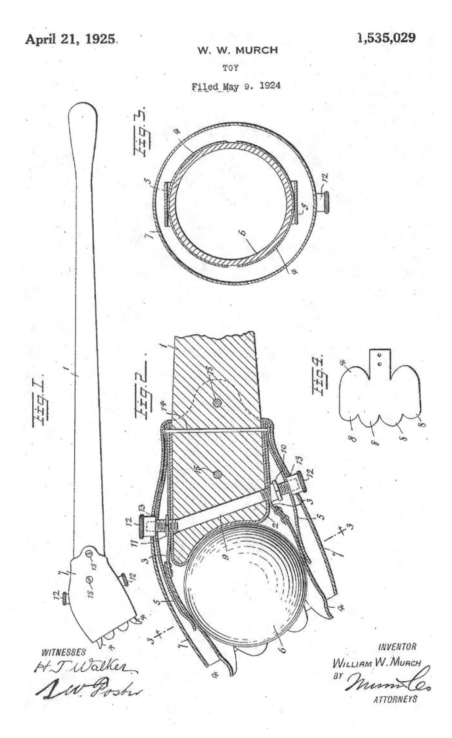

WITNESSES

H. J. Walker

I. W. Poster

INVENTOR

WILLIAM W. MURCH

BY

ATTORNEYS

Chapter 14

BUILDING A BETTER (OR PATENTING A WORSE) MOUSETRAP — PATENT ABUSE

OVERVIEW: BUSINESS METHOD AND SOFTWARE PATENTS

Prior to the issuance of the Supreme Court's *Bilski* opinion,[1] there were high hopes amongst patent critics that the Court would offer a straightforward rejection of the recent proliferation of both software and business method patents in its decision.[2] Most of the traditional legal community was more realistic and was immune to such expectations, but there is a strongly felt dissatisfaction amongst large portions of the software industry and growing segments of general business communities about the abuses of the patent system. In the software industry, vaguely written patent claims[3] can be used as offensive weapons to derail perfectly valid software products through profit seeking litigation. Some examples of unlikely software patents:

- One awarded to security firm Network Associates that gives the company rights to technology that deletes "undesired data" from a computer

- One that gives antispam firm Postini the rights to the process of filtering spam and viruses on a remote e-mail server

---

[1] *Bilski v. Kappos,* 561 U.S. _____, 130 S. Ct. 3218, 177 L. Ed. 2d 792 (2010) (affirming *In re Bilski,* 545 F.3d 943 (Fed. Cir. 2008)). See discussions in Chapter 10 CyberAlchemy, and Chapter 13 FlingWing background sections.

[2] *See, e.g.,* various articles at www.eff.org or www.fsf.org.

[3] *See, e.g., Microsoft has been granted a patent on "Page Up" and "Page Down" keystrokes,* http://www.zdnet.com/news/microsoft-patents-page-up-and-page-down/218626.

The software giant applied for the patent in 2005, and was granted it on August 19, 2008. US patent number 7,415,666 describes "a method and system in a document viewer for scrolling a substantially exact increment in a document, such as one page, regardless of whether the zoom is such that some, all or one page is currently being viewed".

The patent's listed "inventors" are Timothy Sellers, Heather Grantham and Joshua Dersch. However, Page Up and Page Down keyboard buttons have been in existence for at least quarter of a century, as evidenced by this image of a 1981 IBM PC keyboard.

"In one implementation, pressing a Page Down or Page Up keyboard key/button allows a user to begin at any starting vertical location within a page, and navigate to that same location on the next or previous page," reads the patent's summary.

"For example, if a user is viewing a page starting in a viewing area from the middle of that page and ending at the bottom, a Page Down command will cause the next page to be shown in the viewing area starting at the middle of the next page and ending at the bottom of the next page. Similar behavior occurs when there is more than one column of pages being displayed in a row," states the summary.

Microsoft has a long history of applying for, and being granted patents for, inventions that many argue — and can sometimes demonstrate — were based on earlier work carried out by others, or based on a common, self-evident idea.

One example is the company's patent on a mouse wheel that can scroll up and down; another is its patent on double-clicking buttons. The company received its 5,000th patent from the US Patent and Trademark Office in March 2006, and is currently approaching the 10,000 mark.

- Another that gives a California lawyer the rights to the process of assigning professionals a matching e-mail address and subdomain for their websites

- And another that gives Amazon.com the right to charge other website operators for using browser cookies that store data structures.[4]

In the commercial sector generally, patents for business methods can be stretched with similar results, all of which has a very real financial impact on legitimate business and commerce.

The issuance of vague, ill-defined or seemingly facially invalid patents has been most visible in the software and business method patent areas and has resulted in an increasingly common form of patent dispute. The well publicized lawsuit which nearly took Blackberry offline is one example. In that dispute, the plaintiff, a "patent troll"[5] company whose sole business is owning patents and suing successful, deep pocket "infringers," claimed that several of its software patents were infringed by the Blackberry device. In many such cases, regardless of the merit or lack thereof of the claim, the mere instigation of the infringement action will result in an expensive settlement. In the Blackberry case, the suit nearly resulted in several injunctions, any one of which would have taken millions of Blackberry users suddenly off line. Blackberry was able to field its own expensive team of lawyers who were able to prevent any sudden shutdown of the popular devices, but ultimately the case settled for $612.5million.[6]

The basic validity of the plaintiff's patents in the Blackberry case was called into question, and in general, patent trolls often owe their financial success to the existence of broad and vague patents which arguably should never have been granted in the first place. Of course, not all, or even most, patents or infringement actions are the result of these litigation-seeking patent trolls, but the examples of abuse get circulated while boring patents functioning correctly are generally unremarkable and unremarked upon.

---

[4]   Amit Asaravala *Dodgy Patents Rile Tech Industry,* http://www.wired.com/techbiz/media/news/2004/04/62930
[5]   *See* http://www.patentlyo.com/patent/2009/03/what-is-a-troll-patent-and-why-are-they-bad.html.
[6]   http://www.cbsnews.com/stories/2006/03/03/tech/main1368894.shtml.

pended. This "forward and back" movement has been known for generations, and is illustrated in FIG. 1. In contrast to the conventional method of swinging, the present inventor has discovered that much greater satisfaction can be obtained by alternately pulling on one chain to move the swing and the user toward that side, and then pulling on the other chain to move the swing and the user toward that side. This side-to-side oscillatory motion of the swing and the user is thus along an axis that is substantially parallel to the axis of the tree branch from which the swing is suspended, and is illustrated in FIG. 2. This side to side swinging method has the added benefit that it can be continued for long periods of time simply by alternately pulling on one chain and then the other. The importance of sufficient clearance between the swing and any obstructions or threats to the user's safety is apparent.

The present inventor has discovered certain other improvements in the art of swinging on a swing, either or both of which can be used in conjunction with the swinging method described immediately above. The first is that the inventive swinging method can be initiated from a dead stop without pushing, and without the user having to contact the ground. That is, the user can climb onto the swing, and begin from an initial dead stop to pull first on one chain, and then on the other chain, alternately until the user and the swing have begun to swing side-to-side in accordance with the inventive swinging method described herein. This enables even young users to swing independently and joyously, which is of great benefit to all.

Another improvement on the swinging method described above is the induction into the side-to-side swinging movement of a component of forward-and-back motion. That is, by skillful manipulation of the body, the present inventor has found it possible to add a relatively minor component of forward-and-back motion to the side-to-side swinging motion, resulting in a swinging path that is generally shaped like an oval, as is shown in FIG. 3. It is preferred that the magnitude of the forward-and back motion (shown in FIG. 3 as being along the Y axis) be less than the magnitude of the side-to side motion (shown in FIG. 3 as being along the X axis), so that the latter predominates. In this manner, the motion can be more easily continued simply by alternately pulling on one chain and then the other in the manner described.

Lastly, it should be noted that because pulling alternately on one chain and then the other resembles in some measure the movements one would use to swing from vines in a dense jungle forest, the swinging method of the present invention may be referred to by the present inventor and his sister as "Tarzan" swinging. The user may even choose to produce a Tarzan-type yell while swinging in the manner described, which more accurately replicates swinging on vines in a dense jungle forest. Actual jungle forestry is not required.

Licenses are available from the inventor upon request.

Chapter 15

ERSATZ UNIVERSITY — PATENT/ COMBINED IP STRATEGY

EXERCISE

TOPIC: Patent and Combined IP

   i.   Patent Infringement

   ii.   Corporate IP Protection

   iii.   Employee Creation Issues

SKILLS:

   i.   Drafting - Client Communication

   ii.   Critical Reasoning

   iii.   Analysis

ESTIMATED TIME FOR COMPLETING THIS EXERCISE:

Approximately one and a half hours.

ESTIMATED LEVEL OF DIFFICULTY (1–5): 3—Moderate.

Higher education is a rapidly expanding field. Although in the past, experience counted more than an unrelated degree in many professions, now a BA has become a minimum requirement for virtually any white collar job. With the job market remaining tight, waves and waves of applicants are fighting for the opportunity to improve their credentials and skill sets, either to land that all important first job or to qualify for a better one. A side effect of these trends is that on-line education is spreading faster than the latest You Tube clip. The ability to land a degree from an accredited college without having to leave the comfort of your couch appeals to a wide spectrum of people from single moms who face child care challenges to lazy people who don't like to get up.

Your client is Ersatz U, an accredited, for profit, university with no physical classrooms whatsoever.

The school's slogan is "your employer will think you really went to college" and that is emblazoned on Tshirts, ball caps and sweatpants (no polo shirts — the students never get that fancy).

This is the school logo:

The college has hundreds of adjunct professors who are sometimes asked to prepare course materials and sometimes are given prepackaged course materials from which they are required to teach without any derivation.

One of E.U.'s Computer Skills professors, Barry Hakenslash, developed a hidden webcam that allows the professor to see what the student is doing during class by activating the secret web cam in the student's college-issued laptop. It is embedded in the required "Class Chat" software which is loaded onto every student's university-issued laptop. The "Class Chat" software itself appears innocuous; it is the server-based communication system which allows multiparty realtime interface through voice and text during class. Class Chat is a commercial product which EU uses under a limited license. The spy cam feature is disclosed deep in the EULA that all students are required to sign before their first class, so of course none of the students are aware of its existence, although they all clicked "I AGREE" in order to matriculate.

The standard laptop also has a tracking device that allows the E.U. to compile data on which coffee shops are commonly frequented by its students so that it can sell the data to marketing companies and leverage financial arrangements with various Starbucks franchises. This tracking program is based on Lojack and GPS technology. Prof. Hakenslash is very clever and has a fair amount of free time.

The Board of Visitors, the ruling body of the University, recently discussed an article from the *Chronicle of Higher Education* about how many Universities are taking extreme measures to protect their intellectual property. The Board isn't sure what exactly they should be protecting, but they don't want to be left out of any trend, so they called you.

Please think about what you know of this particular school and about universities in general. Prepare a memo addressing the following: What sort of IP is likely to be at issue? What options are there for protection? What advice would you offer with respect to an IP Policy and general strategy for E.U.? Are there any other related legal issues you should raise with your client?

Once your memo is complete, review the Student Assessment in the LexisNexis webcourse.